Organizational Behavior Reference:

20 Books in 1
About Employees and Workplaces

Louis Bevoc

Published by
NutriNiche System LLC

Organizational Culture
Understanding its Importance

Louis Bevoc

Published by
NutriNiche System LLC

Louis Bevoc books...simple explanations of complex subjects

Introduction to culture

Every organization has unique experiences, philosophies, behaviors, norms, and values. They also have specific methods and patterns for interacting with suppliers, customers, employees, and the community. When combined, these attributes define an organization and make up its culture.

Culture starts at the top of an organization and works its way down into the rank and file. Employees can help establish behaviors and norms, but they do not have the same power as those in the upper levels of the established hierarchy. Top ranking members are the only people who have the authority, influence, and control needed to create the overall culture of the organization.

In companies, culture provides guidelines for productivity, performance, service, and quality. It applies to everyone and can be difficult to alter without solid planning.

In short, every culture is distinctive based on the characteristics of the organization. Culture describes an organization and explains its purpose in society. It is also created by the most influential members, establishes policies and procedures, and can be challenging to change without a plan.

Now let's move into a discussion on the ways that culture affects the actions of people in organizations.

Relationship of culture

Organizational culture is associated with many different aspects of organizational behavior. These associations influence employee actions and establish a perception of the organization. Let's take a closer look at these relationships and their impact:

Decision-making

Effective decision-making is critical for the survival of an organization, and that decision-making is almost always influenced by culture. Employees think about their organization's norms and values before deciding the direction to proceed. If they go against those norms and values, they risk bringing about change that might be resisted by coworkers or rejected by higher management.

Let's look at the entire decision-making process and examine how culture plays a role throughout. First, the problem needs to be identified so people can think about potential solutions. If the culture is such that people are disciplined for making mistakes, then they might try to hide the actual problem in fear of the consequences. For example, an employee who breaks a machine might not tell his boss the truth if that boss has a reputation for terminating people who damage equipment.

Once the problem is established, potential solutions need to be generated. Some organizations encourage creative thinking for finding answers, while others have a more strict protocol. The methodology used to resolve problems stems from the culture of the organization. For example, the Catholic Church would not consider abortion as a solution to an overcrowded population problem. Abstinence is a better solution based on their culture.

Now a decision needs to be made. Some organizations have established norms regarding what can and can't be done, and those norms are embedded in the culture. For example, employees who work for an owner who is extremely frugal might know that the best decision is always the one that involves the least amount of money being spent. This is not necessarily the best choice for the company, but it stays within cultural guidelines.

The last part of the decision process involves follow up. Was the decision correct? Once again, this is driven by the culture of the organization. If the end result adheres to the philosophies and values of the culture, then it was a good choice. For example, a bakery might make a decision to throw away 500 donuts because they are more than 12 hours old. If the culture of the company is to put out high-quality products that are always fresh, then the decision was good...regardless of the money spent throwing the product in the trash. However, if the culture of that same bakery is to never waste anything, then the right decision might be to sell the donuts at a reduced cost.

Communication

Employees need to share information in order to accomplish tasks and achieve organizational goals. This can be done verbally (talking, presentation, speeches, videos, etc.) or non-verbally (body language, pictures, signs, symbols, written words, etc.), but it all falls under communication. Good communication keeps organizations healthy, while poor communicating is capable of destroying them.

Communication is an essential part of organizational culture because it influences behaviors, norms, and values. Good communication promotes a positive culture while bad communication creates the opposite effect. Leaders in progressive organizations realize this, and they regularly act to open communication lines. For example, some companies hold company, division, or department-wide meetings with upper management so employees can ask questions and gather information. Employees are able to express their opinions and beliefs to the top decision makers, and this lets them feel like they are being heard. One problem with these gatherings, however, is they can lose focus if they are too large. Due to this, some companies take an additional step and hold smaller meetings with the same goal in mind.

Open communication also leads to trust. Leaders who are aware of this survey their employees to find the level or trust in the organization. Basically, they are looking for employees' perceptions as to what the organization is like as a communication system. Poor communication leads to a lack of trust that can be difficult to restore once it is lost.

One might think that the military has a negative culture because communication is restricted and withheld in many instances. The Army, for example, often keeps information from soldiers. This type of behavior seems like it would lead to a lack of trust, but that is typically not the case. Security is an issue in the Army, and divulging certain facts could result in a crisis. Based on this, soldiers understand and accept that they are simply are better off not knowing some things...and this does not create a negative culture. In fact, the military often has a more positive culture than many of the biggest and best organizations in the world.

The role communication plays in culture is important. However, that role needs to be further broken down for a better understanding of the relationship. The following are critical areas where good communication with employees is needed in order to promote positive culture:

Employee's need for direction

Employees need guidance in order to complete the tasks expected of them and understand their roles in the organization. Without this direction, employees feel abandoned or begin to wander. This creates a culture of indecision and uncertainty.

Organizational example #1

A president of a home builder puts together a team to cut costs within the organization. If this team is assembled without being told why they have been chosen, they might not accomplish the team objectives. An engineer might not realize that he is on the team to make sure the reductions do not compromise safety. Likewise, a salesperson might not realize that she is on the team to make sure the customer will still get a quality house after the cost cutting. The president needs to assign responsibilities to each member to prevent a culture of confusion.

Organizational example #2

Janelle is the owner of a window manufacturing company. She hires Rick to work at the factory because he has management skills that she knows can be utilized. She is not sure exactly what she wants Rick to do, so she tells him to begin work by observing the people and processes. After Rick observes for a while, Janelle wants him to tell her where he thinks his management skills are most needed.

When Rick shows up at work, other employees are confused about his job responsibilities. They don't know what he is doing, and this creates fear, confusion, and resentment for not being told why he has been hired. This also puts Rick in an uncomfortable position because he is unsure of his responsibilities. Janelle should have given Rick specific job responsibilities and made the current employees aware of those responsibilities in order to prevent cultural uncertainty.

Employee's need for honesty

Leaders need to be honest with employees in order to establish good working relationships. Employees want to hear good news and bad news because they have a vested interest in the organization. Management dishonesty leads to a lack of trust, and this results in a negative culture.

Organizational example

A computer company is buying a competitor, and the employees at the company being bought are fearful of losing their jobs during the merger. The new management is aware of these concerns, so they hold a meeting. The new leadership assures the employees that they will all have jobs for at least one year, but some changes might need to be made after that period of time. This is not necessarily good news, but the new management team's honesty allows them to build trust with the workers. This helps establish a positive culture as the merger moves forward.

Employee's need for a voice

Employees want their thoughts and concerns heard by management. Their ideas might be beneficial for the organization, and their involvement will contribute to a positive culture. This being said, discussions are a good idea before implementing workplace changes that impact employees.

Organizational example

A telephone company decides that all service personnel must wear a tie during visits to customers. They did not ask for employee input, they simply made a change because the CEO thought a dress code would create a professional appearance.

This attire change might look good, but it is not realistic. Service personnel need to run phone wires, climb poles and ladders, and go into attics...and a tie is very impractical for this type of work. In fact, a tie even presents a safety hazard if it is not carefully monitored.

This change completely demoralizes the service personnel. Some quit, some grumble silently, and others protest to management. However, the change has been made, and it is going to remain in effect. This creates a negative organizational culture that will be difficult to change.

Employee's need for praise

People like to be told they are doing a good job. This motivates them, makes them feel good about their work, and produces a positive organizational culture that influences the entire workplace. In short, a "pat on the back" goes a long way.

Organizational example

Joe works as a salesman for a barber and hair salon supply company. He normally does a good job, but last week he made a major mistake. His customer ordered 11 new custom razor blades, but Joe mistakenly entered 111 blades in the computer.

When the blades reach the warehouse, the owner Valerie calls Joe since this does not seem accurate. Joe checks his records and realizes that he made the mistake. However, the blades cannot be returned because they are custom made for a specific barber. Valerie is now stuck with $1900 worth of custom blades that none of her customers need.

Joe is upset over his mistake. However, instead of reprimanding him, Valerie tells him that this one mistake does not offset the good job he has done for the company. She thanks him for the good job he is doing and reassures him that, in time, all of the blades will be sold to the barber who uses them.

Valerie's praise makes Joe happy about his work. Her words motivate him to try harder, and they create a positive organizational culture. If she had chosen to reprimand Joe, the effect would have been the opposite.

Employee's need for emotional intelligence

Employees have needs for empathy and compassion at work, and astute leadership has the proper skills to meet those needs. The most important aspect of those skills is emotional intelligence. Emotionally intelligent leaders have the ability to understand and communicate with their employees, and this leads to a positive organizational culture.

Organizational example

Darlene is a driver for a hazardous waste transportation company. She just found out that her father has terminal cancer, and she is visibly distraught when she shows up for work in the morning. Edwardo, the owner of the company, immediately senses her pain. He expresses his condolences and talks to her about the situation, and then he tells her to take the rest of the week off to be with her father.

Darlene appreciates Edwardo's sensitivity and understanding. He could have expressed his sorrow for the illness, and then told her to go back to work. Instead, he used emotional intelligence to comfort her in this time of need. Edwardo's actions made Darlene feel appreciated and respected, and this created a positive organizational culture for her and the employees who witnessed his compassion.

Commitment

Employees' commitment to the goals and objectives of the organization is linked to their perception of the culture. Those who perceive the culture as negative are less committed than those who perceive it as positive. Committed employees identify with the organization, and this leads to better workplace culture.

Many factors are involved in the relationship between organizational culture and organizational commitment. Let's examine some of the most important factors and their involvement:

Role conflicts

Role conflicts result when people have conflicting job responsibilities. Employees who are unsure of their responsibilities perceive the culture as stressful and often start looking for employment elsewhere. In short, role conflicts affect the commitment of employees to the organization.

Organizational example

Mary is an accounts receivable person at website designer. Martin, the owner of the company, has told her on several occasions that when there is a dispute in payment, the customer is always right. However, whenever a customer wants to take a deduction from an invoice, Martin tells Mary to argue with them about it. He becomes upset with Mary if she gives the discount... even if the customer is clearly right.

This situation is stressful for Mary. Martin tells her to behave in a certain manner, but he gets upset with her when she follows his instructions. The conflicting job responsibilities affect Mary's commitment to the organization and create a negative culture.

Empowerment

Employees who have the proper knowledge and resources to perform their work with limited supervision are empowered. They take ownership of their jobs and the processes within them, and this results in a positive perception of the culture and a strong commitment to organizational goals.

Organizational example

Marshall is a welder at an automotive assembly plant. His boss Yolanda knows that he is capable of performing his job without assistance. Yolanda simply makes sure that Marshall has the proper tools and supplies for his work, and then she leaves him alone to perform his job.

These conditions motivate Marshall to perform to the best of his ability. He works with little supervision and takes charge of all of his job-related responsibilities. Marshall is empowered, and that empowerment increases his commitment to his employer and creates a positive perception of the workplace culture.

Autonomy

Autonomy is the freedom employees have within their jobs. This is similar to empowerment, but it involves the liberty to make choices about the job rather than having the proper knowledge and resources to do the job. This results in a positive culture because people develop commitment towards the organization.

Organizational example

Claudine is a graphic artist at an advertising company. She likes to spend Wednesday's shopping and eating lunch with her mother, so she would prefer not to work on that day. Her boss lets her take Wednesdays off and work from home on Saturday to make up the time.

This arrangement gives Claudine freedom to choose where and when she does her job. The autonomy she experiences strengthens her commitment to the company and creates a positive culture for her.

Leadership authority

Leadership authority involves the power of one person or a few select individuals to make all the decisions in an organization. Usually, these people are at the top of the hierarchy, and they limit the authority of lower level employees. When organizations place absolute power in the hands of one or a few people, they decrease employee commitment and create a negative culture.

Organizational example

Reggie is one of twenty salespeople at a lumber company. His boss, Tiffany, is the vice president of sales. Tiffany is very specific that she does not want any salespeople to make decisions without her approval. They cannot discount items, offer sales promotions, or run product advertisements without her authorization. She makes it clear that salespeople will be disciplined if they make unauthorized decisions.

Reggie feels powerless when he is with customers, and he is embarrassed that he cannot make any decisions without Tiffany's approval. This type of work situation demotivates Reggie, lowers his commitment to the organization, and promotes a negative culture.

Values

In organizations, values are very important. They influence people's decisions and behavior, and they establish norms for the entire workplace. They are the foundation of organizational culture, and they establish patterns that employees follow while performing everyday tasks.

Values originate from leadership. Their importance cannot be underestimated because they have a direct impact on significant aspects of organizational behavior including performance and ethics.

For organizations to be successful, leadership needs to align employee values and organizational values. Employees need to identify with the organization if they are expected to work toward achieving its goals and objectives. In short, strongly aligned values result in positive organizational culture.

Organizational example

Olivia works in inventory control for a furniture wholesaler. In her spare time, she volunteers at a soup kitchen close to her house. She strongly believes in giving to the less fortunate in the community.

The company Olivia works for is also philanthropic. They donate tables and chairs to local homeless shelters on a regular basis. This pleases Olivia because she needs to work for an organization that has values similar to her own, and that need is met by the furniture wholesaler.

Olivia identifies with her employer. Her values are aligned with those of the furniture wholesaler, and this enables her to have a positive perception of the organizational culture.

Management style

People are different...and this also applies to leaders. Leaders have distinctive personalities, traits, ideas, beliefs, and philosophies, and all of these factors influence the way they manage people. Management style refers to the specific methods used to manage employees.

Some leaders make decisions by themselves. They seek limited guidance from others and choose to manage using personal experience, established facts, and gut reactions. This works well when they make good decisions by reacting to the needs of the organization and employees, but wrong decisions that go unchallenged can lead to disaster.

Other leaders assume a coaching role. They provide feedback so employees understand what is needed in order to complete tasks and accomplish organizational goals. This motivates top performers, but employees that are not as capable do not always fare as well. These individuals prefer a closer supervisor/subordinate relationship, and they tend to get lost in the coaching process. Think about a basketball team. The starters are interested in the coach's feedback and the goals of the team. However, there are also players on the team who never get to play in games, and they are typically less motivated to listen to the coach and accomplish team goals.

The third type of leader lets employees make choices without interference. There is no autocratic decision-making or coaching, and employees are allowed to make decisions as a team. This works well in many instances because people have freedom to make choices. However, problems can also result. Some individuals tend to take over teams and want to make every decision, while others become social loafers who choose to let everyone else do the work.

All three of these management styles are capable of motivating or demotivating workers, and because of this, they have a direct impact on the organizational culture.

Organizational example

Isabelle and Timothy are part of a team that is working on new packaging designs for dog treats. Their boss wants the team to make all of the decisions and does not want to be involved unless they need support or guidance.

Larry is also on the team, and he is a natural leader. As soon as the group assembles, Larry takes charge. He designates roles and tells members what they need to accomplish in order to produce the new designs. Some members respond well to this takeover, but Isabelle and Timothy do not. They feel left out of the decision-making process, but they are afraid to speak up because Larry is very knowledgeable and confident.

The leadership role assumed by Larry demotivates Isabelle and Timothy. Their interest in the project becomes minimal because they do not feel like their knowledge and skills are being properly utilized. This influences their view of the organizational culture in a negative manner.

Changing culture

As noted in the introduction, culture can be difficult to change without a good plan. This is because cultural change is gradual. Barring major events or disasters, people do not change their perceptions overnight.

In order to change culture, leadership needs to be directly involved. They have to develop a vision for the change, and then implement it by being involved. Their actions will impact others in the organization, and the change will gradually come about.

One major mistake leaders make is to take themselves out of the process. They simply draw up a list of changes and turn it over to managers and human resource personnel for implementation. This does not work because employees need to see people at the top being an active part of the change.

Now that we know leadership needs to be involved and the process will take time, let's discuss what needs to be done to change organizational culture:

Start at the top

Let's revisit the importance of top management involvement. Some leaders implement "do as I say, not as I do" cultural change policies. These do not work and will never be effective because culture involves perception. Employees can be forced to behave in certain ways and conform to new standards, but they cannot be coerced into changing their perceptions. Workplace experiences influence cultural perception, and that perception will be negative if employees see leaders ignoring their own rules. In short, top management needs to change their own behavior if they want others to do the same.

Organizational example

Leadership at a company wants to change the culture to one that cares about the local community. They begin to give money to poor families, and they offer to match any employee donations that are posted on a designated bulletin board. Executives at the company start the process by pledging $200 each on the board. This is a show of good faith and the chance of getting lower level employees to donate increases based on the perception that management is practicing what they preach.

Explain the change

Employees want to know why the culture needs to change. This is completely understandable because work is an important aspect of their lives. Management needs to explain the reasons for the change and get employees involved. Involvement is critical because a change in culture is dependent on a change in behavior, and it is difficult for employees to change their behavior if they are a distant part of the process.

Organizational example

Leadership at a company wants to change the culture to one that is focused on sound ethical principles. They schedule a meeting with all of the employees to explain that certain purchasing agents were taking illegal gifts for preferential treatment of vendors. These individuals have been terminated, but the company wants everyone to be more focused on ethical behavior. To accomplish this, an outside consultant has been hired, and all employees will go through ethical training. Employees are encouraged to ask questions, and management answers them with honesty in order to explain exactly why the change is taking place. In short, the change is explained in a meeting, and the employees will be involved in training.

Communicate throughout

Let employees know how things are going during the entire progress. They need to know what has transpired and what will occur next. This helps maintain focus on the task at hand, and it keeps employees interested. It is achieved by providing information, facts, data, and accomplishments.

Organizational example

Leadership at a company wants to change the culture to one that is more customer oriented. Every month, they send out an email to everyone in the organization to let them know how things are progressing. The following information is always included in the email:

- The number of customer complaints and the percent increase or decrease from the prior month
- The correct order fulfillment rates and the percent increase or decrease from the prior month
- The results from customer surveys and the rating increase or decrease from the prior month

Employees are also encouraged to ask management questions about new developments so they are not left wondering what has transpired. In short, progress of the change implantation is updated throughout the process.

Reward achievements

As employees embrace the change, management needs to highlight their accomplishments using rewards. These rewards do not have to be monetary, but employees who behave in the desired manner need a spotlight put on their actions. Sometimes a simple acknowledgment does the job.

Organizational example

Leadership at a company wants to change the culture to one where everyone arrives for work and meetings in a timelier manner. They schedule an 8:00 am meeting on Monday morning and everyone arrives on time. The manager in charge of the meeting acknowledges this fact and thanks everyone by providing donuts and coffee. This small token of appreciation rewards the achievement of being punctual. In short, this group of employees behaved in a desired manner, and their behavior was acknowledged and rewarded.

After the culture has been successfully changed, it needs to be monitored. Internal audits should be conducted periodically to assure that behavior is not reverting back to old ways. Surveys can be issued to get a snapshot of what is transpiring, but it is often easier and less expensive to ask employees questions during everyday conversation. Under relaxed conditions, people are typically very honest about their workplace perceptions.

Summary

All organizations have unique experiences, philosophies, behaviors, norms, and values that define them and make up their culture. That culture provides guidelines for every employee, and it starts at the top of the organizational hierarchy.

This book examines the concept of organizational culture, the relationship it has with other variables, and the best ways to change it. It provides understanding using insightful analysis, and workplace examples are utilized throughout for real world application. In short, the information provided increases the reader's knowledge about this very significant aspect of organizational behavior.

Industrial/Organizational Psychology
A Basic Introduction

Rachael Collinson and Louis Bevoc

Published by
NutriNiche System LLC

Louis Bevoc books...simple explanations of complex subjects

Introduction

Industrial/organizational (I/O) psychology is a branch of clinical psychology that focuses on workers and workplaces. Essentially, it applies science to organizations to find out what employees enjoy most about their jobs. This information is then used to make work more interesting and increase productivity.

I/O psychologists study organizational behavior using established principles, practices, and theories from the field of psychology. They conduct research designed to improve employee attitudes through training and feedback from management. They also help employees transition into unfamiliar work environments as organizations grow, change, and evolve. Their goal is to improve various aspects of work life including safety, mental health, job satisfaction, productivity, and motivation. In short, they strive to resolve workplace issues and improve the quality of life for employees.

Probably the biggest misconception about I/O psychologists is that they are employed as management consultants. People believe their sole function is to make workplaces more efficient so organizations can be more profitable...with no concern for the well-being of employees. This is simply not true. I/O psychologists are mainly concerned with improving the lives of workers, and often times this costs employers money. However, the application of research findings can have a long-term positive impact on the bottom line because employees find happiness at work and satisfaction with their jobs.

Differences

I/O psychologists are classified as industrial or organizational. These two types have similar goals, but they use distinct approaches for research and problem-solving. A basic description of each is as follows.

Industrial

Industrial psychology was born during World War I. Military leaders wanted to place soldiers in jobs that they were best suited for, so they looked to psychology for answers. Mass group testing was conducted on military personnel, and it worked well.

After the war, the same testing was modified for application to non-military organizations. Management was happy with the results, and the field of industrial psychology gained popularity nationwide.

Industrial psychologists focus on people and their relationships with organizations. The following is an example:

Organizational example

Dr. Radner is an industrial psychologist who works for an automotive supplier. She is currently conducting researching methods for determining the right people for jobs. Specifically, she is studying how the hiring practices and procedures of human resources personnel affect job fit. Factors include previous work history, background checks, and personality. Her findings are obtained by interviewing human resources employees (qualitative research).

Organizational

Organizational psychology started in the 1920s and has gained popularity since that time. The birth of this profession is largely attributed to the now-famous Hawthorne Studies.

The Hawthorne experiments took place at the Western Electric plant in Hawthorne, Illinois. Researchers lowered and raised the level of lighting to see if the various levels influenced worker productivity. Findings showed that any change in lighting increased productivity...regardless of whether the lights were dimmed or made brighter.

After the Western Electric plant research ended, productivity decreased to the levels it was before the studies were conducted. It was later determined that the actual lighting changes had nothing to do with workers becoming more productive. Their increased productivity was simply due to the fact that researchers were paying attention to them as they performed their jobs.

Organizational psychologists focus on the affects organizations have on people. The following is an example:

Organizational example

Dr. Smith is an organizational psychologist who works for a food processor. He is currently researching methods for increasing the productivity of the production workers. Specifically, he is studying how the workplace environment impacts worker productivity. Factors include policies, procedures, and supervisor-subordinate relationships. His findings are obtained by surveying production employees (quantitative research).

As you can see, there are some differences between industrial and organizational psychology. However, both will be viewed as the same in this book. That being said, let's examine the skills that I/O psychologists need to possess for their jobs.

Skills

I/O psychologists are involved in the design, execution, and interpretation of psychological research in organizations. They apply their findings to problems involving people or processes within those organizations. Not surprisingly, a variety of different skills are necessary for these practitioners. All of these skills are related to understanding human behavior in terms of performance, personality, motivation, and ability.

These required skills include the following:

Thinking

Logical and critical thinking are important for all I/O psychologists. They need to identify workplace problems, formulate approaches those problems, and conduct research regarding those problems. After the research is conducted, the findings need to be applied in ways that benefit employees and organizations.

Speaking

Speaking skills are important for I/O psychologists because they talk with people on an everyday basis. They need to convey information verbally in order to complete tasks and achieve goals. Their words, voice tone, and paralanguage affect the understanding of the information they are conveying. I/O psychologists who do not speak effectively leave employees confused. This prevents them from accomplishing their goals and leads to other problems in organizations.

Reading

Reading comprehension is important for many types of professionals. Lawyers who do not understand what they are reading can lose cases for their clients, and medical doctors with poor reading skills can cause physical health issues for their patients.

I/O psychologists must also be able to understand what they are reading. They need to review case studies, hiring procedures, company policies, and legal documents...and then use that information to propose research and makes changes for the better. Without the ability to absorb what they are reading, they are not capable of performing their jobs at the highest level.

Writing

The written word is important for every organization because interpretation of the meaning can be confusing. Consider, for example, the following sentence:

Jim never said Judy stole your book.

Now notice how the meaning changes each time the sentence is read, but a different word is emphasized (the emphasized word is capitalized):

- JIM never said Judy stole your book (meaning Jim did not say Judy stole your book, but another person may have said she stole it)
- Jim NEVER said Judy stole your book (meaning Jim did not say Judy stole your book at all)
- Jim never SAID Judy stole your book (meaning Jim did not say Judy stole your book, but he implied it)
- Jim never said JUDY stole your book (meaning Jim did not say Judy stole your book, but he did say someone else stole it)
- Jim never said Judy STOLE your book (meaning Jim did not say Judy stole your book, but she borrowed it)

- Jim never said Judy stole YOUR book (meaning Jim did not say Judy stole your book, but she stole another person's book)
- Jim never said Judy stole your BOOK (meaning Jim did not say Judy stole your book, but she stole something of yours other than your book)

The above sentence shows how simply reading written words does not always convey the intended message. People who misinterpret word emphasis of the sender may change the context and distort the meaning of what they are reading. The point of this exercise is to show that I/O psychologists need to be able to write effectively or they risk losing the intent of their messages.

Perceiving

This involves the perception of workplace happenings. It is an important skill for I/O psychologists because they need to know what is going on in organizations. Perceiving can be broken down into two basic categories:

Active listening

This is listening to what others have to say by taking the time to understand what they really mean. I/O psychologists need to ask questions for clarification, avoid finishing sentences, and prevent themselves from interrupting if they truly want to understand the key points others are making. Active listening is an acquired skill...and I/O psychologists need to make that acquisition if they want to do their jobs properly.

Social awareness

This is awareness of the reasons for others' behavior. Similar to active listening, it takes time and effort on the part of I/O psychologists. They need to process information and learn from their experiences in order to understand why people react the way they do to workplace experiences. Without this skill, situations can be wrongly analyzed and conclusions can be inaccurate.

Learning

Learning is critical in workplaces all over the world. Virtually every employee needs to learn something about his or her job in order to get better at it...and this general rule applies to I/O psychologists. They must be able to learn or they will not improve their work. In fact, those who are not capable of learning risk losing their jobs. In short, learning skills are not only important for I/O psychologists...they are absolutely essential!

The skills listed above are essential for I/O psychologists. However, they also need to possess certain knowledge, and that knowledge is discussed in the next section.

Knowledge

I/O psychologists also need to possess certain knowledge in order to be effective in their jobs. That knowledge must be in the following areas:

Psychology

This is the most obvious area where I/O psychologists need to be knowledgeable. After all, it makes sense that psychology is the most important aspect of I/O psychologists' jobs. That being said, an understanding of psychological practices, principles, and theories is essential.

Mathematics

I/O psychologists need a good working knowledge of math and statistics in order to design studies and determine results. Their background in this area is far too complex to describe in this book, but it is important to understand that their comprehension of mathematics and statistics must be advanced...far beyond that of a typical employee.

Human resources

Some I/O psychologists are hired mostly for the purpose of working with human resources personnel. They help recruit, hire, train, and retain employees using psychological principles. This benefits HR personnel because they can direct their attention to other matters, and it takes a major burden off the shoulders of management. For this reason, a working knowledge of human resources is important for I/O psychologists.

Management

In order for I/O psychologists to help resolve workplace issues, they must understand how management in organizations works. They need to know what managers do in terms of delegating tasks, motivating employees, and interacting with others in the workforce. They also need to understand various management styles in order to react appropriately to situations and provide recommendations. Without this type of knowledge, I/O psychologists will need to be trained and educated...and they are hired to the opposite (train and educate others).

Conflict resolution

Conflicts occur in every organization. This is good if the conflicts are functional because they inspire the diversity needed to bring about change. However, dysfunctional conflicts typically have no benefits, and they only result in more problems. This is not good...especially when people are attacked instead of problems.

I/O psychologists need to have an understanding of conflict resolution so they can mediate situations when dysfunctional conflict erupts. Since most psychologists are trained in conflict resolution while earning their degrees, this is usually not an issue. That training always comes in handy because their ability to resolve conflicts will be tested at some point in time.

Time management

At first glance, this might seem like a rather unimportant area for I/O psychologists to possess knowledge. After all, what does time management have to do with psychological studies that focus on workplaces and employees? There should never be a rush to find solutions to problems because those solutions can prevent a wealth of headaches in the future. In fact, faculty in psychology departments at universities spend years researching issues in order to make organizations more successful.

While the above paragraph might be true, it must be noted that many I/O psychologists are employed in industry by companies that work off bottom lines. Time is money to these companies...and money is needed for survival. For this reason, I/O psychologists need to have a working knowledge of time management so time and money are not wasted.

Other

I/O psychologists should also possess some knowledge in the areas of advertising, sales, and marketing. These might not be as critical as the areas mentioned above, but understanding them will pay off for research or analysis of consumer behavior.

Now that you understand the basic skills and knowledge required for I/O psychologists, let's move on to the methodology they use for their research.

Methodology

Before beginning this section, it is important to note that it is not designed to encompass the vast array of research methods used by I/O psychologists. It is also not intended to oversimplify the field work of I/O psychologists who spend many years acquiring the skills necessary to properly perform their jobs. This section is merely a brief description and exemplification of a few quantitative and qualitative methods that might be used in organizations. Readers interested in fully understanding the methodologies used by I/O psychologists should read books devoted to the subject.

I/O psychologists study human behavior by applying principles and theories to people in workplaces. Their goal is to make organizations more successful while ensuring the health, happiness, and safety of employees. Often times this involves finding ways to increase productivity and motivation simultaneously.

I/O psychologists use the scientist-practitioner model to conduct their research. Essentially, this involves research and scientific practice. They apply principles of psychology to workplace situations in order to acquire knowledge and establish new methodologies. They also use their findings in future research to create a pattern of continuous learning and application. This helps organizations achieve goals and objectives with motivated and productive employees.

A variety of qualitative and quantitative research methods are used by I/O psychologists. Each method can be used alone or in combination with others for a more effective analysis. The following are examples of the methodology employed:

Quantitative

Quantitative research is implemented to statistically analyze and measure the way in which people think, feel, and behave. It investigates phenomena. More specifically, it investigates *who, what, when,* and *where* using statistics or mathematics.

I/O psychologists use these types of studies to collect numerical data and develop theories, models, and hypothesis pertaining to the phenomena. Findings can be applied to other situations if they have been replicated in different research.

Advantage

Quantitative research provides precise numerical data that is not influenced by the researcher's personal bias.

Disadvantage

Quantitative research produces findings that are often too generalized for application to specific situations.

Quantitative research can involve experimental controls and the manipulation of variables to obtain numerical data. In short:

- A study with a purpose and significance is proposed and defined (demographically).
- Variables are established.
- Relationships are determined from data collected after manipulating some variables while holding others constant.

An example includes the following:

Jessica is an I/O psychologist employed by an automotive manufacturer. She believes money does not motivate hourly employees to work harder. She wants to test this by measuring the relationship between hourly wages and productivity while controlling the type of job being performed. In this study, hourly wages and productivity both change, but the type of job is held constant.

Quantitative research can also involve surveys with structured questions used to collect data. In short:

- A study with a purpose and significance is proposed and defined (demographically).
- Variables are established.
- Relationships are determined after collecting data from surveys measuring the variables.

An example includes the following:

Jessica believes negative comments by supervisors are causing employees to become less dedicated to their jobs. She wants to test her thinking by measuring the relationship between supervisors' verbal aggressiveness and hourly production employees' commitment to the organization. She issues surveys (with rating scales) to hourly production employees that measure perceptions of their supervisors' verbal aggressiveness and perceptions of their own organizational commitment. The results are then correlated to look for relationships.

Qualitative

Qualitative research is broader than quantitative research. It investigates *why* and *how* in addition to *who, what, when,* and *where* using uses interviews, focus groups, observation, and content analysis.

I/O psychologists use qualitative research to understand organizational behavior and the reasons for that behavior. Findings can rarely be applied to other situations because they are usually unique to the people in the study.

Advantage

Qualitative research can be applied to complex phenomena.

Disadvantage

Qualitative research results are often influenced by the researcher's personal bias.

Qualitative research can involve surveys with open-ended questions. In short:

- A study with a purpose and significance is proposed and defined (demographically).
- A survey is distributed.
- Findings are determined by looking for patterns in survey responses.

An example includes the following:

Jessica believes employees do not trust management. She wants to determine if employees are experiencing trust issues and, if so, the reasons for their distrust. She distributes a survey to all employees that asks them if they trust management. If their response is no, then they are asked to write about situations they have encountered that caused them to lose trust in management. Results are then analyzed for patterns that identify common areas where employees lack trust in management.

Qualitative research can involve ethnography. In short:

- A study with a purpose and significance is proposed and defined (demographically).
- Observations are made.
- Findings are determined by subjectively analyzing the observations.

An example includes the following:

Jessica believes employees in the paint department form strong interpersonal relationships with each other, and she wants to know if this can be supported. She observes these employees for two hours a week over a one-year period, and she notes the conversations they have with each other. She then analyzes those conversations to determine if the employees have strong interpersonal bonds with one another.

Now that you understand some of the basic quantitative and qualitative methodology used by I/O psychologists during research, let' move on to their specific job responsibilities.

Job responsibilities

I/O psychologists investigate *who, what, when, where, why,* and *how* of workplace behavior. They use a variety of variables to determine how organizations and the people within them function and communicate. Findings of their research are used to improve workplace situations for employers and employees.

Common job tasks for I/O psychologists include analyzing employee productivity for more efficient methods, designing interview procedures for better applicable, reviewing training documents for higher retention, and consulting with employees for improving communication.

Specific reasons I/O psychologists are hired include:

Job-fit

Job/fit is about finding the best employees for the jobs available. This involves more than simply finding the hardest working people who are motivated to perform. It means matching people to the jobs that fit their personalities and work related goals.

To determine job/fit, I/O psychologists need to understand people's personalities, their reasons for seeking jobs, and the jobs themselves. This requires research that can be time-consuming, but the results are often advantageous for an organization's hiring practices.

Testing

I/O psychologists are often hired to do testing in many different areas of the workplace. They test job applicants for their personality, leadership ability, logic, reasoning, communication skills, and reading comprehension. They also test employees for their levels of motivation, productivity, satisfaction with their jobs, trust in management, perception of communication, commitment to the organization, and management capability. They even test consumers for their perception of products, buying preferences, and behavior at the retail level.

The tests mentioned above are just some of the testing that can be done by I/O psychologists. They can get involved in every aspect of workplaces with the goal always being to make organizations more successful. In terms of testing, I/O psychologists can get very creative.

Recruiting

Leaders are always interested in recruiting the best people for their organizations. They do not want to waste time and money on employees that do not work out, and they are continually looking for new ways to prevent this from occurring.

I/O psychologists work closely with human resources to recruit the best employees. They develop job descriptions and implement testing designed to screen applicants. This is very important to organizations, and sometimes it is the major reason that they hire I/O psychologists.

Training

I/O psychologists are often involved with training employees. They assess the skills necessary to perform specific jobs, and then they design programs to teach those skills.

Interestingly, programs for employees sometimes include their managers. Those managers are taught how to motivate and help the employees being trained in order to facilitate the process. I/O psychologists work with the managers to improve their communication skills, change their supervisory techniques, and make them more supportive. This can save organizations time and money on training.

Work-life balance

Work-life balance involves accomplishing work- related goals while enjoying life outside of work. As people's lives get busier and more hectic, they are realizing the importance of work-life balance. Time is limited, and different things need to take priority at different times in life. People need to work in order to sustain a certain lifestyle...but they also need the time to enjoy that lifestyle.

I/O psychologists are heavily involved with work-life balance. They help employees find happiness at home and on the job by finding equilibrium between these two important aspects of life. They determine what makes employee content, and then they implement programs to help them attain that contentedness. This can be fairly complex because every employee is different, but the effort and time spent by I/O psychologists have taken these programs from concept to reality...and the results have been mostly positive.

Health and safety

The physical health and safety of workers are a major concern of many employers. Injured employees are expensive for organizations because productivity is lost and insurance wages must be paid.

This area is commonly known as ergonomics, and I/O psychologists are involved. Their job is to create environments where employees are safe, and their productivity is maximized. This might include frequent breaks, job rotation, or modified movement of the body. The goal is simply to keep employees working as safely and efficiently as possible.

Structure

Structure of organizations is important because it can affect profitability and the way organizations conduct business. I/O psychologists evaluate organizational structures and look for ways to improve them.

For example, employees might have too many bosses telling them what to do. This causes confusion and negatively affects job satisfaction. Another example is a quality manager reporting to a plant manager in a manufacturing plant. This means the plant manager can ignore quality issues in order to meet production quotas. The quality manager should be on the same level as the plant manager, with both individuals reporting to the owner of the company.

I/O psychologists are hired to identify structural problems in situations similar to the examples listed. They then suggest changes that make organizations more efficient and effective while positively impacting the attitude and commitment of employees.

Performance

Most organizations want their employees to perform to the best of their ability, and I/O psychologists are often assigned the task of making this happen. This involves assessing current employee productivity and suggesting methods for improvement. Many times these methods require change from everyone...not just the employees performing the work. It might seem surprising to some people, but managers need to change the way they supervise and interact with workers in order for those workers to become more productive.

Motivation

Everyone needs motivation at some point in their working career because jobs are not always as inspirational as people would like them to be. Work was never really meant to be fun...but that does not mean it has to be unpleasant or dreaded. Since motivation has been linked to productivity and job satisfaction, it is not surprising that employers want their employees to be motivated.

I/O psychologists are hired by the management of organizations to find ways to improve the motivation of their workforce. This is sometimes done by interviewing or surveying employees to find out what truly motivates them, and then implementing a plan of action that incorporates the findings.

While it can be difficult to accurately measure employee motivation, it can be assessed by measuring factors such as productivity and absenteeism before and after the findings from the surveys or interviews have been implemented. These factors indicate the effect of the changes that were made without asking employees direct questions about motivation. The thinking her is that their actions might speak louder than their words.

Diversity

Diversity means that people are unique based on their physical traits, heritage, culture, spiritual faith, personal beliefs, and social positions. While this uniqueness is not always understood, it needs to be respected and tolerated for people to work together.

In organizations, diversity is a hot topic that is increasing in importance as different kinds of people enter the workforce and organizations move into the global marketplace. I/O psychologists are charged with the responsibility of developing methods for getting employees to accept each other's differences.

Absenteeism

Absenteeism is employees' unscheduled absence from their jobs. The key word here is "unscheduled." Scheduled absences can be planned for in advance, and this helps avoid some of the potential problems that might occur during the employees' time off. However, there is very little time to plan for unscheduled absences, and the necessary resources might not be available at a moment's notice.

When absenteeism becomes excessive, it is a major headache for organizations. If employees do not show up for work, then their jobs need to be performed by other workers. If other workers are not available, then those jobs simply do not get done. This creates difficult and stressful situations for workers and managers, and it occurs far too often in some workplaces.

Since there are problems associated with absenteeism, leaders of organizations need to do whatever they can to minimize it. This starts by gaining a better understanding of the causes and effects...and I/O psychologists are assigned this task. Results are determined by simply measuring absenteeism rates before and after the changes from the research findings are implemented.

Sexual Harassment

Sexual harassment is unwelcome or unwanted sexual comments, advancement, or requests in the workplace. It can be verbal, physical, or psychological. Harassers can be male or female, and same-sex employees can harass each other.

I/O psychologists have the responsibility of preventing sexual harassment, and they typically implement the following to do so:

Training

This starts at orientation and is part of an ongoing process. It is based on psychological principles and focuses on employees and supervisors.

Other training starts as soon as an employee is hired. The goal is to immediately establish acceptable and unacceptable employee behavior. In terms of sexual harassment, orientation training makes workers aware of the rules that are in place and the fact that they are expected to follow them.

Employees must be made aware that there is no tolerance for sexual harassment. Any violations will be dealt with swiftly, and the punishment might include termination from the organization.

Employees must also be encouraged to report sexual harassment that they witness to supervisors. They need to know that their reporting will be taken seriously and kept in complete confidence.

Supervisors also need to be trained. They need to understand that part of their jobs involves keeping employees happy. Happy employees find satisfaction with their jobs, and they are less likely to sexually harass a coworker.

Hiring practices

This is the most important prevention method because, if implemented properly, it stops problem people from becoming employees.

I/O psychologists often recommend background checks on people before hiring them. These checks can find out a lot of information about individuals...including their history of sexual harassment at previous jobs.

Major checks related to sexual harassment include criminal history, employment history, and academic history. Each of these indicates past sexual harassment issues, and they also show different types of problematic behavior that might be related.

Discrimination

Discrimination occurs in organizations all over the world, and it typically involves age, gender, race/ethnicity, and religion. I/O psychologists are hired to prevent discrimination by implementing findings from research they have conducted.

Similar to sexual harassment, training is usually the best way to implement findings and reduce discrimination. Employees need training in order to develop empathy and understanding of the differences of their coworkers. This breaks down invisible barriers and encourages the collaboration that improves job performance.

Training also improves workplace integration. Employees can be taught that they need to work with coworkers who are different in order to learn, grow, and progress within the organization. This opens the door to exchanging ideas and knowledge and helps the organization achieve goals and objectives.

Teams

Teams are an important part of many organizations today. They have replaced individuals in an attempt to satisfy complex customer demands and solve internal problems. In short, teams work toward resolution of issues faster and more accurately than employees working alone.

I/O psychologists are responsible for making sure members of teams are able to work together effectively. This involves assessing employees' strengths and weaknesses to determine the best fit for each team. Teams are also studied as they progress toward problem-solving to see if improvements can be made in the future.

Now that you understand some of the job functions of I/O psychologists, it is time to move on to the next section. This section is one of the most important in this book because is discusses the benefits I/O psychologists provide to their employers.

Benefits

Organizations that hire I/O psychologist want a return for their investment. That leads to a question. What exactly are the advantages of employing I/O psychologists in workplaces? The following are some of the benefits they provide:

Recruiting and hiring

I/O psychologists improve recruiting and hiring methods. They determine which people are best for jobs and organizational cultures by collecting information about the applicants. Methodologies are data driven and provide answers to questions regarding personality, competency, and behavior. This saves management time and money in the recruiting process and allows them to hire the most capable employees for the jobs they have available.

Training and retention

Once employees are hired, they need to be trained and retained. I/O psychologists play a big role here because they define job requirements and assess training needs and objectives based on those requirements. This allows the training to be tailored to a specific job rather than the entire organization.

After the training is completed, I/O psychologists evaluate it for effectiveness, efficiency, and cost. Factors include employee retention of the material, skill proficiency, and feelings about being fed too much material in too short of a time period. Findings are applied to future training to ensure the best instruction at the lowest cost.

I/O psychologists get employees properly trained for the jobs they perform. This eliminates confusion and increases the chance that those employees will remain with their organizations for an extended period of time.

Productivity and efficiency

It's not surprising that productivity is important to organizations. In fact, most leaders put a high priority on the productivity and efficiency of employees because it relates to the survival and growth of their organizations.

I/O psychologists find ways to make workers more productive and happier with their jobs. For example, they implement job rotation programs that reduced boredom and add variety to the workday, and they also introduce job sharing to help employees find work-life balance. Both of these concepts increase productivity because people are more content at work.

In short, I/O psychologists benefit organizations in terms of productivity and efficiency because they help find ways to increase productivity while simultaneously helping employees find satisfaction with their professional and personal lives.

Physical and mental stress

Stress causes many problems for organizations. Major issues include fatigue, anxiety, irritability, and deteriorating physical health. Each of these concerns is examined below:

Fatigue

When stress is too much, it wears on employees. They look tired and feel exhausted. When they go to bed at night, they are kept awake thinking about the issues that are bothering them. In the morning, they wake up well short of refreshed and have to deal with another stressful day.

Anxiety

Excessive stress causes employees to worry about issues. They fret over what might happen or what has already occurred. Worrying is often difficult to control, and sometimes it makes absolutely no sense...like when people agonize about things that might transpire. This worrying is not justified because potential issues are not for certain, and they are beyond people's control. Heavy stress, however, brings worrying to the forefront, and it is can do a lot of unnecessary damage including the hindering of job performance.

Irritability

One of the most common negative effects of heavy stress at work involves anger and hostility. Employees are experiencing difficulties that they cannot seem to overcome, and their unpleasantness toward others is a natural side effect. This hostility can be directed at customers, suppliers, or employees...and it is rarely justified. In fact, most times this type of behavior is based solely on the fact that the person is under a lot of pressure.

Deteriorating Physical health

People under large amounts of stress at work tend to be consumed with their jobs. They spend more and more time trying to overcome obstacles as the list of unresolved issues gets longer. In essence, they are living to work, instead of working to live. This results in health issues such as weight loss, weight gain, and high blood pressure. If left unchecked, those problems can lead to much bigger concerns including malnutrition, heart disease...and possibly even death.

I/O psychologists strive to reduce stress levels in organizations. They council workers and help them work through the personal and professional problems that are causing them to experience the negative emotions that lead to the deterioration of their physical or mental health. This reduces costs to employers in terms of health care and absenteeism, and it helps employees feel better about themselves and their work.

Team building and collaboration

O/I psychologists do a very good job building teams. Using various techniques from their field, they help team members bond and work toward a common goal.

One of the major benefits I/O psychologists provide teams is motivation. They empower members to work through their problems, set goals and objectives internally, and reward the whole group rather than individual members. In this way, the team becomes an independent unit that functions with limited supervision.

I/O psychologists also use their skills to get team members to voice their true beliefs and opinions. By doing this, the team avoids groupthink.

Groupthink is a term established by psychologist Irving Janis to describe a process in which a group can make irrational decisions. In these situations, group members attempt to conform to what they believe to be the consensus of the group. The end result is the group ultimately agreeing on something that each member might normally view as unwise.

Groupthink defeats the entire purpose of teams in organizations because ideas are stymied and synergy is virtually non-existent...and I/O psychologist know how to prevent it.

Motivation and attitude

I/O psychologists understand how to meet the needs of employees...and this is important for maintaining high motivation and positive attitudes. They understand the multitude of variables involved with meeting needs including compensation, fairness, autonomy, and freedom. These variables are utilized to gain a better understanding of employee motivation and attitude in order to improve both and make the workplace better for everyone. In short, I/O psychologists understand the basic psychology of employee motivation...and this makes them beneficial in any workplace.

Conflict resolution and problem prevention

As noted earlier, not all conflict is bad...as long as the problem is attacked instead of the person. Companies that find themselves in continual dysfunctional conflict hire I/O psychologists to resolve the affected issues.

I/O psychologists are often thought of as mediators for disputes. Although partially accurate, this categorization does not paint a complete picture. Yes, these psychologists help resolve disputes by applying concepts from their field. However, they also work toward getting employees to understand and respect each other as they work through their differences.

In terms of conflict resolution, I/O psychologists are beneficial for organizations because they create double-win situations. They help resolve the conflicts that are hindering collaboration, and they also create inspirational relationships that prevent problems from reoccurring. In short, they provide a worthwhile return on management's investment.

Management effectiveness and management behavior

Virtually all organizations depend on decision-making for success. In large businesses, many different layers of management can be involved in everyday decisions. If those managers are not effective, then their employees and their businesses will suffer.

I/O psychologists help managers make more effective decisions using training techniques. This training is unique because it helps managers understand their behavior. It shows them how to properly communicate with others, give appropriate feedback to subordinates, and show empathy toward coworkers in need. This training helps managers adapt to changes in the workplace in order to meet the needs of employees and their organizations.

Management behavior is critical for the survival and growth of organizations. I/O psychologists are beneficial because they monitor and alter that behavior in order to make it as effective as possible. Their role can literally change the way organizations are managed.

Ethical concerns and legal issues

Legal issues can cost organizations a wealth of money. Even if organizations win their cases, they still have to pay court and attorney fees to defend themselves...and their bottom lines ultimately suffer.

Ethical issues might not be as financially damaging as legal battles, but they are still a major concern for organizations. Public perception is at stake, and the last thing leaders want is for their organizations to be perceived as unethical.

I/O psychologists strive to make workplaces better and employees happier. By doing this, they help prevent employees from taking legal action against their employers for being wrongly treated. Happy employees typically do not file lawsuits. Instead, they work toward the success of their organizations.

I/O psychologists also help organizations appear ethical in the public eye. Their goal is to prevent employees from working in under poor conditions, and this prevents them from spreading ill will about the organization. It also keeps workers from contacting the media for stories featuring unethical activity or behavior that will surely get the attention of the public.

Future

The future of I/O psychology is largely based on the three following factors:

Internet

As most people are well aware, the Internet has changed the way organizations conduct business. This is not going to change in the future. The internet will continually evolve, but it will not go away...and it will become even more influential for organizations all over the world.

Before the year 2000, most businesses used the newspaper or magazines to recruit employees. Times have dramatically changed with the wealth of online opportunities available to grow workforces. Technology and innovation have reduced the price of recruiting candidates who meet specified job requirements. This is good for organizations because it means they can be selective about who they hire at a fraction of what it used to cost.

The streamlining of the recruitment process has also been beneficial for I/O psychologists. These individuals now have the opportunity to create more detailed testing to determine the right candidates for jobs. Technology has changed the way organizations recruit and hire employees, and it has also opened the door for the future expansion of I/O psychology.

Globalization

Along the same lines as the Internet, globalization has also had a positive impact on the field of I/O psychology. Organizations have been forced to change policies, practices, and procedures to meet the needs of different cultures. For example, an acceptable policy in the United States might be offensive in the Middle East.

Procedural changes have created a need for I/O psychologists. Their job is to help all employees reach a level of comfort that inspires them to work to their maximum potential. Employee happiness and job satisfaction are paramount in the eyes of I/O psychologists, and this will help organizations find success and retain employees as they expand into the worldwide market.

Conceptualization

Location, location, location! This is a commonly used phrase used in real estate meaning the value of a home is largely based on the area it is located. The same idea relates to I/O psychology, but the phrase is different. The future of I/O psychology will be largely based on conceptualization, conceptualization, conceptualization! In other words, new concepts introduced by the people in this field will determine its future.

I/O psychologists are aware that their concepts will need to change and evolve as organizations move forward with new ideas, products, and services. They are continually thinking of better ways to help organizations, and those thoughts are helping to prepare them for the future.

The field of I/O psychology has already weathered a storm in terms of acceptance...and it is ready for the next challenge.

Summary

I/O psychologists are employed in organizations all over the world. They use principles and practices from their field to conduct the research required to improve workforces in terms of attitude and productivity. Their goal is to help employees find motivation and job satisfaction as their organizations grow, change, and evolve.

This book focuses on the basic skills, knowledge, methodology, responsibilities, and benefits of I/O psychologists. It also examines their future potential as the field continues to grow and expand. The text is informational and educational, and it is written for easy reader understanding at all levels.

Congratulations! You now understand more about industrial/organizational psychologists. These individuals devote their careers to making workplaces better, and they are very important for the study of organizational behavior.

Organizational Design and Structure

Describing and Exemplifying

Louis Bevoc

Published by
NutriNiche System LLC

Louis Bevoc books...simple explanations of complex subjects

Introduction

Organization design and structure define workplace culture. They work together to define management style, establish the working environment, and accomplish the goals and objectives of the organization. They also make sure that work related tasks are completed in an accurate and timely manner.

While design and structure intertwine to create culture, they do have some differences. These differences are as follows:

Organizational design

Design involves management choices that integrate people and processes to accomplish organizational goals and objectives. It is the management style used to support the organizational structure.

Organizational structure

Structure defines the formal authority in an organization, as well as the roles that employees assume. It focuses on the systems in place to create a working environment.

Organizations can be structured in a variety of ways depending on established goals and objectives. This structure is important because it provides a roadmap of how the organization operates as a whole. It also defines the roles and responsibilities of people and departments, and it indicates decision-making power and processes.

In order to be effective, organizational structure depends on three major factors. These are:

Management

Management must properly position employees to accomplish work related tasks.

Employees

Employees must have the necessary skills to accomplish work related tasks.

Processes and procedures

Processes and procedures must create positive workflow to accomplish work related tasks.

As noted earlier, organizational design supports organizational structure. That design is established using certain components of the organization, and the next section will show how this is done.

Design determination

Design is the management style used to support organizational structure. However, questions about the design need to be answered before it can be determined. These questions stem from the following:

Division of jobs

This is where work in the organization is divided into separate jobs. Essentially, all work can be broken down into procedural steps, and those steps are completed by individual employees. The idea here is that employees specialize in doing part of the work, rather than all of it.

This means that employees will have different skills for the jobs they perform. Management directs employees to use their skills in designated areas, and the organization becomes more efficient. For example, an automotive assembly line has many separate jobs. There is a different employee for every step of the process until the finished product is completed. This is much more efficient than having every employee assemble a car by themselves. Additionally, the cost for specialized employee training at one step of the process is much less than the cost of training an employee to build an entire car.

Division of departments

After jobs have been divided, they need to be grouped into departments so they can be coordinated. This is typically done using one of the following three major categories:

Product

In this category, departments are determined based on products. For example, a grocery store might have the following departments:

> Meat – sausage, hamburger, steak, and ham
> Dairy – yogurt, milk, ice cream, and cheese
> Bakery – bagels, bread, donuts, and pastries

Service

In this category, departments are determined based on services. For example, an outdoor maintenance company might have the following departments:

> Lawn care – mowing, edging, weeding, and fertilizing grass
> Pest control – Bird, rodent, bug, and insect control
> Landscaping – Trees, bushes, shrubs, and other outdoor decor

Function

In this category, departments are determined based on functions. For example, a stamping plant might have the following departments:

> Quality assurance – product quality and specification monitoring

Human resources – personnel and benefits administration
Accounting – bookkeeping and financial transactions

Division of authority

After departments have been created, authority over those departments needs to be established. This is typically done using a chain of command with specific authority for each manager in the chain. This streamlines productivity and prevents the confusion that results when employees report to multiple bosses.

Two major factors that need to be taken into account when establishing division of authority are:

Levels of management

Organizations need to determine the ratio of managers to employees. Higher ratios mean more levels of management, and lower levels mean fewer levels of management. Often times, levels of management are based on the skills of the employees. Highly skilled employees typically need less supervision, and this means the organization has fewer management levels. Conversely, employees with low skills often need closer supervision, so there are more management levels in these organizations.

Centralized vs. decentralized decision-making

In centralized organizations, upper management makes all of the decisions. Lower level managers simply make sure the decisions are implemented. An example of centralized management is the military during a war. Generals make decisions, and those decisions are carried out by lower ranking staff.

An advantage of centralized decision-making over decentralized decision-making is there is more assurance that the directives of top management will be implemented. Think about the Catholic Church. The Pope makes decisions that are very likely to be carried out by lower ranking members of the organization.

Decentralized organizations give power to managers at the lower levels. An example is a sports team. The coach is the lowest level of management, but he or she is closest to the action and has the authority to make changes on the spot.

An advantage of decentralized decision-making over centralized decision-making is reaction time to problems is much quicker. Think about Alcoholics Anonymous. Each chapter or division is run by local members with no formal direction from a higher level of management. Ideals and goals are present, but they are organized and carried out at the lowest levels.

Now you understand how organizational structures are designed. In the next section, we will examine some of the more common design types.

Design types

It would very be difficult to describe every type of organizational design in the world. However, there are common organizational designs that can be discussed for a better understanding. Please consider the following design types:

Simple structure

A simple structure has limited departments, limited levels of management, and centralized decision-making. This structure is flexible and cost effective, and management responsibilities are typically laid out well.

In many small businesses, there is only one level of management. That level contains one person...the owner. The owner acts as the centralized decision maker for every aspect of the business, and he or she also performs a variety of other job functions when necessary. Below are some strengths and weaknesses of a simple structure:

Strengths

This type of organizational design works well for small businesses when the owner understands the need of the organization. He or she knows what is best for the business, and that allows him or her to make the right choices. Additionally, employees do not question business decisions because they come from the top of the organization. Finally, there is limited miscommunication because decisions do not have to be filtered through multi-levels of management. Fewer levels of management also allow for faster implementation of ideas and concepts.

Organizational example

Jack founded a small appliance store 12 years ago, and he is actively involved in the business. He makes all major business decisions and runs every aspect of the company. He has survived hard times and economic downturns because he understands his business well.

Jack employs six people at his store. One person answers phones and runs the office, one rotates stock, and the other three are salespeople. Essentially, there is only one level of management (supervision - Jack). The other employees are simply workers.

All six employees communicate with Jack on a daily basis so mistakes and misunderstandings are rare. They also respect the business decisions he makes based on his knowledge and experience.

Jacks designed his business to be a simple structure, and this has worked well for him for many years.

Weaknesses

One problem is with simple structures is the organization can be in big trouble if the only decision maker gets sick, retires, or dies. No one else is capable of making decisions, and this puts the organization in limbo.

Another problem is that some decision makers have difficulty delegating authority as the organization grows. There comes a point when one person simply cannot make every decision, and others are not capable or do not have the authority to do so.

Finally, a few poor decisions by one individual can jeopardize the well-being of the company and its employees. Everyone makes mistakes, but a major decision maker's choices are critical and rarely challenged...and this can be devastating.

Organizational example

Martha owns a small electrical distribution company. She understands the electrical business well, and she makes every major decision that affects the company.

Over the past year, Martha's company has experienced rapid growth. She picked up three major accounts, and the companies' sales have more than tripled. Based on this increase in volume, Martha has had to expand her workforce from eight employees to 26.

The sales expansion experienced by the electrical distribution company is good for business, but it has also caused some problems. Martha is more involved with sales than she ever was in the past, and she no longer has the proper time to manage the day-to-day operations. Combine this with the fact that her workforce has more than tripled, and the business is simply too much for her to handle. Other employees are capable of making decisions, but Martha is unwilling to delegate authority to them, and she will not listen to anyone who tells her to relinquish some of her power.

Martha's inability to delegate authority is causing the business to suffer. She needs to change the design of the business from a simple structure to something a bit more complex, but she does not want to do this and will not listen to anyone who advises her to do so.

Matrix structure

Employees often need to work together in order to complete projects, and sometimes this requires two bosses. A matrix allows employees to have a product manager and a functional department manager (a dual chain of command). This is often implemented in organizations that need to share information between departments in order to resolve problems.

Matrix structures work well in certain organizations, but they not as common as a simple structure or bureaucracy. Organizations need to weigh the advantages and disadvantages of design type before making a decision to implement it. Below are some strengths and weaknesses of a matrix structure:

Strengths

A matrix works well for large organizations with complex interdependent activities...such as universities or government agencies. Communication can be greatly improved and people are able to receive information faster due to structural flexibility. This leads to faster decision-making and problem resolution, and it results in improved productivity and better customer satisfaction

Organizational example

Jane works as a designer for a home remodeling company. Her newest responsibility is to design quality kitchen cabinets out of plastic that resembles wood. The plastic is much less expensive and durable than wood, but it looks "cheap" or "tacky" in some kitchens.

For this project, Jane needs to answer to two different bosses   She answers to the manager of the accounting department to a assure costs are where they need to be, and she answers to the marketing director to make sure customers will like the design.

The structural arrangement Jane is working under works well because she receives immediate feedback from important people about her cabinet design. The project gets completed in less than one week, and it meets quality and cost specifications. In this case, a matrix structure worked well for Jane and the home remodeler.

Weaknesses

The problem with a matrix is it creates stress and uncertainty since people are not always sure whom they report to in the organization. This can create confusion and establish warring factions in the midst of power struggles. The confusion can result in frustrated employees and high turnover rates.

Matrix structures often do not work well in assembly or production environments. Production jobs are very predictable, and the employees perform best when they answer to one boss who gives them the direction needed to accomplish work related tasks.

When thinking about a matrix, it must be remembered that improper implementation can have a negative effect on employee motivation and morale due to the lack of structure. This is rather ironic because the goal of a matrix is to provide structure and make it easier to achieve organizational goals.

Organizational example

Rafael works in sales for a Safeco, an organization that sells safety equipment to companies that handle dangerous chemicals.

Safeco has recently developed a face shield that is virtually indestructible. It will not break or melt under even the most severe conditions, and it is of substantial value to some of their customers.

Rafael wants to sell the face shield, but in order to do so, he needs to answer to two different bosses. The sales manager Peggy wants to get the product out in the field, and she tells Rafael to offer it below cost to get it moving. The COO Timothy wants the item to be highly profitable, and he tells Rafael to sell it at a 30 percent markup.

The discrepancy between Peggy and Timothy causes confusion for Rafael because he is not sure what price the face shield should be offered to customers. Worse yet, Peggy and Timothy are fighting at the office about who has the authority to establish pricing.

One week later, there is no resolution to the problem. Timothy and Peggy are still arguing, and no price has been established. Rafael becomes discouraged and begins to look for new employment. In this case, the matrix structure caused confusion and fighting, and it did not work well for Rafael or Safeco.

Bureaucratic structure

Organizations with bureaucratic structures are typically very inflexible. They have written rules and regulations in place that are upheld by the employees exactly as defined. Clearly established hierarchies, centralized decision-making, and divisions of labor are present at all times. As might be expected, standardized processes and procedures are the norm.

It takes monumental time and effort to change bureaucracies due to the rules involved and the strict chain-of-command protocol. Because of this, people often cringe at the thought of dealing with a bureaucracy in order to implement something new...and city government is a good example. People who want cities to change often face a mountain of a task. This is why the phrase "you can't change city hall" has become so well known.

Below are some strengths and weaknesses of a bureaucratic structure:

Strengths

Bureaucracies have some advantages over other structures. They are very efficient at performing standardized actions. Activities are performed following the same protocol every time, and this allows employees to become very good at their jobs while adhering to safety and quality standards. Additionally, rigid rules and regulations allow less competent lower level managers to be part of the workforce because there is little need for them to make important decisions.

Bureaucratic structures are very important for many United States governmental agencies. They need well-documented rules and regulation in place to make sure the law is being adhered to in the proper manner. Bureaucracies also add assurance that all people are being treated equally, and this is important for democracy.

Organizational example

Jonathon is a firefighter at a fire department operated by a large metropolitan city. The department has strict procedures in place for every fire to avoid chaos and provide safety for the firefighters.

One of the procedures states that firefighters are not allowed to enter buildings that are on fire because the structures could collapse due to the heat and damage. During a recent warehouse fire, Jonathon started to go inside to yell for any people that might be trapped. His boss immediately stopped him because this action does not comply with standard procedures. Three minutes after Jonathon's boss prevented him from entering the building, it collapsed. If Jonathon had gone inside, he likely would have been killed.

In this particular case, the bureaucratic structure in place was successful because a specific protocol was followed. Jonathon was not allowed to deviate from the procedure for safety reasons, and this likely ended up saving his life.

Weaknesses

Disadvantages to bureaucratic structures include (1) they are slow to react to problems and (2) they are difficult to change. Along the same lines, employees within these organizations are fixated on following the rules exactly. They do not deviate from standard procedures, and anything that does not adhere to established regulations is rejected or put on hold. Common sense rarely comes into play because employees do not like to leave their comfort zones.

A bureaucratic structure does not work for creative organizations. A technology based company, for example, would falter under bureaucracy because it would defeat the organization's entire purpose of being innovative.

Organizational example

Michelle works for the United States Department of Agriculture (USDA) as a Consumer Safety Inspector. Her job is to police meat and poultry processing establishments to assure that they are conforming to USDA regulatory standards.

One of the standards in the USDA regulations states that production floors "must be maintained in a sanitary manner and free of debris in order to prevent food safety hazards." Michelle walks into a 100,000 square foot meat processing plant and finds one hairnet on the floor by one of the doors leading into a production area. She documents non-compliance for this hairnet stating that the floor is not free of debris, and therefore not maintained in a sanitary manner.

Michelle's non-compliance infuriates the plant manager. He argues that the floor is spotless except for this one hairnet, and this does not create an unsanitary condition nor does it present any type of food safety hazard. Michelle will not listen to the plant manager's complaint. She follows the rules exactly and does not allow any room for deviation.

In this particular case, the bureaucracy failed. One hairnet on a 100,000 square foot floor does not make it unsanitary, nor does it present any type of food safety hazard. Michelle refused to use common sense because this would have taken her out of her comfort zone by requiring her to deviate from standard procedures. The end result was a documented non-compliance for no legitimate reason.

Virtual structure

Virtually structured organizations are fairly unique. Employees do not share office space, communication is electronic or phone based, and knowledge is much more important than physical assets. Online dating services and auction houses are examples of organizations that can be virtually structured.

Some of the more interesting characteristics of virtual structures include:

Outsourcing

This is by no means a new concept, but virtual organizations typically outsource most of their work. This makes them much more efficient because specialists can be brought in on an "as needed" basis.

Departments

Virtual organizations generally have no need for departments because most jobs are outsourced and do not need to be coordinated. This limits miscommunication and allows for faster decision-making.

Decision-making

Decision-making in virtual organizations is highly centralized. One person often makes the decisions for the entire organization, and that one person might be the only level of management.

Change

Virtual organizations are very open to change and constantly evolving. This is because they are typically small in size with limited levels of management.

Longevity

Virtual organizations are often assembled for the short term. They cease to exist as soon as a project as finished. This is relatively easy to do since they outsource much of their work and employ few employees. An example includes an organization set up to raise money for the medical needs of a sick child.

In short, virtual organizations are essentially the opposite of bureaucracies. They are very flexible with few rules and regulations. They also need competent employees for management positions because important decisions need to be made.

Below are some strengths and weaknesses of a virtual structure:

Strengths

One advantage of a virtual organization is cost savings. Time and travel expenses are reduced or eliminated since people can communicate from anywhere in the world. This benefits employees in terms of work-life balance, and it also positively impacts the organization's bottom line.

Another advantage involves hiring. There are essentially no geographical boundaries when hiring employees, so the best people can be brought on board. An example includes a virtual college that wants to hire all doctoral-level professors as faculty. They have the entire world to choose from for the selection process. Conversely, a traditional university might only be able to hire doctoral candidates within a 50-mile radius of the campus...and this is much more restricting.

Organizational example

Donna works as a website designer for a company located in Arizona. She lives in Texas and is able to complete work with customers all over the world without ever leaving her house. Lately, she has been doing work for several companies located in Brazil, and they are very happy with her service and performance. When she completes a job for one company, they recommend her to another Brazilian firm.

In Donna's situation, a virtual structure works well. She does not need to be physically present at her company's office, and she is able to work from home with customers all over the world. This provides her with good work-life balance, and the organization saves on travel expenses.

Weaknesses

One disadvantage of a virtual organization involves communication since it is mostly done through writing (some phone conversations, but writing is more the norm). The written word (email, text, or letter) works well in many situations, but it can also be easily misinterpreted. Most people who have worked with email understand this dilemma, and they realize that some communication requires face-to-face human interaction. Non-verbal communication, body language, and paralanguage (voice quality, tempo, loudness, and vocal features) are all important for relaying the meaning of messages, and face-to-face contact generally is needed for achieving the full effect. If face-to-face communication is not possible, then employees can lose the ability to effectively communicate. Time is also wasted as people work towards understanding the messages being sent.

Another disadvantage to virtual structures involves hours of work. Employees live in different time zones all over the world, and this makes it difficult to hold meetings or discuss issues "live" online. Meetings might need to be held at 2:00 am for some people, and they simply are not at their best when they should be sleeping. Email can be used for employees to answer questions at their convenience, but this slows response time and hinders productivity.

Organizational example

Marcus is employed at a computer software company as a troubleshooter for computer systems. His job affords him the luxury of working full time out of his home office. For the most part, this works out very well for Marcus. However, it is challenging when he is assigned to a team project.

Currently, Marcus is on a team project with three other employees who physically work at the office. They email back and forth to exchange ideas and information, but sometimes it is hard to understand the true meaning of the messages being sent. For example, Marcus sent out an email with some mild sarcasm that was intended to be humorous and harmless, but one of the team members was offended by it. This created unnecessary stress in the group, and productivity came to a halt until it was resolved with a series of other emails.

Eventually, the team was able to achieve the objectives established by management, but the time needed for completion was twice as much as originally anticipated due to miscommunication. This led management to decide that Marcus will no longer be placed on any teams as long as he works remotely.

The decision to avoid placing Marcus on teams negatively impacts the computer software company because they lose the benefit of his problem-solving knowledge. In this particular situation, the virtual structure was not good for the organization.

Now you understand the common types of designs that make up organizational structures. Let's move forward and discuss the reasons designs differ.

Design differences

Why aren't all organizational designs the same? What causes them to differ? These are both good questions, and the following factors provide some insight into the answers:

Strategy

Organizational goals and objectives drive strategies, so it's not surprising that strategies influence design.

Some organizations' strategies revolve around performing basic functions, such as accounting or engineering. Employees, such as accountants and engineers, have specialized expertise in specific areas. In these situations, division of departments is important for the design so employees can focus on specific job functions. The departments are then coordinated by management to accomplish the overall objectives of the organization.

Other organizations' strategies revolve around customer service. Restaurants and hospitals are good examples. These companies sell consumers products or services, and their designs are based on customer needs. Departments are also needed here, but they are based on products or services.

Last, but not least, some organizations' strategies are based on innovation. Web design companies and advertising agencies are good examples. In this case, they need a design that favors flexibility and decentralized decision-making. Bureaucratic designs do not work well here because they are far too rigid.

In short, strategies are formulated based on the goals and objectives of the organization. When goals and objectives change, so do strategies. When strategies change, they influence the design that makes up the structure.

Size

The size of an organization also impacts design. Large organizations are different than small ones in terms of division of authority (more levels of management), division of departments (more departments), and division of jobs (more specialized skills). They also differ in terms of goals and objectives.

The most interesting point about size is that it affects design less as organizations grow. Think about it...adding 50 employees to a company with 50 employees has a huge impact on design, but adding 50 employees to a company with 500 employees has much less of an impact.

Age

As organizations mature, they typically become more standardized, specialized, and rule oriented. This changes the goals and objectives of the organization, and those changes affect organizational design.

Technology

Technology includes the knowledge, procedures, and resources needed to produce a product or service. Essentially, this encompasses everything involved during the conversion of inputs to outputs. As technology changes, so does the organization's design.

Environment

Environment impacts decision-making. In difficult times, decision-making can change...and this influences the design of the organization.

Summary

Workplace culture is determined by organizational design and structure. These two concepts work together to accomplish the goals and objectives of the organization. Along the way, they define management style, establish the working environment, and make sure that work related tasks are completed in an accurate and timely manner.

This book focuses on organizational design and organizational structure. First, the difference between the two concepts is defined. Next determination of design is discussed. Then common design types are explained. Finally, factors that affect design differences are explored.

Congratulations! You now understand organizational design and structure...two very important aspects of organizational behavior.

Diversity in Organizations
Understanding and Improving

Louis Bevoc

Published by
NutriNiche System LLC

Louis Bevoc books...simple explanations of complex subjects

Introduction

First, diversity needs to be described. It essentially means that people are unique based on their physical traits, heritage, culture, spiritual faith, personal beliefs, and social positions. While this uniqueness is not always understood, it needs to be respected and tolerated for people to live, work, and interact together in a functional society.

In organizations, diversity is a hot topic that is increasing in importance as different kinds of people enter the workforce and organizations move into the global marketplace. Gone are the days when married White Anglo-Saxon Protestant (WASP) men ran businesses while women and minorities were steered away from higher positions in the workplace. Also gone is the thinking that disabilities and sexual preferences need to be hidden, older people are of little value despite their knowledge, and only people with money are important. While the working world is far from perfect, it has come a long way in the past 50 years.

This book examines four major types of diversity in workplaces, highlights the benefits, discusses the challenges, and offers ways to improve those challenges. The types discussed are age diversity, gender diversity, race/ethnic diversity, and religious diversity. Workplace examples are used throughout the text for better understanding.

Let's move forward with analyzing, discussing, and exemplifying different types of diversity in organizations.

Age Diversity

Age diversity is unique because every person in the organization falls into this category. Employees might not look the same, act the same, think the same, possess the same amount of money or education, or belong to the same race, culture, or religion...but they all fall somewhere on the age spectrum. The number of years separating their age creates the diversity factor.

Many organizations employ multiple generations of people. These people grew up in different time periods and did not encounter the same life experiences. That being said, they do not always share similar viewpoints.

Age diversity also affects workplace communication. Technology largely impacts the way employees interact and solve problems, but traditional methods still have value in many situations. When different ages of people work together, they shape the workplace as it moves forward.

Please consider the following concerning age diversity in organizations:

Benefits

Dissimilar viewpoints are good for organizations because they promote discussion that challenges the status quo. If employees do not question the status quo, then the organization can become stagnant with little or no growth. Younger people are assets to organizations because they challenge current methods and encourage change, while older people's knowledge and experience rationalize whether or not that change will be for the better.

Technology sparks change in virtually every organization. It makes communication faster and easier, but it can also distort the intent of the message. Workplace age differentials help determine the best ways to communicate based on individual understanding of the situation.

Organizational example

Heather and Leroy work for an engineering design firm. Leroy has been with the company for over 25 years, and Heather started working there two years ago after she graduated from college.

These two employees are working on a project, and they have some design ideas they want to present to the customer. In the past, designs ideas were always hand delivered to customers, but Heather thinks this is an outdated way of doing business. She believes a power point presentation should be made with a link for the customer to click on to access the ideas. Leroy disagrees and believes the designs should be hand delivered to avoid the misunderstanding that can occur when nobody is present for added explanation.

After some debate, Heather and Leroy agree to develop a power point presentation. However, they will deliver that presentation in-person at the customer's business in order to maintain an interpersonal relationship.

In short, Heather and Leroy had dissimilar viewpoints. Heather challenged the status quo by suggesting new technology, and this changed the way business was done. However, Leroy understood the importance of interpersonal relationships, so face-to-face contact was also maintained.

Challenges

Dissimilar viewpoints are good for generating discussion, but they also produce conflicts where people focus on position instead of principle. This can lead to arguments between people of different ages that are sometimes difficult to resolve.

In terms of technology, some older people do not want to change simply because it takes them out of their comfort zone. Along the same lines, younger employees sometimes want to change just because the technology is new.

The example involving Heather and Leroy resulted in a solution that was beneficial to the employees, customer, and organization. However, not all workplace disagreements go this well...as we will see in the following example.

Organizational example

Fernando and Eileen are attorneys at a law firm. Fernando is a 25-year old recent law school graduate, and Eileen has been a lawyer for almost 30 years.

These two attorneys are working with a client who is suing her former employer for sexual harassment. They have some video clips from workplace cameras that they want to share with the client, and Eileen wants to hand deliver them as she has done many times in the past. Fernando thinks the personal delivery is inefficient and believes the files should be uploaded to a cloud storage site where anyone can view them. Eileen disagrees because she thinks it is better to visit the client in person to show more interest in the case. She does not see any value in the technology suggested by Fernando.

An argument between Eileen and Fernando ensues, and it starts to get heated. Fernando tells Eileen that she is a "dinosaur" who in incompetent when it comes to technology. Eileen becomes angry and tells Fernando that he has no idea how to handle clients and should not have been hired by the law firm. Both attorneys leave the room upset with each other, and they tell the partners of the firm that they cannot work together on future cases.

In short, Eileen and Fernando had dissimilar viewpoints. Fernando challenged the status quo by suggesting new technology, but ended up insulting Eileen when she did not agree with his idea. Eileen did not want to change the way she traditionally conducted business, became defensive, and insulted Fernando. Both attorneys left the room upset and decided that they could work with each other again.

Improving

In the law firm example, the problem between Eileen and Fernando could have been avoided if they each took the time to clarify the benefits and worked toward some type of compromise. Fernando should have indicated the simplicity of uploading a file to a cloud, the time savings involved, and the fact that many people prefer information being transferred electronically. Eileen should have explained in more detail that people appreciate personal visits, and she should have added the fact that electronic often communication needs to be clarified because it is misunderstood.

Additionally, both attorneys should have avoided any type of personal attacks. This did absolutely nothing to resolve the conflict, and it caused damage in their working relationship that might not be repairable. Personal insults are non-productive, and they lead to a negative workplace environment for everyone. This prevents organizations from attaining goals and objectives, and it causes people to look elsewhere for employment. Eileen and Fernando should have attacked the problem instead of the other person, and they should have avoided verbally aggressive language.

If Eileen and Fernando had clarified the benefits of their ideas, worked toward a compromise, and avoided person insults, they could have found a successful solution similar to the one reached by Heather and Leroy.

In summary, age diversity occurs in every organization with employees. It is beneficial in many ways, but it also faces challenges. The best way to overcome these challenges is to take the time to explain the thinking behind ideas or changes and avoid any type of verbally aggressive language in the process.

Gender Diversity

Traditionally, the term gender has referred to men and women. However, this has recently changed to add a third category known as transgender. For the sake of simplicity, this section will only focus on males and females.

In organizations, gender diversity refers to the representation of male and female employees in the workplace. Up until the 1960s, jobs were classified for men and women. The positions available to women were limited, and higher level management jobs were designated for men only. Times have changed since then, and the government is now involved in preventing gender bias in organizations.

Male and female employees work together to accomplish tasks and achieve organizational goals, but they have different perceptions about the jobs they perform and are not always treated equally. These factors raise questions about the importance of work/life balance and gender equality, and they complicate many workplaces since there is no "one size fits all" answer.

Please consider the following concerning gender diversity in organizations:

Benefits

Gender perceptions of jobs differ, and this is good for the organization. Different ideas lead to better problem solving and prevent gender specific thinking. Quite simply, men and women have different job skills, product knowledge, and personal experience that inspires creativity and helps accomplish organizational objectives.

Gender diverse workplaces are also an asset for sales and marketing because customer bases are more diverse today than they ever were in the past. Add to that the fact that half of the potential employees are male and the other half are female...and it's rather obvious that organizations cannot disregard either gender if they want to hire the best people and be competitive with their products and services.

Based on the above arguments, gender diversity should be an important aspect of every organization's growth strategy. However, it is sometimes merely treated as a shift in personnel designed to meet government regulations.

Organizational example

Nikki and Veronica are female chemical engineers at an oil refinery. They are both very competent employees, and part of their job involves traveling with sales people to provide technical support to customers.

Nikki and Veronica are welcome at the businesses they call on because they are knowledgeable about their company's products and services, and they are genuinely concerned about the well-being of the customer's employees on a personal and professional level. Additionally, some of the customers have female purchasing agents who enjoy dealing with women due to the things they have in common and the bond they establish.

Nikki and Veronica are top-notch engineers who understand their products and customers. Upper management at the oil refinery understands the importance of these two women and realizes that diversity helps the organization grow and positivity affects the bottom line.

Challenges

One of the major issues with gender diversity is that CEOs typically do not get personally involved with its implementation and maintenance. They tend to delegate this task to specialized committees or teams so they can focus on other "more important" tasks. When this happens, the significance of gender diversity is reduced, and it gets placed on the organizational "back burner."

Another challenge is the fact that, regardless of the advancements that have been made, a "glass ceiling" still sometimes exists for females...and even for some males. Glass ceilings prevent organizations from reaching their full potential because new ideas, thoughts, and concepts are stifled.

Organizational example

Shelia is an executive at a hazardous waste removal company. She has been promoted three times during her 17-year career, and she is now being recommended for the CEO position by the CEO after he retires next month.

The board of directors realizes Sheila has done a great job for the organization. She has been in charge of several successful projects, and her cost savings track record is one of the best in the company. However, men have always been in the top position of this company, and the board believes a male is necessary for this job because the hazardous waste industry is very male dominated. Based on this thinking, they promote a male executive to the CEO position.

The man promoted to the position is a very competent manager, but he does not have the cost savings background that Sheila possesses. This is a problem for the company because one of their major goals is to reduce costs by 15 percent over the next three years.

In short, Sheila does not get the CEO position due to the board of directors' thinking that the job should be filled by a man. This "glass ceiling" also prevents the organization from being its best in terms of cost cutting because Sheila was the most qualified person for achieving that goal.

Improving

In the hazardous waste removal company example, the current CEO should have been involved in the decision-making process. He knew Sheila was the right person for the position, and that is why he recommended her. However, Instead of staying actively involved in the selection process, he left the decision up to the board of directors.

The glass ceiling also held Sheila back. The board of directors thought that the position was best suited for a man, and this sealed Sheila's fate...regardless of her qualifications. Again, involvement of the current CEO could have made a difference. He could have prevented the glass ceiling by questioning the decisions of the board members and forcing them to focus on qualifications instead of gender.

In summary, gender diversity is the equal distribution of males and females in a workplace. This balance benefits the overall health of the organization by generating new insight and ideas that positively affect the bottom line. Gender diversity also faces challenges in the form of glass ceilings and limited involvement from top decision makers. The best way to overcome these challenges is for CEOs to be part of the implementation and maintenance of solid gender diversity programs.

Racial/Ethnic Diversity

This type of diversity is based on people and their linkages. These people include Asians, Blacks, Latinos (Hispanics), Native Americans, and Whites who are associated with their skin color, ancestry, culture, or nationality.

In organizations, racial/ethnic diversity refers to the representation of the groups mentioned above in the workplace. Similar to gender diversity, many of the best jobs in the past were only available to white people, and minorities were forced to take lower paying positions. Once again, the government stepped in and now monitors workplaces to prevent racial/ethnic bias in organizations.

Today, people of all different colors and backgrounds work together every day in many organizations across the United States. They strive to accomplish the same objectives, but their ethnic and racial differences play a role in their perception of the workplace and the way they are treated by management. These variances lead to major debates on best business practices, and there is no universal solution.

Please consider the following concerning racial/ethnic diversity in organizations:

Benefits

Teams benefit the most from racial/ethnic diversity in organizations. The combined skills, knowledge, and cultural understanding of members creates synergy that cannot be found in homogeneous teams. Differing viewpoints contribute to overall effectiveness and improve decision-making, and this works well for complex projects that involve innovative thinking.

Racial/ethnic diversity in organizations also helps employees gain a better understanding of each other's roles in the workplace. Subconscious barriers of cultural judgment and racial intolerance are broken down as employees become more empathetic towards their coworkers.

Organizational example

Dhar and Jamie work for an international trading company that exports goods to Europe. Dhar immigrated to the United States from India, and he practices Hinduism. Jamie has been a US citizen her entire life, and she is not a member of any organized religion.

Over the past year, Dhar and Jamie have worked together on several different projects. In the beginning, Jamie would establish a position during the decision-making process and defend it vigorously. If anyone disagreed with her ideas, she would argue with them until they sided with her or the problem was resolved by someone in higher management. Dhar, on the other hand, has always followed the Hindu thinking that he must appreciate his adversary's point of view because there is no absolute truth. There are multiple solutions to the same problem, and more than one person can be right.

Dhar's behavior establishes great respect for him from other team members, and this is impressive to Jamie. After observing his actions for a while, Jamie begins to change her ways. She starts to listen to other team members' viewpoints, and this leads her to accept ideas and thinking that is different from her own.

Jamie's behavioral change greatly improves the problem-solving ability of the team. Her acceptance of other members' thoughts and ideas creates an environment of innovative thinking, and it is due to the actions of an employee from a different culture.

Challenges

One challenge associated with racial/ethnic diversity involves communication. Employees from different cultures or nationalities do not always understand each other, and this can lead to confusion and ineffective job performance.

Another issue with racial/ethnic diversity involves integration. Employees from different races or ancestries often form social groups in the workplace. These divisions develop naturally and prevent employees from leaving their comfort zones. Consequently, the cross-cultural exchange of knowledge and information is hindered because coworker relationships are limited to those with the same racial or ethnic classification.

Organizational example

D'Andre and Juan are production workers at a food processing plant. D'Andre is a Black male, and Juan is a Hispanic male. They are both good employees and have worked their way up to line leaders in the same department.

During company breaks, D'Andre sits at a table with all Black employees, and Juan sits at a different table with all Hispanic employees. This makes the breaks more enjoyable for each man due to commonality factors, but they never converse with each other or discuss ways to make their jobs easier, better, or more efficient.

Essentially, the cultural differences between D'Andre and Juan prevent them from leaving their comfort zones and exchanging knowledge. This hinders the growth of both employees and the food processor.

Improving

Training is the best way to improve racial/ethnic diversity in an organization. This might seem cliché, but it works.

In terms of communication, employees need training in order to develop empathy and understanding of the differences of their coworkers. This breaks down invisible barriers and encourages collaboration that improves job performance.

Training also improves workplace integration. Employees can be taught that they need to work with coworkers who are different in order to learn, grow, and progress within the organization. This opens the door to exchanging ideas and knowledge and helps the organization achieve goals and objectives.

If D'Andre and Juan undergo some type of training, then they will learn to leave their comfort zones and discuss workplace happenings with each other. This will benefit them and the organization as they share ideas and learn more about their jobs.

In summary, racial/ethnic diversity in organizations involves Asians, Blacks, Latinos (Hispanics), Native Americans, and Whites who are linked together by physical characteristics, nationality, and culture. This type of diversity is beneficial because it promotes unique and innovative thinking, but it also divides employees and keeps them from leaving their comfort zones. Training is the best method to overcome the challenges involved with racial/ethnic diversity because it teaches people how to interact, transfer information, and learn more about the work they perform.

Religious Diversity

This type of diversity is based on people's religious affiliations. Examples include Christianity, Islam, Judaism, and Buddhism...but this is by no means an exhaustive list, and sub-religions fall within each major category. A conservative estimate is that there are more than 1000 religious denominations in the United States.

In organizations, religious diversity refers to the variety of religions found in the workplace. This diversity might seem insignificant at first glance, but it actually drives change in the workforce...especially as companies compete in the global marketplace and employ people from different cultures all over the world.

Another reason religion has entered the workplace is that faith and spirituality are no longer restricted to employees' private lives. They take their religion to work with them, express it freely, and even let it define them as people. In fact, some people consider religion to be the most important aspect of their lives and would not work at an organization that does not respect their spirituality. This is in sharp contrast to the not-so-distant past when religion had no place in corporate America.

In short, employees with many different religious beliefs work together every day to accomplish objectives established by their organizations. Their spirituality affects their perception of the workplace and the way they are perceived by others. These variances lead to disagreements about best business practices regarding faith, and so far there has not been a perfect resolution to the problem.

Please consider the following concerning religious diversity in organizations:

Benefits

Religious diversity allows employees to express their freedom in the workplace. Their spiritual beliefs cannot be controlled, and this is particularly satisfying in a place where performance is measured and activities are monitored on a regular basis.

Religious diversity also promotes peace in organizations. Religion is very important to some employees, and they become upset is their spiritual faith is disrespected. This can lead to workplace conflicts and disruption that hinder productivity. Tolerance and acceptance of religious diversity reduce hostility and conflict because people feel respected.

Most importantly, religious diversity in organizations promotes trust in management. This trust leads to increased morale and retention of valuable personnel. Additionally, employees who trust leadership will work harder to achieve the objectives established by the organization, and this positively impacts the bottom line.

Organizational example

Haleema works as a cashier at a grocery store. She is Muslim and wears a facial scarf as part of her religion. The owner of the grocery store respects Haleema's religious beliefs and encourages her to wear the scarf as she services customers.

The owner's respect motivates Haleema to work hard every day. She truly believes that the grocery store is a good organization and strives to be the best cashier possible.

Ultimately, Haleema trusts the owner due to his acceptance and support of her religious values. This increases her morale, inspires her to work harder, and positively impacts the grocery store's bottom line.

Challenges

Religious diversity is beneficial in many workplaces, but it also faces some challenges that can be upsetting to some employees.

One challenge involves organizations with religious overtones. Some owners try to push their personal religious beliefs on their employees, and this can be offensive to workers who are not of the same faith or are non-religious. Some employees might not even want to participate in celebrations for religious holidays such as Christmas.

Another challenge is the fact that paid holidays are geared towards specific religions. For instance, employees get paid for Easter that is celebrated by many Christian denominations, but they do not get paid for Greek Easter that is celebrated by the Greek Orthodox faith.

Organizational example

Bernie is a Jewish purchasing agent at a paper mill. He has been with the company for seven years and is thought of as a very good employee by coworkers and management.

Bernie asks to schedule off two days to celebrate Rosh Hashanah, also know known as the Jewish New Year. His employer denies his request because Rosh Hashanah occurs at a busy time for the paper mill, and they do not recognize the Jewish New Year as a holiday.

This denial infuriates Bernie because he has strong ties to the Jewish faith, and he believes it is being disrespected by management at the paper mill. Based on this, he decides to quit his job because he considers his faith to be more important.

In short, management at the paper mill recognizes religious holidays for some employees, but not for others. Bernie feels disrespected and reacts by quitting his job. As a result of religious intolerance, the company loses a valuable employee.

Improving

There are actually many ways to improve religious diversity in the workplace. The following are a few ideas that work, but they might be impractical for some organizations:

- Organizations should implement policies regarding prayer and practice of religious observances. For instance, a room could be provided for employees to use for religious purposes. This meets the religious needs of employees and builds a positive relationship with management.

- Organizations should be aware of all religious holidays and try to avoid scheduling important events during those times. For example, they should not schedule a mandatory meeting for all employees on a known religious holiday. This is considered disrespectful and insensitive by affected employees. Along the same lines, organizations should honor requests of people who request time off for religious reasons. In the example involving Bernie, the paper mill should have approved his time off. This would have made him happy and prevented him from leaving the company.

Here are some ideas that can be implemented in any workplace:

- Organizations should plan celebrations that do not exclude any employees. Consideration should be given to the choice of decorations, speeches, prayers, and entertainment. For example, the company "Christmas party" could be changed to the company "holiday party," and the theme could focus on happy holidays instead of merry Christmas.

- Organizations should encourage employees of different religious backgrounds to interact and work together. This helps them learn about each other, and it acts as a catalyst for accepting different behavior. For example, teams can be assembled with religiously diverse members. The common goal of finding solutions to problems inspires members to work closely with each other.

In summary, religious diversity occurs in most organizations. It is beneficial because it promotes freedom, peace, and trust, but it also faces challenges due to disrespect and lack of tolerance. The best way to overcome these challenges is to make accommodations for religious practices, become aware of religious holidays, include all religions in celebrations, and encourage interaction between employees with different faiths.

Summary

Workplace diversity is not always understood because it involves unfamiliar customs and cultures from a wide variety of different people. Regardless of the understanding involved, it needs to be respected in order for people to work together and successfully achieve organizational goals and objectives.

This book examines and discusses the concept of diversity in organizations, the four major types of diversity in organizations (age, gender, racial/ethnic, and religious), the challenges involved with the four major types of diversity in organizations, and the best ways to improve the four major types of diversity in organizations. Workplace examples are used for clarification in every section, and academic jargon is avoided to make learning easier.

Congratulations! You now have a better understanding of diversity in organizations.

Job Satisfaction

**Effects on Employee Motivation, Performance, and Pay
and Suggestions for Improvement**

Louis Bevoc

Published by
NutriNiche System LLC

Louis Bevoc books...simple explanations of complex subjects

Introduction

Job satisfaction is a fairly complex subject because it is based on people's perceptions and attitudes. One employee might find a work environment very satisfying, while another is quite unhappy in the same scenario.

It is also difficult to establish an all-encompassing definition of job satisfaction due to the number of variables involved. Compensation, status, promotion opportunities, work environment, communication climate, culture, and workload are all examples of factors that play a role. However, for the purposes of this book, job satisfaction is simply defined as:

The amount of satisfaction that employees derive from their job

Measurement of job satisfaction is typically done using a survey. Questions address employee perceptions of many different aspects of working in the organization, and results indicate the extent to which the employee is satisfied with those aspects. Management can use the findings to make changes that keep people happy.

Organizations also need to understand job satisfaction in order to reduce employee turnover. A transient workforce is a problem because it results in repeated training and quality issues. This adds stress for managers and causes product, process, and service mistakes since new employee are unsure how to properly complete tasks.

Essentially, job satisfaction is important to organizations, and that is why a wealth of attention is paid to it in industry and academia. It has been linked to lower turnover, and it has also been found to motivate employees. Motivation is a very important aspect of organizational behavior, so let's take a closer look at its relationship to job satisfaction.

Job satisfaction and motivation

There is an association between job satisfaction and motivation. Satisfied employees tend to be more optimistic than unsatisfied employees. Optimism leads to increased motivation on the job, and this helps the organization achieve goals and find success. In short, organizations benefit when employees experience job satisfaction and motivation.

Let's examine some specific aspects of organizational behavior that improve when employees experience job satisfaction and motivation:

Commitment

Commitment refers to employee's identification with and involvement in their organization. It encompasses people's psychological attachment to their jobs, and it is important for achieving organizational goals and objectives. Employees who experience job satisfaction and motivation are more committed because they are happier with their work environment.

Organizational example

Vicki is employed as a receptionist at a doctor's office. She needs to earn income, but she also has two small children that require care while she works. The doctors at the practice understand the problems associated with child care, so they have trained another person to take over Vicki's position if she needs to be with her children for illness or other reasons.

Vicki is comforted by the fact that she can attend to her children if necessary, and the doctors' understanding brings her job satisfaction. She is motivated to do her best at her job, and she has a strong commitment to making the practice successful.

Trust

Trust involves integrity, honesty, and character. In organizations, employees need to trust management if they are going to follow through on established goals and objectives. Job satisfaction and motivation lead to an atmosphere of trust due to the positive effect they have on employee-management relationships.

Organizational example

Pete works as an electrician for a home builder. He has been with the company for 90 days. As he was promised when he was hired, his boss gives him a $2 per hour raise and health insurance for his family.

Pete is very happy with the raise and the fact that his family is now insured. He is satisfied with the way he has been treated by his employer. This satisfaction motivates him to do his job well, and it establishes a trust that his organization will deliver on promises.

Communication

Communication is the process of using words or behavior to express thoughts or exchange information. Organizational communication is needed for employees to complete tasks and accomplish goals. Job satisfaction and motivation improve organizational communication because happy employees interact well with others and are willing to share information.

Organizational example

Juanita is an accountant at furniture wholesaler. She mostly works independently at her job, but her boss has recognized the fact that she has great interpersonal skills and gets along well with others. Due to this, she has been chosen to represent the office on a committee that will meet weekly and research ways to improve employee morale.

Juanita is happy about this opportunity. She talks to employees, asks questions, takes notes, and prepares for every meeting. She experiences satisfaction from her selection, and this motivates her to communicate with employees so she can accomplish the committee objectives.

Enthusiasm

Enthusiasm occurs when people feel excited or inspired. In organizations, employees are enthusiastic when they get involved with work they enjoy doing. Job satisfaction and motivation lead to enthusiasm because people feel upbeat about their jobs and related tasks.

Organizational example

Tim is a supervisor in a welding shop. He is selected by the owner to be part of a team that will oversee the benefit packages for everyone in the company. Tim was chosen over nine other supervisors because of his leadership skills and understanding of employee needs.

Tim is excited because he enjoys working on teams and will be directly involved in making decisions that influence an important aspect of the business. He experiences a great deal of satisfaction from being chosen by the owner, and this motivates him to be an upbeat and enthusiastic team member.

Sense of belonging

When people that feel like they are an important part of something, they experience a sense of belonging. In workplaces, sense of belonging helps employees feel connected to the organization and entices them to perform their jobs effectively and efficiently. Job satisfaction and motivation lead sense of belonging because they establish comfort for employees.

Organizational example

Salina is a marketing person at a radio station. She has just been recognized for ten years of service at the station. As a token of appreciation, she receives a company pin and gets to select a gift from a catalog.

Salina is proud of her longevity. She experiences satisfaction because the company recognizes her accomplishment, and that satisfaction allows her to feel comfortable in her role as an important member of the organization.

Now that you understand some of the way organizations benefit from job satisfaction and motivation, we need to examine job satisfaction's relationship with other variables. Let's look at performance, another important aspect or organizational behavior, and its association with job satisfaction.

Job satisfaction and performance

The vast majority of full-time workers spend more waking hours at their jobs (driving to work, working, driving home from work, traveling for work, etc.) than anywhere else. Based on this, it makes sense that they should be happy at work, and this happiness should help them perform at a higher level. However, is this really what happens? This relationship needs to be explored in more detail, and it leads us to the premise of this section...a discussion about the relationship between job satisfaction and performance.

Are these job satisfaction and performance linked? The short answer is yes. However, this answer needs to be explained in more detail. To do this, we need to separate job dissatisfaction and job satisfaction for a better understanding of the impact of each on performance.

Job dissatisfaction

First, let's discuss job dissatisfaction. When people are not satisfied with their jobs, they do not care about the organization. They miss work, lower their quality standards, and ultimately produce less. In other words, dissatisfied workers perform at a low level.

Organizational example

Mitch is an engineer at an aerospace company. His favorite part of his job is coming up with new ideas for making products safer and less expensive. However, his boss has assigned him to a production supervisor's job for the last month due to a staff shortage.

Mitch dislikes production work and is very unhappy in this position. He repeatedly tells his boss that he wants to move back into engineering, but she tells him that he must remain in production until further notice because that is where he is needed.

Mitch dreads coming into work and begins to call in sick. He isn't really physically ill, but he cannot stand the thought of working in a job he disdains. On the days Mitch does work, he is not concerned with production quotas. When quotas are not achieved, he states that there is nothing he can do about it.

Mitch is dissatisfied with his job transfer to production, and this causes him to take time off and not care about meeting the job expectations. The end result is a decrease in performance that affects the company in a negative manner.

This example shows a relationship between job dissatisfaction and lower performance. However, it does not address job satisfaction and performance. We need to look at job satisfaction and see if it results in employees performing at a higher level...as many people believe it does.

Job satisfaction

Happy employees stay in their jobs, but they are not necessarily more productive. Sometimes they are content because they do not have goals or responsibilities, and they are able to do minimal work to get by at their jobs. These individuals are not considered more productive and their value to the organization is questionable.

Organizational example

Angela works for the United States Department of Energy. She is guaranteed pay raises, gets five weeks of yearly paid vacation, and never has to work weekends. Additionally, her 21 years of seniority have earned her the job as a backup for employees who are absent. She is a capable replacement for all of the jobs she fills in for, but major issues are always put on hold until the permanent employee returns. This shields Angela from difficult or stressful situations.

Angela is very happy with her job. She has few direct responsibilities, minimal stress, and a stable work environment. If she is ever asked to do something outside of her government classification, she has the right to say tell people that it is not her job. She can essentially pick and choose the work she wants to get in involved with because she has earned that right to turn down undesirable jobs based on her seniority.

Angela only does what she has to do, and this makes her work day enjoyable. While this is good for Angela, it is not good for her employer. Her satisfaction lowers her work performance, and this negatively impacts the efficiency of the Unites States Department of Energy.

This example shows how there is a relationship between job satisfaction and performance, but that relationship does not necessarily result in higher performance levels. In reality, organizations are more effective without these types of satisfied employees. In order to grow and prosper, businesses need people who are eager to learn and take on new responsibilities.

What does this mean?

It means that Job satisfaction and performance are linked in organizations, but not the way many people believe. Dissatisfied employees perform at lower levels, but satisfied employees do not necessarily perform at higher levels. In fact, satisfied employees can perform at lower levels than dissatisfied workers.

So what makes employees perform better? The answer involves their relationships with their jobs. Specifically, employees increase productivity when they are engaged in their work. This is because they take ownership of the task at hand and feel empowered. Employers need to recognize the engagement factor if they want their people to perform at higher levels.

Now, we will explore job satisfaction's relationship with other variables. Let's start with pay since monetary compensation is at the top of many employees' lists of important work needs.

Job satisfaction and pay

Money is very interesting. We need it to prevent some problems, but it causes other problems. Some people are unable to accumulate it, some can't hold on to it, some won't spend it, and others will do almost anything for it. Thousands of books have been written on the subject, yet people never lose interest. Money does not necessarily buy happiness, but lack of it can create misery.

In organizations, money is also important. People work in exchange for money that they use for living. However, employees' perception of money is often different. Some people see it as the absolute most important reason for working, while it has less value to others. It's difficult to determine the exact importance of money, but we do know that in some way, shape, or form, it is important to all employees.

Money is the focus of this section. More specifically, it examines the relationship between job satisfaction and pay. This might like a relatively simple analysis, but it is actually rather complex...as you will see.

Is pay associated with job satisfaction? Many times the answer is yes, but this is not always the case. This question needs further analysis, so let's discuss specific situations that show why a linkage does not always exist:

Executives vs. middle management

Most people rank pay as important, but as noted earlier, that importance is not always the same. Employees in middle management typically rank pay fairly high in terms of job satisfaction, but executives have often cited opportunities to use their skills as more important than money. This makes sense because executives typically do not need money as much as middle managers due to the generous compensation they receive. Money might rank much higher on executive's lists if they were to lose the salaries and bonuses they receive.

Organizational Example

Ken is a production supervisor in a soap manufacturing company. He earns $75,000 per year and has a good benefit package. He has two children in college with annual costs of $35,000 per year. Ken needs to drain his savings to pay for his kid's college or they will amass a student loan debt of more than $70,000 each when they graduate. Money is very important to Ken's satisfaction with his job.

Linda is a director at the same soap manufacturing company. She earns $250,000 per year with a $30,000 to $40,000 bonus every Christmas. She has two children in college win annual costs of $35,000 per year. Linda can pay for her kid's school every year with her bonus alone. She does not have the same financial worries as Ken, so opportunities for growth are more important to her job satisfaction.

Money is important to Linda. However, she does not have the same financial burden as Ken, so she can focus on the importance of other work aspects. If Linda took a wage cut down to Ken's salary, pay would likely have a much closer association with her job satisfaction.

Economic implications

Economic situations also affect the relationship between pay and job satisfaction. If the economy is in bad shape, many employees are simply happy to have a job, and pay is not as directly linked to job satisfaction as it is during good economic times. Additionally, people who are the second income in a household might place more emphasis on health insurance, time off, autonomy, creativity, or freedom.

Organizational Example #1

Brianna has worked at a book publisher as a sales representative for the past ten years. When she started with the company, the economy was in rough shape. She was satisfied simply to have a job at that time because many of her work acquaintances and friends were not able to find work.

Now, however, the economy has recovered. Brianna is no longer satisfied simply to be employed since she can find comparative jobs elsewhere. Her satisfaction is now derived from monetary compensation in the form of base pay and commission.

Brianna's job satisfaction was not linked to pay when she started, but that changed as the economy went from bad to good.

Organizational Example #1

For the past eight years, Darnell has been an artist at an advertising agency. Before he began working for this company, his goal was to find a job where he could work from home instead of going into an office. Money was not an issue at the time due to his wife's sales job, so Darnell took the artist's position at a fairly low salary because he was allowed to telecommute. He experienced great job satisfaction due to the freedom his job provided.

Now, however, Darnell's life has changed. He and his wife just had a child, and his wife wants to reduce her role in the workforce to part-time so she can spend time with the baby. Darnell now finds that his job satisfaction comes from his paycheck, and he is willing to go into the office five days a week in order to make more money.

Darnell's job satisfaction was not linked to pay when he started, but that changed after the birth of a child and his wife's move part-time status.

Non-monetary rewards

Some organizations offer non-monetary rewards that stem from the culture of the organization. Employees feel that their work makes a difference in the world because it helps others. They are proud of their accomplishments, and that pride is more closely linked to job satisfaction than their wage.

Organizational Example

Heather works for a food bank that collects canned food and donates it to developing countries to feed poor people. She has always wanted a job like this because if makes her feel like she is making a difference in the world by helping others. When the job was offered to her, she immediately accepted it and did not even attempt to negotiate compensation. Her pride brings her job satisfaction, and the pay is simply a means of survival.

Non-monetary rewards, however, cannot be overestimated. Organizations still need to compete, and sometimes that requires paying better wages for the people they hire. Heather might find a different organization that also helps poor people in developing nations but offers a higher salary for the same job. If she does, then she might choose to work for that organization.

Pay satisfaction vs. job satisfaction

Last, but not least, some people are satisfied with their pay, but not their job. They believe they are being fairly compensated for the work they perform, but they are not happy with the work itself.

Organizational Example

Larry attended college immediately after high school. During his summer breaks, he worked on an automotive assembly line. After college graduation, Larry was unable to find a job that paid more than his assembly line position, so he stayed at the automotive plant.

Larry has now been working on the assembly line for 15 years. He is paid $35 an hour with excellent benefits and yearly bonuses. His job is not stressful, and he feels he is well compensated for the work he performs. However, Larry has very little job satisfaction because he performs the same repetitive tasks every day and does not feel like his work is very important. He never used his college degree and would need to take a major pay cut if he were to begin using it at a different organization.

In Larry's situation, job satisfaction and pay are not linked. He believes he is fairly compensated for the assembly line work he performs, but he is not satisfied with the job itself.

What does this mean?

It means that Job satisfaction and pay are not always linked in organizations. The relationship is dependent on employees' financial situations, personal needs, and perception of their work situation.

So why do we need to be paid for our work? The answer is because we need money to survive and do things that are important to us. Money is essential for certain things in life, but it is not always associated with job satisfaction.

Now you understand the relationship that job satisfaction has with some major variables in organizations. Since job satisfaction is an important aspect of organizational behavior, we need to understand how to improve it. That takes us to the next section that focuses on ways to make people happier with the jobs they perform.

Improving job satisfaction

Leaders who are truly concerned about employee job satisfaction need to find ways to make it better. Let's explore some way that this can be done.

Rewards

People like to be rewarded or acknowledged for their accomplishments. Obvious rewards are monetary in the form of raise or bonus, but money can't be given out every time any employee does something noteworthy. That being said, a simple thank you or pat on the back works well in many situations.

Simple rewards might seem cliché or unimportant, but they really can build job satisfaction by helping people feel appreciated for their contributions to the organization. Consider the example below as support for this thinking.

Organizational example

Roger is a shipping manager in a distribution warehouse. On a normal day, his department ships out 700 packages to 400 different customers. Order accuracy is monitored and, on average, there is a .2% error rate. That means that Roger's department makes mistakes on less than two packages per day. However, Roger is held accountable for those packages by the director of distribution. He has to research every error, report why it occurred, and document what can be done to prevent it from happening again.

The CEO has a different perspective on this situation. She notices that Roger's department fills 99.8% of all orders correctly, and wants to use this to motivate him. She makes a point of telling him that his department is doing a great job, thereby increasing his job satisfaction. The CEO's praise for a job well goes a long way here because Roger normally only hears about the few problems that occur in his department...not the vast majority of things that are done correctly.

Trust

Trust is critical in any organization. If employees do not trust management, then they will not believe what they are told...regardless of how true it might appear to be on the surface. This lack of faith prevents employees from identifying with the organizational objectives and goals of their employer and ultimately contributes to their job dissatisfaction.

Ethics are also associated with trust. Employees who witness unethical actions at their organization lose faith in leadership, and this leads to job dissatisfaction.

Management needs to build trust within the organization. This is done by following through on the statements and promises that are made to employees. Leadership also needs to behave ethically and root out unethical employee behavior in order to establish faith that leads to job satisfaction.

Organizational example #1

Cynthia works in an office with outdated computers. Management stated that they will replace the entire system within the next year, but the office workers are skeptical because it has been six months and nothing has been updated.

Cynthia asks the president of the company if he is serious about replacing the computer equipment within the designated time frame. Money is tight due to unexpected expenses that have recently surfaced, but the president wants to establish the trust of the employees. In an act of good faith, he borrows money and updates the computer system within the next three weeks. This motivates Cynthia and the rest of the office staff and restores their trust in management.

The president believes employees need to have faith that management will follow through on promises because that faith results in trust that leads to greater job satisfaction.

Organizational example #2

Martin is an accountant at a beverage manufacturer. On a routine check of accounts payable, he discovers that a vendor has undercharged his company by more than $8000. He reports this error to the vice president of purchasing, and she immediately calls the vendor and informs them of the mistake. The vendor is very grateful and makes the necessary changes to the invoice.

Martin is happy about the decision of the vice president to report the error to the vendor. He wants to work for a company that is ethical, and now he knows that this is the case. Martin has faith in the management of his organization, and this promotes job satisfaction for him.

Empowerment

Empowerment results when employees take initiative and make decisions in order to solve problems. Essentially, they become responsible and accountable for their actions by taking ownership of their jobs. The resulting freedom helps them develop a sense of belonging that promotes job satisfaction.

Organizational example #1

Lynette is the president of a paper mill. She has put together a team to work on quality issues in production. She takes a very "hands off" management approach by encouraging the team to create their own roles, norms, and structure in a way that allows them to reach a comfort level with each other. She monitors the overall team performance to make sure they are meeting objectives, but only interferes if she needs to resolve an issue or conflict.

Lynette's management style empowers the team to make decisions that help them solve problems and meet established goals. The roles and norms they develop help them adapt to each other and function effectively. The freedom and responsibility within the team promote a sense of belonging that leads to job satisfaction for every member.

Organizational example #2

Charles is in charge of the packaging department at a meat processing company. His company recently bought a new vacuum packaging machine, and Charles needs to determine the best area to position it the department.

Lucille has worked in the packaging department for the past five years. She has done almost every job and knows how to operate most of the machines. Based on Lucille's experience, Charles asks her for advice on where to put the machine. She tells him where to place it based on production efficiency and product flow, and Charles agrees. The machine is set up in the area recommended by Lucille, and she is elated that her opinion is considered valuable by the organization.

Charles asks Lucille for input on the placement of the new packaging machine, and this empowers her. She takes ownership of the job, and the responsibility she experiences allows her to feel an important part of the packaging department. Ultimately, this leads to her experiencing job satisfaction.

Communication

Employees want to know what is expected of them. They need direction so they can accomplish tasks and obtain organizational goals. They also want to know when and why their organization is making changes. These answers can only come from management, and the only way to do this is through communication.

Good management-employee communication can be challenging. It takes awareness and effort to reach the intended audience and avoid being misunderstood. Management needs to be aware that employees want to understand job expectations and workplace changes. They also need to make an effort to explain the reasons for those expectations and changes. Once open communication is achieved, employees will experience job satisfaction.

Organizational example

Michelle works for a cable company. The company offers several benefit options for their employees, and the choices are confusing. Michelle is stressed out by this since she provides the benefits for her family and wants to make the best selection based on their needs.

Fortunately, management at Michelle's company is aware that employees find the benefit packages confusing. Because of this, they have scheduled two different meetings with benefits administrators where employees can ask questions and discuss their personal situations. This makes Michelle happy because she feels like the company cares about her needs, and it leads to her experiencing job satisfaction.

Growth

Employees have a need to grow within their organization. A common way to grow is to get promoted, but this is not the only way. People also like to learn through new and different experiences. This broadens their knowledge of the workplace, and it also helps them develop empathy for the jobs that others perform.

Management needs to be aware that people want to grow, and they need to find ways to help them do so. Growth leads to happiness, and happiness leads to job satisfaction.

Organizational example

Trollick Toys is a company that makes stuffed animals. Wanda is a production supervisor and Jerry is a salesperson at the organization.

Jerry meets with Wanda and other plant supervisors once per month to discuss customer issues. In the meetings, Jerry talks frequently about problems his customers are experiencing with products. Wanda listens to Jerry's concerns, but she often feels like he just likes to complain.

During one particular meeting, the plant manager suggests that Wanda to out on the road with Jerry so she can hear what the customers have to say. Wanda and Jerry both like this idea, so they go out the following day.

After talking with the customers, Wanda understands why Jerry is complaining. When she returns to her job at the plant, she makes sure she addresses the problems that she heard about on the sales calls.

Jerry is appreciative of Wanda's new attitude. After working with her for the day, he realizes that she also faces issues that he did not know about. Because of this, he begins to handle some of the customer's problems on his own without complaining in the meetings.

After Wanda and Jerry gained a better understanding of each other's jobs, they developed empathy for each other. This led to an increase in job satisfaction for both of them.

Summary

People who are satisfied with their jobs are assets to the organizations that employ them. They show up for work on a regular basis, are committed to organizational goals, trust management, communicate well with others, express enthusiasm for their work, and feel like they are part of the culture.

Based on the above paragraph, it's obvious that job satisfaction is important to leaders of organizations. This book examines job satisfaction's relationship with motivation, performance, and pay using real world examples for support. It also suggests ways to improve job satisfaction in the workplace. In short, it increases your knowledge about a very important aspect of organizational behavior.

Work-Life Balance
Benefits, Challenges, and Improving

Louis Bevoc

Published by
NutriNiche System LLC

Louis Bevoc books...simple explanations of complex subjects

Introduction

Let's begin with a question. What exactly is work-life balance? Is it progressing in the organization? Is it spending time with family? Is it maintaining friendships? Is it spending time alone? Actually, it is all of the above. For the purposes of this book, work-life balance is defined as:

Accomplishing work related goals while enjoying life outside of work

As people's lives get busier and more hectic, they begin to realize the importance of work-life balance. Time is limited, and different things need to take priority at different times in life. People need to work in order to sustain a certain lifestyle...but they also need the time to enjoy that lifestyle.

Technology has completely changed work-life balance. People can now work and communicate with others from just about anywhere in the world. This means employees do not have to physically be at work in order to perform certain aspects of their jobs...they can simply telecommute.

Telecommuting helps eliminate stressful, costly, and time-consuming aspects of people's jobs. Travel, for example, is often minimized with the advent of teleconferencing. A 20-hour plane flight is no longer needed to meet people across the globe, and the company saves money on travel costs. One thing to keep in mind, however, is the fact that telecommuting will always have some limitations. For example, most people would not feel comfortable with a virtual doctor or dentist performing surgery on them.

Some aspects of work-life balance have little to do with technology. For example, company day care centers provide a very desirable service for some employees. Parents have piece-of-mind when they can check in on their children while they are at work, and this allows them to focus on performing their jobs to the best of their abilities.

As noted in the definition above, work-life balance is about meeting work objectives while enjoying life outside of the organization. For the most part, this is possible to accomplish, but people need to understand that absolute work-life balance is unrealistic. The goal is to find a balance that works most of the time...and that balance might need to be tweaked periodically to adjust for changes in life or priorities.

Now you understand the definition of work-life balance. Next, we will move into the benefits that it provides.

Benefits

There are many benefits of work-life balance, and this is why progressive organizations have implemented programs. Let's examine some of these benefits in more detail using workplace examples for clarification and support:

Reduced stress

In order to understand the benefits offered here, it is best to first obtain a better understanding of the negative effects of stress in the workplace. These include:

Fatigue

When stress is too much, it wears on employees. They look tired and feel exhausted. When they go to bed at night, they are kept awake thinking about the issues that are bothering them. In the morning, they wake up well short of refreshed and have to deal with another stressful day.

Anxiety

Excessive stress causes employees to worry about issues. They fret over what might happen or what has already occurred. Worrying is often difficult to control, and sometimes it makes absolutely no sense...like when people agonize about things that might transpire. This worrying is not justified because potential issues are not for certain, and they are beyond people's control. Heavy stress, however, brings worrying to the forefront, and it is can do a lot of unnecessary damage including the hindering of job performance.

Irritability

One of the most common negative effects of heavy stress at work involves anger and hostility. When employees experience difficulties that they can't seem to overcome, their unpleasantness toward others is a natural side effect. This hostility can be directed at customers, suppliers, or employees...and it is rarely justified. In fact, most times this type of behavior is based solely on the fact that people are under a lot of pressure.

Deteriorating physical health

Employees under large amounts of stress at work tend to be consumed with their jobs. They spend more and more time trying to overcome obstacles as the list of unresolved issues gets longer. In essence, they are now living to work, instead of working to live. This results in health issues such as weight loss and high blood pressure. If left unchecked, those problems can lead to much bigger concerns including malnutrition, heart disease...and possibly even death.

Employees experiencing work-life balance are able to step away from their jobs and enjoy life. They worry less, and this helps them go to sleep without thinking about work related problems. In the morning, they awake refreshed and ready to meet new challenges.

Work-life balance also makes employees less hostile and irritable because they focus on enjoyable aspects of their lives rather than the problems they experience at work. This reduces dysfunctional conflict in organizations and promotes better physical health by reducing worry and apprehension.

In short, work-life balance produces happy employees, and happy employees are typically less stressed than those who are unhappy.

Organizational example

Fran works as a cancer nurse at a children's hospital. The hospital has a program in place called MEDTALK where trained counselors are available three days per week to listen to the problems the hospital employees are experiencing. These problems can be work or home related and can involve just about anything. The idea is to provide employees with someone who will act as a sounding board and provide advice when needed.

MEDTALK is very important to Fran. She observes a lot of serious problems associated with innocent children, and sometimes this is stressful and difficult for her to handle. She has to be strong with parents in order to show support, but she is affected mentally and needs someone to talk with about her internal grief.

Every Wednesday, Fran meets with a counselor to talk about her internal feelings. These discussions enable her to find the strength required to deal with sick children and their parents. In short, Fran's stress is relieved due to the work-life balance program the hospital has in place.

Reduced absenteeism

Employees whose jobs are dependent on others to complete their work know how difficult it can be when the employees they depend on are not at work. Job tasks become more time consuming and difficult, and sometimes they simply cannot be completed.

Individual employees are not the only ones affected by absenteeism. It impacts the entire organization by making it less efficient. Employees are hired for a reason, especially in today's lean times, and their absence breaks a link in the organizational chain that can be difficult to repair. In short, absenteeism is very important to organizations because the bottom line is negatively affected when employees are not at work.

Absenteeism improves when employees find work-life balance. They enjoy their lives more and want to show up for work. They also have a stronger desire to achieve the goals and objectives of the organization.

Organizational example

Terrell is a broker at a mortgage company. He relies on other brokers to complete portions of his work, and without them, he comes to a standstill. Fortunately, management at the company is aware that the brokers need each other to complete job-related tasks, and they have taken preventative measures to reduce absenteeism.

One of these preventative measures is designed to improve the broker's physical health. A nurse is available two days per week to measure employee blood pressure and address other health-related health concerns.

Additionally, a nutritionist comes to the office once per week to set up programs for employees who want to eat healthier. She tailors the programs for individual needs and charts employee progress on spreadsheets.

The brokers at the firm enjoy the benefit of having qualified personnel available to help them with their physical health needs. Since the program began two years ago, absenteeism has been reduced by 13 percent, and this results in increased productivity for the mortgage company.

Absenteeism is important to the mortgage company because it impacts the bottom line, and the work-life balance program works well to prevent physical health issues.

Reduced turnover

Turnover is the process of losing and replacing employees. It is a concern for many organizations because it adds cost to an employer's bottom line. Employees who leave an organization typically need to be replaced, and those replacements need to be trained. There is a cost to that training, and that cost becomes higher as turnover increases.

Another concern with turnover involves errors. During training, mistakes happen...and those mistakes can be very expensive. Experienced employees tend to make fewer mistakes, and this helps an organization function more efficiently.

Work-life balance reduces turnover by addressing the needs that employees have outside of work. Employers who show interest in the personal lives of their employees benefit because those employees choose to remain employed at the organization. Their experience is valuable, and the cost of replacing it negatively impacts the bottom line.

Organizational example

Beatrice works as a cashier in a grocery store that only hires full-time employees. Many of the cashiers at the store are mothers with young children at home. In the past, these mothers had to make a choice between working full time or staying home with their children. Consequently, many women chose to stay home, and this resulted in the store losing good workers.

Recently, the grocery store has added a job sharing program. Cashier jobs are still full time, but employees are now allowed to share the position's responsibilities. Cahiers can work out their own schedule as long as the required hours are covered.

This program works well for mothers with young children because they can establish schedules that allow them to earn money and spend time with their children. It has also benefitted the grocery store because they no longer lose good workers simply because those individuals do not want to spend the entire week away from their children. Additionally, hiring and training costs are reduced because cashiers remain in their jobs and do not have to be replaced.

Job sharing has allowed cashiers with young children the option to spend more time at home, and this has reduced turnover at the grocery store. This work-life balance program works well for employees and the organization.

Increased morale

Employee morale is defined as the outlook employees have about their workplace. It involves their thoughts about the work they perform and their job satisfaction. When employees' morale is lowered, their drive to achieve organizational goals decreases, and their job satisfaction diminishes.

Work-life balance programs improve employee morale by addressing their work related and non-work related needs. The end result is a win-win for the organizations and their employees.

Organizational example

Lloyd works as an agent for an insurance company, and he is consistently one of the best performers. He is currently experiencing a challenging personal issue because his mother is ill and cannot care for herself. Since Lloyd and his sister do not want to put their mother in a nursing home, they take turns caring for her at her house. Lloyd's job flexibility allows him to attend to his mother in the day, and then his sister watches her at night. When his sister arrives in the evening, Lloyd performs all of his job-related tasks.

Lloyd likes his job, and the fact that his employer cares about him increases his morale. He knows that he would not be able to work for the insurance company if they did not allow him to have a flexible schedule. Lloyd's work-life balance creates job satisfaction for him, and it allows the insurance company to retain him as an employee.

Increased productivity

Productivity increases when employees have work-life balance because they feel more committed to the goals of their employer. When people believe they are being treated fairly, they want to give back...and the best way to give back to an organization is to become more productive.

Organizational example

Maryanne is a college math professor in Minnesota where the winters are very cold. She enjoys her job, and this is partly due to the fact that her employer cares about her personally. As part of a work-life balance program, the college owns condominiums in California and Florida that can be used free of charge by any faculty member. Instructors simply sign up for their condominium of choice and then head to a warmer climate where the lodging is free.

The college's treatment of Maryanne motivates her to be a better teacher. She is always available for students, and she makes it a personal goal to engage them in the learning process. This makes the process of education more enjoyable for everyone.

Maryanne is appreciative of her work-life balance, and it entices her to give back by becoming more productive. This results in a better learning environment and overall college experience for the students, and it positively impacts the image of the college.

Based on what you have read so far, it is rather obvious work-life balance is beneficial for employees and organizations. It produces happier and more productive employees while reducing absenteeism and turnover. However, this raises a question. If work-life balance is so advantageous, then why doesn't every organizational embrace it in some form? The answer is because there are some drawbacks involved, and they will be discussed in the next section.

Challenges

Every program, policy, or procedure implemented by an organization has some shortcomings. Work-life balance programs are no exception to this rule as they create problems for employees and organizations. Let's discuss a few of the challenges involved with work-life balance using organizational examples for a better explanation:

Expenses

This drawback applies to organizations rather than employees. Quite simply, some work-life balance programs are expensive and difficult to justify. For example, a gym takes up a lot of space, equipment is costly and needs to be replaced over time, and safety of the employees is a concern. In terms of safety, who is responsible if an employee is injured while working out? Does it turn into a worker's compensation case? All of these questions need to be considered and the answers might indicate that the disadvantages end up outweighing the advantages.

Organizational example

Halverson Engineering is looking into providing a dare care center for children of their employees. They realize some parents will find this very beneficial and take comfort in knowing that they can check on their children during the work day.

However, after looking into the necessary requirements for the day care, Halverson management has a change of heart. The costs associated with such a program are staggering. To begin, there needs to be a suitable location within the building to house the children. This requires more than just space because there are also government requirements that need to be fulfilled. Eating, sleeping, and play space need to be considered, and the area needs to have restricted access for security reasons.

Another hurdle is the fact that background checks need to be conducted on every employee hired into the day care. If there are problems with personnel, Halverson will be responsible, so this means additional insurance is necessary to protect the company financially.

Due to the risk associated and the costs involved, Halverson Engineering scraps the plans for an employee day care center. In this particular case, the negatives outweighed the positives for implementing a work-life balance program.

Communication

Often times the major form of communication for employees working remotely is the written word (email, text, letter). This works well in many situations, but it can also be easily be misinterpreted. Most people who have worked with email understand this dilemma, and they realize that some communication requires face-to-face human interaction. Non-verbal communication, body language, and paralanguage (voice quality, tempo, loudness, and vocal features) are all important for relaying the meaning of messages, and face-to-face contact generally is needed for achieving the full effect. If face-to-face communication is not possible, then employees can lose the ability to effectively communicate.

Organizational example

Milton is a website designer who works at a computer software company. His job affords him the luxury of working full time out of his home office. For the most part, this works out very well for Milton. However, it is challenging when he is assigned to a team project.

Currently, Milton is on a team project with three other employees who physically work at the office. They email back and forth to exchange ideas and information, but sometimes it is hard to understand the true meaning of the messages being sent. For example, Milton sent out an email with some mild sarcasm that was intended to be humorous and harmless, but one of the team members was offended by it. This created unnecessary stress in the group, and productivity came to a halt until it was resolved with a series of other emails.

Eventually, the team was able to achieve the objectives established by management, but the time needed for completion was twice as much as originally anticipated due to miscommunication. This led management to decide that Milton will no longer be placed on any teams as long as he works remotely.

The decision to avoid placing Milton on teams negatively impacts the computer software company because they lose the benefit of his problem-solving knowledge. In this particular situation, the work-life balance Milton achieved was not good for the organization.

Career progression

This is likely the biggest negative of work-life balance. People who are not involved in the day-to-day activities of the organization can be passed up by others simply because they are not physically noticed. This is a major threat for employees whose jobs are completely remote.

Organizational example

Helen works for a large aerospace company. She lives and works in the United States, but the company headquarters are in London, England. Helen truly likes her remote status, but it does result in some problems for her. She is not part of the culture at the aerospace company, and this results in "out of sight, out of mind" thinking. That thinking is not always bad, but it does not work well for rewards. Promotions, bonuses, and raises are more plentiful for employees working physically at the headquarters, and this results in Helen being left behind in terms of financial compensation.

Helen's distance from the headquarters of the aerospace company restricts her ability to receive promotions, bonuses, and raises. In this situation, the work-life balance she has attained presents some major drawbacks.

As you can see, there are some challenges involved when workplaces want to incorporate work-life balance programs. However, these challenges are easily overshadowed by the benefits, and the end result is happier employees and more successful organizations. That being said, ways for improving work-life balance need to be discussed...and that is exactly what will be done in the next section.

Improving

An interesting fact about work-life balance is that employees can improve it with little or no help from their employer by making simple changes. This involves some planning and effort, but it can be done, and it does pay dividends.

The following are specific ways that employees can improve their work-life balance:

Focus on important work goals

Workers who worry about everything on their plate put themselves in a position to become easily stressed...and this can lead to them disliking their jobs. Sometimes it is difficult to do, but work related goals can be prioritized. This method for improving work-life balance involves addressing important job aspects while moving those of lesser importance to the back-burner. This allows employees to eliminate small problems in order to focus more completely on larger ones.

Try this method for yourself. It really does work, and you will likely find that some aspects of your job were not as important as you originally thought.

Document accomplishments

Employees need to record the good things they have done for the organization. Detailed notes and dates of accomplishment need to be documented and stored where the information can be easily retrieved. This helps during performance reviews because it shows your employer what you have been doing on the job.

This leads to a question. How does this documentation improve work-life balance? The answer is that it can be used as leverage for rewards. Employees who document their accomplishments typically get good reviews. This opens the door to discuss rewards for good performance, and some of those rewards can come in the form or work-life balance.

Instead of asking for money, employees can ask for things that make their life easier such as flexible work schedules, telecommuting, or time to go to the gym during the day. They can improve the quality of their lives through non-monetary compensation...and it can lead to them becoming more dedicated and productive.

Eliminate wasted time

Procrastination is an issue for many people, and this results in precious time being wasted. That time, if properly harnessed, could be put to much more constructive use. One way to harness it is to make a list of goals for the day. Check off those goals as you achieve them and move forward. Each check will provide motivation for you to continue progressing in a positive direction, and your procrastination will diminish over time.

This method might seem simple or cliché, but it does work. When you accomplish small goals, you feel better about yourself and want to keep moving forward in a positive manner...and this puts you on the right path to finding work-life balance.

Take time off

Use your vacation time...even if it means hanging around the house. Some employees think they appear more committed to management when they don't take any time off. This might be true in certain situations, but it also leads to being abused. Over time, it becomes expected that you will not take vacations, and this is not good for your mental or physical well-being.

Time off is a critical element of work-life balance. If you have time available, then use it to make yourself a happier employee.

Maintain health

This includes mental and physical health. In terms of mental health, find something that is interesting, enjoyable, or relaxing. This can be as simple as working crossword puzzles or meditating, but the key is to find something you like to take your mind off the pressures of your job.

For physical health, it is often best to start exercising. This can be done at a gym or in your basement, but the key is to work out and prevent health issues such as high blood pressure, diabetes, heart disease, and obesity. If hard-core exercise is not for you, then try walking or performing Yoga. These activities also work to prevent physical disease, and they also do wonders to stimulate the mind.

With some time and effort, employees can improve their work-life balance. This is important because work-life balance is becoming necessary for organizations to grow and prosper....as leaders all over the world are beginning to realize. This leads us to another question. What does the future hold for work-life balance? Let's explore this question in the next section.

Future

Work-life balance is gaining momentum as management and employees understand its value and importance. It helps employees enjoy their personal lives and excel in their careers. It also helps organizational achieve the goals and objectives that they have established.

The future of work-life balance is rather simple because it is good for everyone involved. It will be much more significant in the future, and the need for organizations to implement related programs, policies, and procedures will increase. Work-life balance was not a big part of the past, but it will be a big part of the future.

Summary

The focus of this book is work-life balance. It examines the advantages and disadvantages of the phenomenon and then discusses ways to improve it along with thoughts about its future. Workplace examples are used throughout the text to promote a better understanding of the subject matter.

The significance of work-life balance cannot be underestimated. It provides a variety of benefits as it helps organizations grow and prosper. There are some challenges involved, but those challenges are easily overshadowed by the positive end results.

Work-life balance is more significant now than it has ever been in the past. This trend will continue as people's lives become more complex and they realize the importance of being happy at work and at home.

Congratulations! You now understand work-life balance...an important aspect of organizational behavior.

Absenteeism
in Organizations
Causes, Effects, and Prevention

Louis Bevoc

Published by
NutriNiche System LLC

Louis Bevoc books...simple explanations of complex subjects

Summary   107

Introduction

Absenteeism is employees' unscheduled absence from their jobs. The key word here is "unscheduled." Scheduled absences can be planned for in advance, and this helps avoid some of the potential problems that might occur during the employees' time off. However, there is very little time to plan for unscheduled absences, and the necessary resources might not be available at a moment's notice.

Leaders in organizations are not naive enough to think employees are going to be at work on every scheduled day. They expect workers to miss some time because they are not feeling well or want to attend to personal matters that conflict with the times they are supposed to be at work. This is acceptable and does not present a problem...unless it becomes excessive.

When absenteeism becomes excessive, it is a major headache for organizations. If employees do not show up for work, then their jobs need to be performed by someone else. If no one else is available, then those jobs simply do not get done. This creates difficult and stressful situations for workers and managers, and it occurs far too often in some workplaces.

Absenteeism has a greater impact on smaller organizations than it does on larger ones due to the size of the workforces. For example, a business with 100 employees will function close to normal if five people are absent. However, a business with eight employees might operate if five workers are missing.

Regardless of the number of employees in a workplace, excessive absenteeism causes problems. It stresses out the employees who are forced to take on additional workloads, lowers morale, and affects productivity. Ultimately, it impacts the financial well-being of organizations as they struggle to meet the needs of their customers.

Since there are problems associated with absenteeism, leaders of organizations need to do whatever they can to minimize it. This starts by gaining a better understanding of the causes and effects.

This book examines the causes and effects of absenteeism. It explores the reasons employees miss scheduled days of work and analyzes the problems this causes for organizations. It also offers suggestions for preventing workplace absenteeism so the negative effects can be minimized.

Now that you have a basic understanding of workplace absenteeism and the scope of this book, let's move on to discussing the causes of this problem.

Causes

As noted in the introduction, absenteeism is employees' unscheduled absence from their jobs. Unscheduled absence can be intentional or unintentional as shown in the following examples:

Intentional absenteeism

Manny comes home from work on Wednesday night and finds an envelope in his front door. As a surprise, one of his best friends leaves two baseball tickets to the Atlanta Braves home opening game that starts Thursday at noon. Manny is thrilled, and he texts his friend that he will be at the game.

The next morning, Manny calls his employer and tells them that he will not be into work. He says he has some "personal business" that he needs to attend to, and he will return on Friday.

Manny's decision to miss work in order to go to the baseball game is an example of intentional absenteeism.

Unintentional absenteeism

Juanita and George are married with two children under the age of five. They both work full-time jobs, and her husband frequently travels. This week he is away on a business trip.

George's business trips are normally not a problem for Juanita because drops her children off at a daycare in the morning before going into work. However, this morning she wakes up to find her daughter vomiting. This child will not be able to go to daycare today and Juanita is the only person who can care for her. She calls work and tells them that she will not be in today due to a sick child.

Juanita's decision to miss work in order to take care of a sick child is an example of unintentional absenteeism.

In the view of an employer, Juanita's decision is much more legitimate than Manny's for missing work. However, regardless of the intent, unscheduled absences do not allow organizations to plan for handling missing employee's work that needs to be completed. For this reason, it is important to understand the causes of absenteeism so attempts can be made to eliminate them and minimize absences on scheduled work days.

It is virtually impossible to list every cause of absenteeism due to the fact that every employee is unique. However, the following are some major causes of these unscheduled absences:

Stress

Work related stress can lead to mental and physical health problems if it is not dealt with in some manner. Employees use a variety of different techniques to deal with stress including yoga, exercise, meditation, relaxation, massage, and therapy. However, workers also deal with stress by not showing up for work...and this is why it is a cause of absenteeism.

Family care

Family care has changed considerably since the 1960s. Mothers used to stay home to take care of children while fathers worked to financially support the family. However, this has changed. Today many, if not most mothers, are employed in some capacity. Children go to day care and are picked up after the parent's workdays are finished.

The dual income family works well financially for many families, but this arrangement poses a problem when children get sick. One of the parents needs to stay home to care for the child, and this means that he or she needs to miss work. Although this absence is unintentional, it is still unscheduled and therefore classified as absenteeism.

Family care absenteeism does not end with care for children. Employees today are part of the "sandwich generation" where they need to help young children and aging parents. When a parent needs assistance, one of their children needs to miss work to provide the necessary care...and the end result is an unscheduled absence. So, the same people who miss work for their children can also miss work for their parents.

In short, family care today is a major cause of absenteeism based on dual income households and the needs of various relatives. This will continue to present a challenge as long as working couples have young children and aging parents.

Bereavement

An old saying goes, "two things people have to do during life are die and pay taxes." The taxes part is debatable...but the part about dying is an absolute fact.

When people die, friends and family need time to grieve over the loss. However, it is difficult to specify how long employees should mourn because everyone is different. Some workers need more time than others and therefore end up missing more days of work. Since this missed time is unscheduled, it is considered absenteeism.

Illness

Essentially, illness can be physical or mental. Physical illness can be as simple as the common cold or as serious as terminal cancer. Mental illness often involves some type of depression, but it can also involve issues such as paranoia or schizophrenia.

The following examines the two types of illness in more detail:

Physical illness

It is not uncommon for employees to become physically ill. Their illnesses often require them to miss work, and the number of days they are absent depends on the time required for healing.

Management expects employees to miss some time at work due to physical illness, but that time is not scheduled in advance and is therefore deemed absenteeism.

Mental illness

Mental illness is not as common as physical illness, but it does affect employees in every type of workplace. This illness often requires people to miss work, and they are not able to return until their conditions are cured or controlled.

Management typically does not expect employees to miss work due to mental illness, but they do understand that it does occur. However, the time missed is unscheduled and is therefore considered absenteeism.

Bullying

Employees who are bullied by coworkers might choose to stay home rather than come to work and take the abuse. This type of situation is unfortunate because bullying can lead to depression and long-term negative effects. Bullying might not be one of the most common causes of absenteeism, but it is one of the most important due to other problems that can result.

Poor supervision

Poor supervision is a problem in many organizations, but only the more severe cases result in absenteeism. Employees simply cannot bear to see their supervisors, so they decide to call in sick. They become overwhelmed with negative thoughts and choose to avoid the situation rather than deal with bosses that they disdain.

Workload

Workloads can be so excessive that employees choose to stay home rather than go to work. Ironically, the absenteeism resulting from workloads is often an indirect consequence of other absenteeism. This is because employees miss work and their coworkers have to do their jobs. Those coworkers then have much larger workloads, so they also decide to not show up for work. Unfortunately, this cycle can repeat itself until the overworked employees burn out and permanently leave the organization.

Working conditions

Working conditions have a big impact on absenteeism. Workplace temperature, sanitary conditions, and ergonomics all play a role in determining if employees will show up for work. Please consider the following examples:

Cold temperatures (workplace temperature)

Cold temperatures create discomfort and cause workers to lose focus. All they think about is getting to a warmer environment, and that in itself is enough to make them not show up for work.

Dirty workplaces (sanitary conditions)

Unsanitary conditions result in mental disgust for some employees. They would rather be home than in a dirty workplace and decide not to come to work.

Poor lighting (ergonomics)

Dimly lit areas cause eye strain. This makes it difficult to complete work and causes headaches. Due to the pain, employees call in sick.

Travel

Some jobs require employees to travel. This is not a problem unless the travel becomes excessive. Employees do not want to constantly be on the road because they miss out on many aspects of their personal lives. When they finally get home, they want to spend time with family and friends rather than going right into the office...so they tell their employer that they will not be in. This is understandable, even in the eyes of some employers, but it is still considered absenteeism.

Personal reasons

There are times when people do not go to work for personal reasons. They choose to attend a daytime sporting event, catch a matinee movie, go on a day trip with a friend, or just relax in front of the television at home. This is also known as "playing hooky," and it happens in workplaces all over the world.

Employers typically do not view personal reasons as legitimate excuses for missing work. However, they realize that employees are going to "play hooky," and there is not much that can be done about it. This form of absenteeism will likely occur in some capacity as long as people work for organizations.

Injury

Injuries are legitimate reasons for missing work. When employees are hurt, they cannot perform certain aspects of their jobs, and therefore need to be off work.

As far as employers are concerned, there two basic types of injuries including:

Work related

These injuries result from accidents that occur on the job. Workers' compensation pays for the employees' time missed because the injury occurred while working. This is bad for the employer for two different reasons because (1) their insurance premiums increase due to the claims and (2) their employees are not able to perform their jobs.

Non-work related

These injuries result from accidents that do not occur on the job. Employers are not required by law to compensate employees who are not injured at work...although some provide short-term and long-term disability benefits. Employers save money by not paying injured employees, but they still lose because these individuals are not able to perform their jobs.

Employers realize that injuries are going to occur. However, these claims can be abused. Workers who do not want to come back to work can often get doctors to extend their excused absence regardless of whether or not they are healed. If this happens, then absenteeism is even more costly to employers...especially if workers compensation is being paid to the injured employees.

Other employment

Some employees miss work because they are working other jobs. This is usually not acceptable to employers...and some even consider it grounds for termination. However, regardless of the rules in place, other employment is a cause of absenteeism that occurs in many workplaces.

Job searches

This involves missing work to (1) look for another job or (2) interview at another organization. Obviously, most employers would frown upon this because they are on the verge of losing employees...and those employees might be going to competitors. However, in reality, missing work for job searching is fairly common because interviews are typically conducted during normal working hours.

Transportation

Most people need some type of transportation to get to their jobs. If that transportation is not available, then they are unable to show up for work. This type of problem is more common for employees who rely on public transportation, but personal vehicles also break down.

Transportation issues are usually beyond the control of employees. However, they are still considered unscheduled absences and a cause of absenteeism.

Excessive hours

Employees who work too many hours sometimes miss work just to get some personal time away from the job. For example, a production plant might be working seven days a week. After two or three weeks without a day off, employees decide to stay home and rest instead of going into work. This rest is obviously justified, but it is considered absenteeism.

Strange hours

Some employees miss work because they work strange shifts or hours. For example, third shift employees might never get to see their families or friends, so they decide to not come into work in order to attend special events in their lives. This type of absenteeism is more likely to happen to employees who work when most people are at home or out socializing.

Religion

Leaders in organizations are beginning to realize that employees need time off for designated religious occasions that might not be recognized by the government. However, this type of management thinking is in its infancy, and it will be a while before employees are excused for the days they consider sacred. Until that time, workers will not show up for work for religious reasons, and their unscheduled absences will be considered absenteeism.

Drugs and alcohol

Substance abuse is an issue in many workplaces, and this is likely to continue as long as drugs and alcohol are readily available to employees. In some cases, management is required by law to allow employees time to deal with their addictions...and these absences are not part of absenteeism since they are scheduled. However, hangovers and other substance related aftermath are considered absenteeism, and they will likely never be accepted as legitimate by leaders of organizations.

Attitude

Attitude is a major cause of absenteeism. Employees who have negative attitudes about their place of work tend to show up less frequently than coworkers with positive attitudes. Attitude is about perception...and perception truly is reality.

Age

Age is also a cause of absenteeism. Typically, younger workers miss time because they are out socializing or having fun. Older employees often miss time for health concerns or family situations.

Younger and older employees miss work for different reasons, but all of those reasons result in unscheduled absences.

Seniority

Long-term employees sometimes feel a sense of entitlement when in terms of taking unscheduled time off from work. They have been with the organization for a long time and believe their seniority gives them the right to be absent without notice. Unfortunately, this is still considered absenteeism...and it requires other employees to do extra work.

Boredom

Repetition makes jobs mundane. Employees lose the motivation to work after repeating the same task throughout their work day, and this leads them to take unscheduled days off work. In short, boredom is a cause of absenteeism because it does not provide employees with challenges.

Some causes of absenteeism are specific to certain groups of employees such as immigrants. These include:

Family businesses

Some employees miss work because they need to work at seasonal family businesses. For example, they might need to leave to help their family work the fields during harvesting periods.

Absenteeism caused by family businesses can be a big problem for organizations if too many workers leave at the same time. Mass exodus of employees can cripple productivity and even force some organizations to cease operations.

Unrecognized holidays

Similar to religious occasions, some holidays are not recognized by organizations in the United States. Examples include Cinco de Mayo, Greek Easter, and Rosh Hashanah.

Management **is** beginning to realize that employees need time off for designated holidays, but it will be a while before they are formally excused. Until that time, workers will not show up for work on days they consider holidays, and their unscheduled absences will be considered absenteeism.

Homeland visits

Some employees miss work because they go back to their homelands to visit friends and family. These visits are very important to these workers, and they leave regardless of whether their absences are approved by management.

This type of absenteeism is difficult to prevent because employees have strong ties to people from their countries of origin.

Now you understand some of the major causes of absenteeism, and this is important in order to develop methods of prevention. However, before exploring ways to prevent absenteeism, the effects that it has on workplaces needs to be examined.

Effects

Absenteeism negatively affects employers and employees in a variety of different ways. Some of the major ways include:

Costs

There are high costs associated with absenteeism. Some of these costs are:

Wages and benefits

In many cases, especially those involving worker's compensation, absent employees still receive wages and benefits until they are able to return to work. In some cases, these payouts can go on for years...and possibly even the rest of the employees' lives.

Overtime

As noted earlier, absent employees leave work behind that still needs to be done by coworkers. Those coworkers need to work longer hours to complete the designated tasks, and they are paid overtime for those hours.

Training

Absent workers sometimes need to be replaced by new employees. These new employees need to be trained…and that training has a cost associated with it.

Administrative

Many people are not aware that there are administrative costs for managing absenteeism. For short-term absences, letters need to be sent to the offenders detailing disciplinary action. For long-term absences such as those involving workers' compensation, massive amounts of paperwork need to be filled out…and this takes time and resources. Additionally, meetings need to be conducted with insurance companies, medical providers, and attorneys to discuss specifics of the case.

In short, absenteeism impacts the bottom lines of organizations. This impact is never good, and it can lead to some companies permanently shutting down.

Productivity

Absenteeism results in decreased productivity. This is due to the fact that experienced employees are missing from the workplace, and coworkers who are less familiar with their jobs need to fill in.

Morale

When employees are forced to take on more work due to absenteeism, they often become frustrated with their jobs. They resent management for the increased workload, and their morale decreases.

Trust

When employees are forced to take on more work due to absenteeism, they lose trust in management. The absenteeism is not their fault, yet they are paying the price. The worst part about issues involving trust is the fact that it is very difficult to restore once it is lost.

Stress

When employees are forced to take on more work due to absenteeism, they experience job stress. Over time, this causes them to burn out...and burnout causes their absenteeism to increase. It is rather ironic, but absenteeism results in absenteeism.

Turnover

When employees are forced to take on more work due to absenteeism, they start to dislike their jobs. This causes them to leave their organizations for other positions. In short, absenteeism results in turnover.

Now that you understand some of the more important effects of absenteeism, it is time to move into the next section that discusses methods of prevention.

Prevention

Once absenteeism starts, it can snowball and quickly get out of control. This is why the best way to stop it is to prevent it from occurring.

Some of the best methods of prevention include:

Hiring practices

Effective hiring practices are likely the best way to prevent absenteeism because (1) they prevent problem employees from entering the workplace and (2) they prevent employees from becoming problem employees.

The following are some important aspects of effective hiring practices:

Check references

It's always a good idea to call past employers to determine if potential employees have a history of absenteeism. It is illegal for employers to divulge certain facts about past employees, but they can release attendance records if policies were in place. This allows organizations to find out if potential employees were terminated for absenteeism related reasons.

Emphasize attendance importance

The importance of showing up for work should be stressed at the time of hiring. This makes it clear to employees that they are needed on the job and expected to show up when they are scheduled.

Orientation training

This occurs after the employee is hired. Orientation training talks about absenteeism and details the attendance policies in place...including disciplinary actions for violations. Training can be expensive, but it is well worth the cost if it is properly conducted.

Rewards

Rewards are a good way to prevent absenteeism because they provide goals and motivation for employees to show up for work.

There are several different types of rewards including:

Awards

Awards are typically certificates that reward good employee attendance. They are motivational because employees are recognized in front of the entire organization. They can also be used by employees for negotiating raises and other perks at a later time.

Incentive pay

This involves paying employees for good attendance. In other words, the incentive for reducing absenteeism is a cash reward. Typically, these are paid out on a monthly basis, and they can be in the form of an annual or bi-annual bonus.

Paid time off

Some organizations reward employees for good attendance by giving them paid time off. Certain workers prefer this over cash incentives because they value time more than additional income.

Lotteries

This involves lotteries for workers with good attendance. These individuals are entered in periodic (often monthly) lotteries with cash prizes that go to the selected winners.

All of the above rewards can be based on attendance systems put in place by organizations. For example, a system that issues employees points for unscheduled or unexcused absences could be utilized. Employees who reach a specified number of points are progressively disciplined...up to the point where they are terminated for extreme absenteeism.

Rewards can also be used to create peer pressure. Team or organization-wide absenteeism systems can be put in place that document employee absenteeism as a whole. This results in employees monitoring each other's attendance because one employee's absenteeism can prevent everyone from receiving rewards.

Job rotation

This prevents absenteeism by (2) reducing the boredom of performing only one job and (2) empowering employees because they are more involved in the operation of the organization.

Another benefit is the fact employees know each other's jobs when someone is absent. This reduces mistakes and saves time in terms of training.

In short, job rotation reduces absenteeism because employees want to come to work, and they understand each other's jobs.

Communication

If absenteeism is an issue, management should ask employees why it is occurring. They might be surprised by the answers they receive from workers, and those answers can be used to prevent reoccurrences.

For example, some employees might indicate that they are missing time because other employees are always absent... and management does nothing about it. If this is the case, then an attendance system needs to be implemented.

As the saying goes, "a little communication goes a long way."

Summary

Absenteeism is employees' unscheduled absence from their jobs. Leaders of organizations generally do not have a problem with absenteeism unless it becomes excessive. Excessive absenteeism creates headaches for organizations because job tasks still need to be completed with fewer employees.

This book examines the causes and effects of absenteeism. It explores the reasons employees miss scheduled days of work, and it analyzes the problems this causes for organizations. It also offers suggestions for preventing workplace absenteeism so the negative effects can be minimized. Simple explanations are used for easy reader comprehension and understanding.

Congratulations! You now understand more about workplace absenteeism...and important aspect of organizational behavior.

Employee Empowerment
Understanding and Implementing

Louis Bevoc

Published by
NutriNiche System LLC

Louis Bevoc books...simple explanations of complex subjects

Introduction

Introduction

Leaders all over the world want their organizations to operate efficiently. This is traditionally accomplished using supervisors to oversee the work of others. Supervisors make sure their subordinates follow established procedures and strive towards accomplishing organizational objectives and goals.

While supervisors often do a good job, some organizations do not need them to oversee the work of other people. Instead, they implement a process of empowerment where employees have authority over their own jobs. Empowered employees understand the needs of the organization and know what they must do to accomplish their designated tasks. Management has faith that they will make the right decisions and move towards achieving organizational goals and objectives.

Employees who are empowered are skilled in specific areas. They improve the efficiency of the organization because decisions are made faster when a supervisor's permission is not required. Management only steps in if they need to overrule something that they know is not right.

Empowered employees are also encouraged to make suggestions about improving products, processes, and procedures. This participation makes them feel like they are making valid contributions, and it results in them taking ownership of their jobs.

Now that you have a basic understanding of employee empowerment, let's move into some of the benefits.

Benefits

Not surprising, some organizations are skeptical about empowering employees. Management questions the ability of this process to work properly because they are not sure if employees will make the right decisions. Essentially, employees will make the right decisions if they have the proper skills...and it is up to management to provide them with those skills through training.

Employees who are empowered provide many benefits to organizations. Some of these benefits include:

Improved idea generation

Employees who are empowered expose their thoughts about improvements that can be made throughout the organization. This is advantageous because everyone has different ideas based on their experiences that can be used for bettering the organization as a whole. Employees also discuss ideas with each other to generate feedback and create synergy that would not exist without empowerment.

Organizational example

Mel is a meat cutter in a grocery store that is part of a chain with over 100 different locations. He has recently undergone employee empowerment training that was initiated by corporate management. In the training, he learned about company specifications for pork, beef, lamb, chicken, and turkey products that he prepares on a daily basis.

Mel now has the authority to reject any meat or poultry that does not adhere to company specifications. He no longer needs to involve the meat department manager for permission.

Due to his empowerment, Mel takes ownership in his job. He watches product closely for non-conformance issues and takes pride in putting out top-notch meat and poultry products. His newfound interest has also inspired him to suggest ways of improving quality. For example, his experience has shown him that beef starts to lose color after four days in the meat counter. Due to this, he suggested that management buy beef twice per week instead of the normal once per week. Management accepted his idea, and now the meat only stays in the counter for three days because it is rotated more frequently with fresh stock.

Mel's idea brought about change for the better of the store. The meat is now fresher, the customers are happier, and sales have increased by three percent. The situation was a "win" for everyone, and it happened because Mel's empowerment motivated him to come up with a good idea.

Improved performance

Empowerment motivates employees to perform optimally. Optimal performance is advantageous because productivity increases as costs decrease, and the end result is a more efficient operation.

Organizational example

Katherine is one of six dental hygienists who work for three different dentists in the same office. The hygienists' jobs involve cleaning patient's teeth, performing oral exams, and assisting the dentists with more detailed work.

The hygienists work on hundreds of patients each year with a variety of different tooth and gum issues. They each have their own patients that they know well, and this gives them a sense of comfort. However, it also prevents them from learning different experiences.

This year, the dentists decided to empower the hygienists. They now allow them to make more of their own decisions during teeth cleaning and oral exams. The dentists also encourage the hygienists to come up with new ideas to make the dental practice better.

Katherine suggests that the hygienists rotate jobs so they can be exposed to different issues and learn about each other's patients. Her suggestion is implemented, and it is very successful. The change experienced by the hygienists during rotation turns out to be very motivational, and productivity starts to increase due to their understanding of each other's jobs and involvement in the organization. As productivity increases, the costs of the dental office go down, and this impacts the bottom line.

Katherine's suggestion resulted in improved performance of the hygienists, and it was a direct result of the empowerment she received from the dentists.

Improved customer service

Employees who are empowered pass that empowerment on to the customers in terms of service. Their involvement in decision-making processes makes taking care of customer needs an important priority. This benefits the organization because customers who believe they are being properly serviced are more likely to continue buying products or services.

Organizational example

Rosemarie is a college professor who has taught at the same school for the past 15 years. Her favorite part of her job is when her students apply the concepts they learn to the real world. This brings Rosemarie job satisfaction because she believes a combination of education and application is necessary for complete understanding of classroom material.

Administration at the college has recently empowered the professors by giving them more control over teaching decisions in their classrooms. This motivates Rosemarie because she is able to implement more real world application of the theories she discusses. Instead of tests, she has her students write essays that apply the concepts being studied to their current jobs or the jobs they would like to obtain in the future. This inspires the students because they are personally involved when they write about themselves, and they comprehend more from this type of learning structure than they do taking tests.

In Rosemarie's situation, her students are the customers. The customers perceive her service as improved, and the end result is better learning. In short, Rosemarie's empowerment inspired changes that resulted in improved customer service.

Improved employee commitment

Empowered employees buy into the process, and this results in higher levels of commitment to their work. This is very beneficial to the organization in terms of absenteeism and turnover because employees like their jobs and look forward to performing them.

Organizational example

Orville is an automotive assembly line worker in a manufacturing plant. He has worked at the plant for ten years and does the same job every day. He is assigned the task of putting together taillights for SUVs.

Orville used to have little motivation to do his job other than a paycheck. He was not allowed to make decisions and needed approval for everything from his supervisor. For example, if he ran out of a part, he was not allowed to stop the line or substitute another part with the permission of his supervisor. Based on his lack of motivation, he missed work on a fairly regular basis.

Over the past six months, Orville's job has changed substantially, Management implemented an empowerment program and, after detailed training, he is now able to make decisions on his own without input from his supervisor.

Orville is now motivated to perform his job. He shows up for work every day and takes charge of assembling the taillights. He enjoys his new responsibility and likes the fact that he has the power to make decisions. Orville's commitment to the company has increased, and this is a direct result of his empowerment.

Improved change acceptance

Sometimes, it seems like the only change employees want to accept is an increase in their paycheck. Empowerment changes this outlook by making them part of the change. They are able to suggest ideas for change and change implementation, and this promotes acceptance because the employees are involved in the process.

Organizational example

Delores is a cook in a for a high school cafeteria. She dreads the bi-annual menu changes because she has to learn to cook several new menu items and the students always complain. Administrators in the school system realize their cooks dislike the menu changes, but they need to be made in order to keep up with the Food and Drug Administration's (FDA) nutritional requirements for students.

This year, the superintendent implemented an empowerment process in the cafeterias of every high school in the district. Cooks will now have a voice in menu changes. They can decide what items they want on the menu, as long as they meet FDA requirements.

Delores is very happy about this change. She talks to the students every day, and she is aware of the foods they like and dislike. She can now make choices that meet nutritional requirements and satisfy students.

The end result is a win for everyone. Delores no longer dreads the menus changes because she has decision-making power, students complain less because they get to eat food that they like, and administrators know the food meets FDA requirements. All of this is due to the empowerment program that was implemented.

Improved culture

Employees who have the proper knowledge and resources to perform their work with limited supervision are empowered. They take ownership of their jobs and the processes within them, and this results in a positive perception of the culture and a strong commitment to organizational goals. Empowered employees also spread the word about the positive culture they work within, and this allows the organization to attract better people.

Organizational example

Robert is a welder who works for a mobile home manufacturer. His boss Vicki knows that he is capable of performing his job without her assistance. Vicki simply makes sure that Robert has the proper tools and supplies for his work, and then she leaves him alone.

These conditions motivate Robert to perform to the best of his ability. He works with little supervision and takes charge of all of his job-related responsibilities. Robert is empowered, and this empowerment increases his commitment to his employer and creates a positive perception of the workplace culture.

Improved teams

This might be the biggest advantage of empowerment. When empowered employees are placed on teams, they all want to contribute to the discussion in order to accomplish the team objective. This results in a variety of ideas that can be used for solving problems.

Organizational example

Sidney is the president of a paper mill. He has put together a team to work on quality issues in production. He takes a very "hands off" management approach by encouraging the team to create their own roles, norms, and structure in a way that allows them to reach a comfort level with each other. He monitors the overall team performance to make sure they are meeting objectives, but only interferes if he needs to resolve an issue or conflict.

Sidney's management style empowers the team to make decisions that help them solve problems and meet established goals. The roles and norms they develop help them adapt to each other and function effectively. The freedom and responsibility within the team promote a sense of belonging that leads to better problem solving, and it is all because the members are empowered.

Now you understand some of the positive aspects of empowerment. Obviously, organizations have a lot to gain by empowering their employees. However, this leads us to a question. If the benefits are so great, then why do some organizations choose not to implement empowerment processes? The answer is because challenges exist, and these will be discussed in the next section.

Challenges

Inadequate training

Employees must be properly trained before they are allowed to make decisions related to their jobs. Lack of training can result in problems because employees make decisions based on hunches, instincts, or perceptions. If these decisions are wrong, they will cause the organization to become less efficient and the bottom line will be negatively impacted.

Organizational example

Betty is an agent at an insurance company. She has only been in her job for three months when management announces that they are going to implement an empowerment program.

Betty undergoes one day of training, and management considers her ready to make her own decisions. The next day, a new customer named Bart asks her for a quote on life insurance. He smoked for most of his life, but he has not smoked for the past five years. Since Bart does not smoke now, Betty writes him up as a non-smoker, and he gets a discounted rate. Bart signs the policy, and it will be valid for the next 20 years.

Later, an auditor at the insurance company notices that Bart's smoking history was not documented. If Betty had done more diligent research, she would have found out that he smoked two packs a day of cigarettes for 32 years. Bart should not have received the discounted rate based on his history of smoking, but the policy has already been signed and now the company cannot make any changes.

Betty made a decision that could potentially have a negative on the impact the bottom line of the insurance company, and it was due to the fact that one day of training was inadequate.

Inadequate oversight

Empowerment works well when decisions are made correctly. However, like any other business activity, there is the potential for making mistakes. This in itself is not a major concern...as long as qualified employees monitor the decisions being made and step in when necessary. Management cannot be completely "hands-off" because their guidance is sometimes necessary.

Organizational example

Trish works in sales and marketing at an art studio with an empowerment program in place. Employees at the studio can now make many of their own decisions.

Trish decides to run an inventory reduction sale where all prints will be marked 30 percent lower in price. She begins the sale, and it is going very well. Almost 90 percent of the targeted print stock is sold to customers. However, when the owner Rick looks at the profit margin, he realizes there is a big problem. Every print in the studio was sold below cost, and this is not good for the business.

Trish made a mistake on the pricing of the prints, and this was costly to the art studio. If Rick had been monitoring her sale, he would have noticed the mistake and changed the pricing so it was profitable.

Unwilling management

Some managers do not want an empowered workforce. They might (1) feel threatened by the shift in power, (2) think their employees are not competent enough to make decisions, or (3) resist the change due to fear of the unknown. Whatever the reason, unwilling managers impede the empowerment process and prevent its success.

Organizational example

Dennis is a foreman in a vegetable processing plant who thinks employees are incapable of making decisions for themselves. He strongly believes that supervisors are hired to make all decisions, and this should never change.

Laura, the president of the company, has recently implemented an employee empowerment program. She wants the plant employees to feel an important part of the organization by making decisions by themselves.

Despite the change, Dennis continues to cling to the old style of management. When one of his employees make a decision, he overrules it...regardless of whether it is right or wrong. Then he tells other supervisors that the empowerment program is not working.

Dennis is a supervisor who stands in the way of the empowerment program's success, and this is a direct result of him being an unwilling manager.

Confusion

Empowerment can cause confusion in the workforce. Employees have different ways of handling situations pertaining to their jobs, and these variances can create misunderstanding. What works as a solution for one person, might not work for another. For example, some employees like to involve others using team approaches to problems solving, while others prefer to work individually. This can create chaos for organizations...especially when customers are involved.

Organizational example

Sheena and George work in customer service for an online sporting goods distributor called Living Sports. Sheena gets a call from a customer who is unhappy that her son's football cleats were defective. She tells the customer to return the cleats for a refund plus 10 percent. The customer is happy with this resolution because she believes she is being reimbursed for her inconvenience. She has plenty of time to buy new cleats because her son's team, the Badgers, does not have a game for two weeks.

Another mother whose son plays for the Badgers ordered the same type of cleats from Living Sports, and these shoes were also defective. This time, however, George takes the call. He tells the customer to send the cleats back, and he will send out a more expensive pair from a different manufacturer with free shipping. The customer accepts George's resolution to the problem and is happy that her son will get better cleats out of the deal.

The two parents see each other while picking up their sons from practice. They discuss the cleats they purchased from Living Sports. Since they bought the same type of cleats, they don't understand why the refund/exchange policy was different for each of them. They are both happy with the resolution to their problems, but they are baffled as to why they were not offered similar compensation.

Empowerment resulted in Sheena and George offering different resolutions for the same problem, and this created confusion for their customers.

Selfishness

Selfishness occurs when empowered employees disrespect their coworkers' efforts. Since they are in charge of their own decision-making, they believe other employee's work is not of equal importance. This results in a lack of respect and disregard for workplace courtesy, and it can cause the organization to run less efficiently.

Organizational example

Pricilla is a hair stylist at an upscale hair and nail salon where the owner Rolando has recently empowered all of his employees. She is now able to suggest any type of haircut to customers without the approval of Rolando. In the past, Rolando did not want hairstylists to make such suggestions to elite clientele in fear that they might be offended or scared off from the salon.

Pricilla has been doing well with making suggestions to her clientele. In fact, her customer base has increased at the salon...and that means more money for her and Rolando. However, she has also begun to show less respect for the nail technicians. She does not see their work as nearly as important as hers, and this shows by her lack of respect for them. She takes their supplies without their permission and never worries about leaving a mess for them to clean up.

Pricilla's behavior causes problems at the salon. The nail technicians dislike her, and they go out of their way to avoid helping her. They have also complained to Rolando, and two technicians have left the company for positions at a competitor.

Pricilla's empowerment led to her becoming selfish, and this resulted in efficiency problems for the salon.

Confidentiality risks

When organizations empower employees, they share important information so those employees can make justifiable decisions. This is good...but it can also be bad if employees freely exchange that information with others and risk confidentiality. Competitors, for example, can use that information to their advantage.

Organizational example

Reginald is a teller at a bank that recently empowered its employees. He is now authorized to see more of people's personal information than he ever had in the past. This helps him make decisions, but it also caused him to make a bad mistake.

A big celebrity was using Reginald's bank and wanted her name to remain anonymous to avoid problems with the paparazzi or other people intent on finding out personal information about her. When Reginald discovered who she was, he was excited and divulged it to a security guard at the bank. This turned out to be a big mistake because the security guard told several other people. Eventually, the celebrity found out, became upset, and changed banks.

Reginald exposed confidential information about a celebrity customer who wanted to remain anonymous. This was upsetting to the customer, and she took her business to another bank.

Overstepping boundaries

Sometimes empowered employees let their newfound decision-making power "go to their heads." When this happens, employees believe they no longer need management in any decision-making capacity, and the end result is people doing whatever they think is best without considering the objectives of the organization.

Organizational example

Sandra is a nurse in a hospital where employees have recently been empowered to make more of their own decisions. Sandra is very comfortable with her new authority because she is very good at her job. Today, however, she made an important error. She gave a patient certain medication that doctors had determined was no longer necessary. She did this because she believed she knew what was best for the patient and made a decision...without reading the doctor's notes on the computer. Fortunately, the medication did not cause any health issues for the patient, but the doctor was very upset.

Sandra's decision-making freedom led her to believe that she did not need the help of management. Because of this, she overstepped her boundaries and risked the health of a patient.

You can see that there are some challenges to empowerment programs. However, the benefits will overshadow these challenges if the program is implemented properly. This leads us to the next section on successfully implementing empowerment programs.

Successful implementation

You now have a basic understanding of employee empowerment, and this leads to a question. How should the program be implemented so that is will be beneficial to the organization? The following are some general rules that need to be followed for successful implementation:

Employees need to be involved from the beginning

Empowerment programs need to have employees involved from day one if management wants them to be successful. This does not mean that employees are told about the process, and then it is implemented. It means employees need to actively participate and have their thoughts heard. This can involve something as simple as setting up a suggestion box for employees to provide ideas. It can also be more complex where meetings are held for employee input and feedback about the organization. Once the findings are gathered, management can make an honest estimate of what is needed for successful implementation of the program.

There is one more key point for getting employees involved. Regardless of the involvement method chosen, management needs to make sure that employees are not afraid of retaliation for their comments. If this is the case, workers will not be honest about their thoughts.

Management needs to be committed throughout the program

Management involvement is critical for implementing employee empowerment programs. They cannot simply start the program and walk away to focus on other matters. They need to be involved throughout the entire process. If management does not show genuine interest, then employees will not view the program as important.

Another part of management commitment involves trust. Employees need to be able to trust managers to follow through on the claims they have made. If this does not happen, employees will lose faith that the program will work.

Training needs to be conducted before the implementation

Training needs to be complete and thorough. Management that does limited or ineffective training is "shooting themselves in the foot" before the program takes root.

Employees need to understand what is expected of them if they are going to help meet organizational goals. They also need to be educated and informed on how to make proper decisions that apply to their jobs Organizations should strongly consider hiring outside trainers to make sure all employees are effectively trained.

Time needs to be sufficient for the process to take effect

Time is very important for successful implementation of empowerment programs. Management must understand that proper time needs to be allotted for employee input, employee training, and start-up glitches. Goals can be set for the implementation, but nothing should be written in stone. There will be unforeseen issues, and organizations that refuse to allow for these issues will not be able to effectively implement the program.

Summary

Employee empowerment is about getting employees involved in the management of an organization. It eliminates the need for supervisor approval on every decision made by their subordinates. It is also very beneficial for the survival and growth of an organization.

Specifically, employee empowerment improves idea generation, performance, customer service, employee commitment, change acceptance, culture, and teams. It faces some challenges, but the positives outweigh the negatives once the program is up and running.

The key to a prosperous employee empowerment program is successful implementation. This entails employee involvement, commitment from management, proper training, and sufficient time for the program to gain momentum.

Congratulations! You now understand employee empowerment in organizations. Think about implementing it during your management career.

Employee Pay and Compensation
In Organizations
Types, Advantages, and Disadvantages

Louis Bevoc

Published by
NutriNiche System LLC

Louis Bevoc books...simple explanations of complex subjects

Introduction

Introduction

Some people do not need to work. They are financially independent and do not need to earn additional income to live within the means of their current lifestyle. Unfortunately, this is not the case for the majority of the population. Most people need to earn money so they can provide for themselves and their families.

People who do work tend to put a high priority on their compensation. This compensation can come in many different forms including pay, bonuses, commission, retirement plans, profit sharing, stock ownership, and benefits. Employees want job satisfaction, and money always seems to play a role in finding that satisfaction. In fact, money is typically one of the most important aspects of employment, and it is a major reason why workers remain at their current employer or leave for other positions.

This focus of this book is employee pay and compensation in organizations. It examines various types of pay structures and benefits. Specifically, it looks at salary pay, hourly pay, commission pay, bonus pay, piece-rate pay, merit pay, skill pay, profit sharing programs, gain sharing programs, employee stock ownership programs, work-life balance programs, and benefit packages. Each type of compensation is described, discussed in terms of pros and cons, and illustrated using a workplace example.

Let's move into the next section to discuss the types of pay and compensation mentioned above.

Types

This section is the main focus of this book. It discusses employee pay and compensation using workplace examples for illustration and real world application. The writing is rather easy to follow and comprehend, but please note that the advantages and disadvantages are based on the employee rather than the employer. Employer advantages and disadvantages are generally different depending on the situation.

The following are the various types of pay and compensation noted in the introduction:

Salary

This type of pay involves a set amount of money for a certain period of time. Typically, the money is based on one year of work. This wage does not normally change until management decides a change is justified. Usually, employees' salaries go up based on their increased value to the organization. However, salaries can also go down if management believes employees are not producing enough to warrant their wage.

Organizational example

Rocco is a store manager at a submarine sandwich shop. His job is to manage all aspects of the business for a fixed wage that is paid every Friday. He does not have set hours that he has to be at the store, but he needs to make sure it is operating efficiently every day. In short, Rocco receives a weekly salary as compensation for his job responsibilities regardless of the number of hours he works.

Below are some pros and cons of salary pay:

Employee advantages

- Salaried employees are not required to punch a time clock. There is no need to track every minute worked due to the expectations involved. Salaried workers have a job that needs to get done, and, within reason, management will not interfere if it is getting done.

- Salaried employees can easily budget their expenses because they know what they are getting paid. They do not have to wait to see how many hours they worked in a given week or worry about making less money during slow periods.

- Salaried employees experience high job satisfaction. Workers sometimes associate salary with prestige since this is the most common type of compensation for management personnel in organizations. Hourly employees often rank lower in the hierarchy, and they perceive salaried positions as promotions.

Employee disadvantages

- Salaried employees do not get paid overtime when they work more than 40 hours a week. In this respect, they can be taken advantage of by management when they are told they need to complete a job regardless of the time it takes.

- Salaried employees can go long periods of time without pay increases. There are typically no unions to guarantee more money, and management is not required to give raises.

- Salaried employees often have higher workloads than hourly employees. Salaries are a fixed cost...meaning they get paid out regardless of organizational sales. During slow periods, salaried personnel might be perceived as not doing enough work to support their wage, so management adds more responsibilities to their jobs.

Hourly

Employees who are compensated hourly receive an agreed upon amount of money per hour of work. There is no guaranteed amount of money that these employees make in a year because the number of hours worked depends on organizational needs or customer demand. However, unions have changed the rules for many workplaces by guaranteeing minimum hours per week for hourly employees.

Typically increases in money per hour for hourly employees are based on time intervals or the ability to perform certain job functions. Again, unions have intervened and implemented rules that need to be followed in some workplaces. These rules guarantee employees wage increases after a certain amount of time with the organization. Rarely do hourly wages go down, but this can happen if concessions are implemented.

Organizational example

Katrina is a production worker at a forklift assembly plant, and she earns 14 dollars per hour. When she works over 40 hours in a week, she receives 21 dollars per hour. In short, Katrina's compensation is a pre-determined wage for every hour she works assembling forklifts.

Below are some pros and cons of hourly pay:

Employee advantages

- Hourly employees get paid overtime (typically 1.5 times their normal hourly wage) when they work more than 40 hours a week...and sometimes when they work more than eight hours a day. In this respect, they get paid for every minute they are on the job.

- In general, hourly employees have designated pay increases. For example, management might give them a raise after 90 days to show that they are valued. Unions are often used to guarantee higher wages for these workers, and management has no choice other than to comply once changes in compensation have been negotiated.

- Hourly workers often have less stressful jobs than salaried workers. They have designated work that they must perform, but that work is done under controlled conditions with established productivity requirements.

Employee disadvantages

- Hourly employees are usually required to punch a time clock. Every minute that they work is tracked, and they do not get paid if they are not punched in.

- Hourly employees find it difficult to budget their expenses because they do not know how much money they will earn in a pay period. They have to wait to see how many hours they worked and be concerned about making less money during slow periods.

- Hourly employees lack power. They often rank low in the hierarchy, and they have limited say in the direction of the organization. This can cause job dissatisfaction and lower morale.

Commission

Commission pay is typically used for salespeople. Often times it involves a base salary plus a commission that is based on the total sales achieved. In short, increased sales result in increased commission.

Commission does not necessarily have to be monetary. Depending on the leadership of the organization, it can also be used for purchasing:

- A company vehicle
- An upgrade of a benefit package
- Additional time off or vacation
- A contribution to a retirement plan
- Company stock

Organizational example

Bert is employed as a salesperson for a solar energy company. He receives a base salary, and he gets two percent of his total sales volume as commission. Last year, Bert's sales were $2,000,000, and this resulted in a $40,000 commission for him.

Below are some pros and cons of commission pay:

Employee advantages

- Commission employees are motivated because they are rewarded for reaching goals.

- Commission allows employees the opportunity to live more comfortably. Many organizations have commission plans in place that can be very lucrative for salespeople.

- Commission employees can earn more than their salary without receiving a raise. In this respect, they control some of their own destiny in terms of income.

Employee disadvantages

- Employees who do not achieve commission based goals can end up demotivated. Their efforts are not rewarded, and this can lower their morale.

- Some employees cannot live comfortably without their commission pay. Since organizations want salespeople to perform, they tend to make it difficult for them to survive off only their base pay.

- Employees control some of their financial destiny with commission, but management is watching their earnings closely. If salespeople begin to earn too much money, some organizations lower their commission rates.

Bonus

Bonus pay is money given to people at the end of a specific amount of time. It is typically based on performance, and there are a variety of ways to calculate the amount of money paid out. The bonus can be a percentage of employees' pay, an amount based on profitability of the organization, a number based on employees' goal achievements, or an arbitrary figure determined by management. Regardless of the method used for determination of the dollar value, the objective of a bonus is to reward employees with additional income.

Organizational example

Tabitha has worked as a nurse in a doctor's office for the past six years. She earns a competitive salary, but the main reason she stays at this office is her year-end bonus. Doctors distribute bonuses to every employee based on their length of service with the organization.

Below are some pros and cons of bonus pay:

Employee advantages

- Bonuses motivate employees by providing a "carrot at the end of the stick." This opportunity for reward entices people to work harder to achieve goals.

- Bonuses can be paid to teams. This is good because every member shares in the success of the group, and it promotes teamwork throughout the organization.

- Bonuses are a nice yearly addition to income...especially if they come during the holidays when they are needed.

Employee disadvantages

- Bonuses are motivating due to the "carrot at the end of the stick", but the size of the "carrot" makes a difference. Employees who receive smaller amounts than expected can actually be demotivated by this added compensation.

- Bonuses based on team accomplishments can cause problems because some members do more work than others. If social loafers get the same bonus as everyone else on the team, then the members who did the majority of the work can become resentful.

- Employees often take bonuses for granted, and they become upset if they do not receive them...even though management does not make any guarantees.

Piece-rate

This form of compensation pays employees a pre-determined amount of money for a specific amount of work. People earn income based on their total output regardless of the amount of time they spend doing the job.

Organizational example

Gary works as an assembler at a cell phone company. He does not receive an hourly wage or a salary for his efforts. Instead, his entire compensation is based on the number of cell phones he assembles, regardless of the amount of time it takes him.

Below are some pros and cons of piece-rate pay:

Employee advantages

- Piece-rate provides a unique opportunity for earning income. Workers who produce quickly can earn more money than people who are paid hourly to do the same work.

- Employees take pride in their productivity because they are responsible from start to finish. They do not need others to help them do their jobs.

- Less supervision is needed because employees know exactly what they need to do to accomplish tasks. Workers make all job-related decisions, and they essentially manage themselves.

Employee disadvantages

- Employees who move too quickly can lose focus on quality and end up producing inferior products. They know that slowing down costs them money, so they are willing to sacrifice quality for quantity.

- Piece-rate pay discourages teamwork because employees prefer to work alone in order to earn money for themselves. This prevents people from collaborating with each for new ideas and concepts.

- Piece-rate pay does not help employees build skills outside of speed and productivity. They lack the ability to solve unique problems because their focus is limited.

Merit

This is a traditional type of compensation. Essentially, employee performance is evaluated using an appraisal system, and compensation is adjusted based on the results.

Organizational example

Isabelle is an inventory control manager at a book publisher. She is evaluated by the president of the company once per year, and any increase in her pay is based on that evaluation.

Below are some pros and merit pay:

Employee advantages

- Top performing employees are rewarded for their efforts. They find this motivating because lower performing employees do not receive the same pay increases.

- Merit pay is virtually unlimited in terms of rewards. There is no firmly established "top of the pay scale" because rewards are based on management perception of employees.

- Merit pay is beneficial for people who participate in successful team projects. Members are rewarded for their efforts based on the success of the team.

Employee disadvantages

- Economic conditions can prevent wage increases for employees regardless of their performance. This is demotivating and might cause some workers to stop performing at a high level.

- Equal pay for team members can cause problems because members who did most of the work can become resentful about not being recognized. Management typically rewards the group as a whole rather than recognizing individual members for their achievements.

- Unions typically resist any type of merit pay. Unions are designed for the progression of an entire group rather an individual, and this hurts top performers because they are not rewarded for their efforts.

Skill

This compensation is based on employee expertise rather than more traditional factors such as seniority or specific achievements. Essentially, skill pay is based on worker performance in relation to core competencies such as multi-tasking and leadership.

Organizational example

Jermaine is employed as a general manager in an upscale restaurant. His pay is based on his ability to lead his employees, rather than his accomplishments in areas such as cost savings or profitability.

Below are some pros and cons of skill pay:

Employee advantages

- Seniority has no bearing on compensation. New employees have an opportunity to be well compensated regardless of their experience or years with the organization.

- Employees can focus on their performance as related to specific job attributes. They know they will be rewarded if they do well in certain areas, and they do not have to worry about other unrelated aspects of their jobs.

- Skill-based pay promotes self-improvement. Focusing on specific competencies motivates employees to continually improve because they know they are compensated for getting better in those areas.

Employee disadvantages

- Skill-based pay can promote a sense of entitlement. Employees who are guaranteed money based on their expertise can become complacent.

- Objectivity is sometimes missing. Evaluation of competencies such as multi-tasking and leadership is very subjective because it is based on personal interpretation.

- Employees can feel unfairly treated if they find out that lesser valued employees received larger monetary increases. This can happen with any type of employee compensation plan, but it is more prevalent with skill-based pay due to the subjectivity involved.

Profit sharing

This type of compensation is provided in addition to salary, hourly wages, bonuses, and commissions. It is based on the profitability of the organization, and management determines the amount of the contribution. The money is often paid out when employees leave the organization or retire.

Organizational example

Candice is employed as a stewardess for an airline. She earns a salary and has a benefit package that includes health, dental, and life insurance. Additional compensation for Candice includes a profit sharing retirement plan that the airline contributes to after profitable years.

Below are some pros and cons of profit sharing programs:

Employee advantages

- Profit sharing plans are essentially free compensation. Employees have a retirement plan in place without contributing any of their own money.

- Profit sharing plans promote teamwork. Employees work together and focus on making the organization profitable because they share in the rewards.

- Profit sharing plans help employees identify with the organization. Employees feel like they are an active part of the company because their contributions matter.

Employee disadvantages

- Employees have a retirement plan in place that does not consist of their own money, but management determines the amount and time of the contributions. There is also no guarantee that contributions will be made.

- Employees sometimes focus only on profitability... regardless of the consequences. Lower quality or less expensive products might be more profitable in the short-term, but they can have long-term ramifications that negatively impact the organization.

- Profit sharing plans can be demotivating when contributions are not made. People become dependent on these plans for their retirement, and they lose morale when the organization chooses not to contribute.

Gain sharing

Gain sharing is similar to profit sharing with some distinct differences. Both programs are designed for employees to share in the success of organizations. However, contributions to gain sharing programs are not based on profitability. Instead, employees need to meet designated goals in order to receive payouts. Typically these goals involve productivity increases from one period to the next.

Organizational example

Felix is an auto mechanic at a car dealership. He earns an hourly wage and has a benefit package that includes health, dental, and life insurance. Additional compensation for Felix includes a gain sharing plan where management measures the mechanics productivity every quarter and compares it to the previous quarter. If productivity increases, the mechanics receive a payout from the dealership.

Below are some pros and cons of gain sharing programs:

Employee advantages

- Gain sharing is motivational. It inspires employees to increase productivity and improve their financial well-being.

- Gain sharing is paid out regardless of profitability. Employees are paid as long as they reach designated goals.

- Like profit sharing, gain sharing rewards employees for performance. However, gain sharing payments are more frequent because progress is measured and rewarded several times per year.

Employee disadvantages

- Gain sharing motivates employees, but it also has the potential to decrease morale because it is not guaranteed. Employees begin to expect payouts, and they are demotivated when money is not paid out because designated goals were not achieved.

- Gain sharing is not directly based on profitability, but it can disappear if organizations are not profitable. Organizations that are struggling financially need to cut costs, and gain sharing is often one of the first things to go.

- Similar to profit sharing, gain sharing employees sometimes focus only on increasing productivity. When they do this, quality can be lowered to the point where it negatively impacts the organization.

Employee stock ownership

This type of compensation is part of a benefit program where employees can purchase stock. The price of the stock is typically below the market value, and this makes it easier to purchase for workers.

Organizational example

Felicia is a foreman at a gutter and siding company. She is paid a salary and has medical and dental benefits for her family. Felicia also has an opportunity to own part of the company. Every year, her employer offers her the option to buy company stock at 20 percent below the market value. The only stipulation is that this stock cannot be sold until she leaves the company or retires.

Below are some pros and cons of employee stock ownership programs:

Employee advantages

- Employees are interested in the success of the company because they are stock owners. In short, they have a financial interest and want to see it grow.

- Employees tend to become more motivated when they own stock. They want to get involved in ways that help the company grow and prosper because they identify with it through ownership.

- Stock value grows as the organization grows. Employees can accrue large amounts of money as the value of their investment increases. Best of all, they can do this without the stress or headaches of managing the company.

Employee disadvantages

- Stock ownership is not always enough for employees to stay motivated. They also need to be informed of the company status and progress in order to feel involved, and sometimes management fails to address this concern.

- Stock ownership programs are often designated for retirement. If the company performs poorly and the value of the stock decreases, then employees who relied on it for their retirement can end up with little or nothing.

- Often times the stock issued to employees is non-voting in status. This means employees own stock, but they have no voice in the direction of the company.

Benefits

Employee benefits are compensation in addition to an agreed-upon wage. They encompass a variety of different components and are based on many factors. However, the major benefits referred to in this section are health insurance, dental insurance, life insurance, vacation, paid days off, and retirement programs.

Organizational example

Quinton just accepted a job as an engineer with an aerospace company. He agreed upon a salary, but the company also offers a benefit package as additional compensation. This package includes health insurance, dental insurance, life insurance, two weeks of paid vacation, three paid days off, and a 401K program with a 25 percent company match.

Below are some pros and cons of benefit packages:

Employee advantages

- Benefit packages often allow employees to make choices, and this is good because people have different needs. They can select the benefits that are most beneficial and pass on the ones that are not essential.

- Good benefit packages are an added incentive to remain with an organization. In fact, benefits are more important than wages for some employees.

- Benefit packages allow employees to monitor and maintain the health of themselves and their families. This is good for the employee and the employer.

Employee disadvantages

- Benefit packages often allow employees to make choices based on their needs, but the wrong choice can create financial problems. Quite simply, it is hard for employees to know what benefits will be needed in the future.

- Good benefit packages can force employees to stay at jobs that they dislike. They might want to move on to something that pays a higher wage or is more interesting, but they cannot make a change because they need the benefits offered by their current employer.

- The costs of benefits are constantly rising for organizations, and they need to pass some of this onto the employees. This means employees are required to pay for their benefits, and some opt out if they cannot afford to do so. When this happens, the benefits offered by the organization are no longer beneficial to the employee.

Work-life balance

Work-life balance involves accomplishing work-related goals while enjoying life outside of work. As people's lives become busier and more hectic, they begin to realize the importance of work-life balance. Time is limited, and different things need to take priority at different times in life. People need to work in order to sustain a certain lifestyle, but they also need the time to enjoy that lifestyle.

Organizational example

Jaquelin works as a pediatric nurse at a hospital. The hospital has a work-life balance program in place where trained counselors are available to listen to the problems the hospital employees are experiencing at home or at work. This program provides employees with someone who acts as a sounding board and offers advice when needed...and it helps Jaquelin cope with the stress of her job.

Below are some pros and cons or work-life balance programs:

Employee advantages

- Stress is reduced. Work-life balance programs such as counseling and therapy help relieve stress and prevent the consequences that result from it.

- Physical health is improved. Gym memberships and exercise areas help employees maintain physical health at work and at home.

- Telecommuting is a huge benefit for many employees. They can perform their job from home and not have to worry about traffic or restrictive work schedules.

Employee disadvantages

- Career progression is hampered. Telecommuters who are not involved in the day-to-day activities of the organization can be passed up by others simply because they are not physically noticed. This is a major concern for employees whose jobs are completely remote.

- Telecommuting can cause communication issues. Typically the major form of communication for employees working remotely is the written word (email, text, letter)...and written words can easily be misinterpreted.

- Cost is a concern. Expenses can force organizations to eliminate work-life balance programs, and the loss of these programs can be demotivating to the employees who found them useful.

Now you have an understanding of the basic types of pay and compensation available for employees. Leaders in organizations need to figure out which types work best for their workforces in order to keep people content and productive. Ultimately, this requires finding and maintaining a balance between satisfied workers and a financially stable organization.

Summary

Compensation is very important to employees. It affects their motivation and commitment, and it is a major factor in determining their longevity with organizations. People want to find happiness at work, and compensation always seems to factor into that happiness.

This book focuses on employee pay and compensation in organizations. It examines various types of pay structures and benefits including salary pay, hourly pay, commission based pay, bonus pay, piece-rate pay, merit pay, skill pay, profit sharing programs, gain sharing programs, employee stock ownership programs, work-life balance programs, and benefit packages. Each type of compensation is described, discussed in terms of pros and cons, and illustrated using a workplace example.

Congratulations! You know have a better understanding of employee pay and compensation...two importance aspects of people's jobs that affect their organizational behavior.

Toxic Leadership
in Organizations
Understanding and Surviving

Louis Bevoc

Published by
NutriNiche System LLC

Louis Bevoc books...simple explanations of complex subjects

Introduction

The term "toxic leader" was originally established by Marcia Whicker in the mid-1990s to describe leaders that failed miserably in their positions at the top. She described these individuals as selfish, deceitful, controlling, and non-productive. Many of them had successful careers, but that success came at the expense of others.

Over the years, other people have written about toxic leadership. They expanded upon Whicker's work using well-known examples...and the Wall Street scandals of the not so distant past gave them a lot to write about. As might be expected, all of these writers agreed that toxic leadership is bad for employees and organizations.

This book provides a broad overview of toxic leadership. It examines the characteristics that make up these leaders, the tools they use to maintain their positions, and the effects that their actions have on workplaces. It also suggests ways to survive working in an organization with toxic leadership.

Toxic leadership occurs when leaders abuse the relationships they have with employees and others associated with the organization. These individuals are often aware of their actions, but they simply do not care about the damage they do to others because their only concern is personal advancement.

Please consider the following example of toxic leadership:

> Salvatore takes over as the CEO of a publicly traded computer hardware manufacturing company. The company is surviving, but it has not been profitable for a few years, and the stockholders are demanding better performance.

> Within six months of taking over the organization, Salvatore lays off ten percent of the management staff because he claims the company is top heavy. He also eliminates 15 percent of the manufacturing jobs after his analysis determines that the production plants are overstaffed.

> These cuts save the company over 15 million dollars a year. Profitability returns, and the stock price increases 25 percent. This looks good for Salvatore, and he is rewarded with a three million dollar bonus at the end of the fiscal year.

> However, 18 months later, the company starts to lose money again. The stock price goes below its value before Salvatore took over as CEO, and the stockholders are furious. Salvatore is terminated from his a position with a two million dollar severance package.

> In short, Salvatore was paid over 5 million dollars to reduce the market value of the computer hardware company. He profited while employees lost jobs and the company faltered.

The above example is not a true story, but is indicative of the fallout from toxic leadership. Typically, these individuals leave an organization in worse condition than it was when they took over the top management position. Sometimes the damage they do is so severe that companies are forced to shut down.

Now that have some basic understanding of toxic leadership and have seen an example, let's move to a discussion on specific characteristics of these individuals.

Characteristics

Toxic leaders have definitive characteristics associated with them. Certain traits, such as being competitive in their style of management, produce some positive effects in workplaces. However, most toxic leader characteristics negatively impact employees and organizations.

In general, toxic leaders are:

Autocratic

Toxic leaders essentially are in a style of management all by itself. They do not fall into the traditional leadership categories that consist of authoritarian, democratic, laissez-faire, paternalistic, transactional, and transformational. However, they have some traits in common with autocratic leaders because they:

- Act as a dictator in the sense that they use fear to establish power
- Communicate from top to bottom with limited communication in the reverse direction
- Focus on control and maintain close supervision so they do not lose control
- View other types of leadership style (such as democratic) as inefficient because control is limited

Unlikeable

Toxic leaders are in control of their employees, but this does not mean they are liked by those employees. In fact, workers typically dislike toxic leaders because:

- They are afraid to argue or question decisions due to the fear of jeopardizing their jobs.
- Their creativity and diversity are stifled.
- They are not entitled to opinions, and there is no room for debate or disagreement.
- There is only one right answer...and it comes from the toxic leader.

Untrustable

Trust builds relationships, and lack of trust deteriorates them. Since toxic leaders do whatever is necessary to accomplish their goals, they often violate the trust of their employees. Those employees then lose their commitment to their organization because they no longer identify with its values....and the workplace begins to spiral downward.

The worst part about a loss of trust is that once it is gone, it is difficult to restore. However, many toxic leaders are not concerned with getting that trust back as long as they have achieved their personal goals.

Arrogant

Arrogance comes naturally for many individuals. In workplaces, some employees do not even realize they are displaying arrogance because they are unaware of their behavior. They are trying to do their job to the best of their ability, and they unintentional display conceitedness or superiority.

Arrogance is acceptable for some employees, but it produces problems for leaders because they create a barrier between themselves and their employees. That barrier prevents the flow of communication and restricts the exchange of ideas and information.

Many toxic leaders are arrogant. They often realize their arrogance, but they simply do not care. They have an agenda that is going to move forward regardless of who is upset or offended. Unfortunately, that agenda is about personal gain rather than organizational growth and prosperity.

Competitive

Competition is good for organizations. It makes sense because the best positions are often very lucrative, and employees work hard to attain those positions. In short, they compete with each other to reach the top.

Toxic managers push competition to another level. They are over competitive and will do whatever they need to do to get to the top. This is not good because dishonest and unethical activities are often part of their game plan. Competent people get passed over for positions because rules are bent or broken, and this prevents the best employees from rising to the top. Ultimately, the organization suffers...and so do the employees within it.

Micromanagers

As noted in the introduction, toxic leaders are controlling because they need to make sure their agenda is moving forward. One method used to ensure control is micromanagement.

In the case of a CEO, the employees most often micromanaged are top ranking executives. These executives then lose their motivation to work hard, and the negativity slowly trickles down into the rank and file employees.

Micromanaging is not good for an organization at any level. If the CEO is guilty of this type of management style, then it is only a matter of time before the entire workforce culture is impacted.

Bullies

Some people might find it difficult to believe that top leaders of organizations are bullies. After all, these individuals have reached positions where their word is the law, and they should not have to coerce others to behave in desired ways. In many cases, this is true...but not if the top person is a toxic leader.

Toxic leaders rise to their positions by intimidating and mistreating others, and they have no intention of changing their tactics. In fact, once they reach the top they believe they are even more justified to bully others simply because they are the top authority. Bullying also prevents rivals and dissenters from becoming threats and helps toxic leaders maintain their position of dominance.

Inflexible

Good leaders know that they need to be flexible in order to adapt when it is best for their organization. Toxic leaders view flexibility as a sign of weakness and instead choose to remain firm on their decisions...regardless of whether they are right or wrong.

Inflexibility is another tactic used by toxic leaders to prevent dissenting employees from becoming threats to their power. When workers realize that their leaders will not change their minds under any circumstances, they stop opposing them because that opposition is pointless.

Insecure

Confidence is an important trait for leaders. Employees expect those in charge to be confident, and leaders who fail to live up to that expectation lose the respect of the workforce. This is not a problem for most good leaders because they are competent individuals who have worked hard to achieve their position. They understand their job responsibilities and the employees in their workplace, and this leads to happy workers and organizational success.

Toxic leaders do not fit into the good leader category, but they attempt to imitate them by portraying a high level of self-confidence. Some are successful in this portrayal, and it leads to the illusion that they are competent. Others fail to create that illusion...and their insecurity is quite transparent.

In theory, insecurity should be an expected trait of toxic leaders. After all, these individuals reach their positions through deceitful rather than honest behavior...so why would anyone expect them to be competent or confident?

Narcissistic

Narcissistic people are self-absorbed. They admire themselves over everyone else, and their ego controls many aspects of their behavior. Based on this, it is rather easy to see why toxic managers are narcissistic because they value themselves over all other employees. Worse yet, they view themselves as more important than the organization they are responsible for overseeing...and this is never good.

In regard to narcissism, always remember the following:

Narcissistic employees can damage organizations...but narcissistic leaders can destroy them.

Discriminatory

As more businesses compete in the global marketplace, diversity becomes increasingly important. Good leaders understand this point and diversity their employees. They establish heterogeneous workforces that stimulate creativity and innovation during problem-solving. They want the synergy that evolves from different minds.

Toxic leaders do not value diversity and would rather discriminate. They prefer people like themselves so they can further their agenda...which is to benefit personally from the organization that they oversee. Workforces under toxic leadership are not creative and innovative, but this is not a concern for the leaders because they typically make important decisions themselves.

Condescending

Toxic leaders are often critical. They tear employees down rather than build them up because criticism maintains control while praise leads to the empowerment that breeds independent thinking. This is why so many toxic leaders exhibit condescending characteristics.

The following are some organizational examples of how toxic leaders display their associated characteristics in the workplace:

Organizational example #1

Victoria owns a bakery. When she makes business decisions, she does not trust or consult anyone else. She makes choices based on her perception of the situation, and she is not open to people who challenge her decisions.

There are problems associated with Victoria's leadership style. She has made some decisions that her managers knew were wrong, but they did not challenge her due to the fear of retribution. They know Victoria does not take kindly to disagreement or criticism, and she does not allow people to debate her choices. This is demoralizing to Victoria's managers because they feel like they have no freedom and their opinions do not matter. It has also resulted in some costly mistakes that could have been prevented with some discussion.

Victoria's toxic leadership style is such that she is inflexible and does not trust others to help her make decisions. Her tight control suppresses the individuality of her managers, negatively impacts their moral, and prevents them from engaging in healthy debate.

Organizational example #2

Mark is the CEO of a pest control company owned by venture capitalists. His organization services retail establishments in 21 different states. The hierarchical structure of the company consists of a CEO, two vice presidents, one general manager, one office manager, ten office workers, 24 area managers, and 380 licensed pesticide applicators.

Mark does not let any management employees approach the venture capitalist owners with suggestions or ideas for improving the company. He makes it clear that he is the only person who is allowed to talk to these individuals, and there will be consequences if anyone goes over his head. This demoralizes Mark's managers and causes them to dislike him as a boss.

Mark's micromanagement is based on his concern that he might not receive credit for an idea generated by someone else in the company. His toxic leadership style shows his insecurity and demotivates his workforce.

Organizational example #3

Tonya is the president of an office equipment distribution company. She decides to establish a team of employees to find ways to lower shipping costs. The team consists of the office manager, purchasing manager, safety manager, quality manager, inventory control manager, and shipping manager. Tonya chose these individuals based on their skill levels and areas of expertise, but she is not confident that they will make the right cost-cutting decisions for the organization. She believes she knows best what needs to be done, so she monitors their activities closely and makes sure she has the final say on any decisions made by the group.

The team comes up with three new cost-cutting ideas, but Tonya rejects them all. She tells them their ideas make no sense, and she lets them know that she expects better ideas from them as a group. She states that they have embarrassed themselves and the company, and this is not acceptable. The team wants to abandon the project, but they meet again because Tonya requires them to do so.

Tonya is a micromanager, and her critical comments demotivate the team members. They know that regardless of their findings, Tonya will react in a condescending manner and override their ideas because she believes she knows best. Tonya truly is a toxic leader.

Now that you understand some of the characteristics of toxic leaders, let move into the tools they use to control others and personally benefit.

Tools

Toxic leaders use specific tools for their jobs. Unfortunately, these tools are mostly used to maintain control over employees rather than to make organizations grow and prosper.

The toxic leader's tools include:

Power

Most leaders control people's decision-making power for the benefit of their organization, but toxic leaders use this tool for personal gain. They make decisions that affect their control of the organization, and they appoint "puppets" to make less critical decisions. Please consider the following example:

> Gertrude is a toxic leader. She runs her organization with an iron fist and will not allow employees to make decisions without her approval. She does this to maintain strict control over all aspects of the workplace.
>
> Gertrude needs a marketing manager to replace the one she recently terminated. There are several qualified candidates in the marketing department, but none of them are people that Gertrude wants in charge. Instead, she chooses a production supervisor named Arthur for the job. Arthur knows very little about marketing, but this does not concern Gertrude because he is a "yes man" who will only make decisions that help her maintain control of the organization.

In the above example, Gertrude arranges the decision-making power structure for her own personal gain. She is only looking out for herself, and there is nothing beneficial for the organization or employees.

Games

This tool utilizes mind games. It is a form of bullying where potential rivals or dissenters are assigned tasks that they cannot possibly complete. Please consider the following example:

> Ronald is a toxic leader who sees Janet, the human resources director, as a potential threat to his control of other employees. In a well-planned move, he puts Janet in charge of a construction project. He tells her that she is a skilled employee who can handle the task.
>
> Unfortunately, Janet has no engineering, building, or architectural experience. Ronald knows this and purposely assigns her to the task because he knows that she will not be able to complete it.

In the above example, Ronald is setting up Janet to fail so she will not be considered for other opportunities.

Discipline

Toxic leaders look for rule violations to discipline people they do not like or do not want to see advance. Please consider the following example:

> Leslie is a toxic leader who views Mitch, the director of finance, as a threat to her control and authority. Leslie knows that Mitch has been using his company vehicle for personal use, so she disciplines him with an unpaid suspension.
>
> Mitch's personal use of his company vehicle is technically a violation of company policy. However, other managers do this on a regular basis without facing any disciplinary action.

In the above example, Leslie appears to be adhering to company policy rather than singling out a rival or dissenter. However, the reality is that she wants to punish Mitch to make him look bad.

Status

This involves the power to control work-related privileges that symbolize authority. Executive parking lots, private bathrooms, and catered lunches are examples of status tools that many leaders have at their disposal. Toxic leaders remove these privileges from individuals that they consider to be a threat, and this is demeaning. Please consider the following example:

> Patrick is a toxic leader. He considers the vice-president of production Mary to be a threat to his control. He wants Mary to leave the organization, so he removes some of her perks. Specifically, he takes away her parking space in the covered garage and announces that all production employees must park in the manufacturing plant lot for security reasons.
>
> In reality, Patrick sees no legitimate security reason for all production employees to park in the manufacturing plant lot. He implements this rule because he wants to discourage Mary so she will leave the organization.

In the above example, Mary lost a privilege. On the surface, this might not seem significant. However, privileges indicate status and achievement and are therefore important to employees.

Structure

This refers to the structure of work relationships in the organization. Employees have certain likes and dislikes when it comes to coworkers, and this causes them to prefer working with some people more than others.

Toxic managers use this tool to monitor or control employee work relationships for their own personal gain. Please consider the following example:

> Larry is a toxic leader. He is insecure about his position and constantly monitors his employees to eliminate potential threats to his authority and control.
>
> Rhonda is one of Larry's favorite managers. She does whatever he asks, and keeps him informed of workplace happenings. Larry knows that Rhonda supports him, and he uses her for many of his undermining activities. Rhonda is not liked by many of her coworkers, but this is fine with Larry as long as she feeds him information.
>
> Larry is suspicious that the office personnel might be plotting against him behind his back. Since he is not always around them, he moves Rhonda's desk into the office to monitor their conversations and report back to him. The office employees are not happy about this move, but they cannot stop it.

In the above example, Rhonda has no reason for her desk to be in the office other than the fact that she can be a snitch for Larry. In this sense, Larry uses the structure tool to maintain his control as a toxic leader.

Now that you understanding of some of the tools used by toxic leaders, let's move into the effects that their actions have on workplaces.

Effects

Toxic leadership has a variety of different effects on employees and organizations. Unfortunately, almost all those effects are negative, and some of the major ones are listed below.

Trust

Toxic leaders almost always violate trust because they destroy workplaces while furthering their own agenda. Unfortunately, this lack of trust often goes beyond the toxic leader. Many workers lose trust in the organization as a whole...even after the toxic leader is no longer a part of it.

As was noted in the characteristics section, the worst part about lost trust is the fact that it is very difficult to restore. Good leaders realize this and work toward being sincere and honest so their employees have faith in their actions.

Turnover

Once employees have had enough of toxic leadership, they look for employment elsewhere. This means good employees are lost because toxic leaders are only interested in furthering their own agenda. In certain situations, the exiting of workers is welcomed by toxic leaders...but it is rarely welcomed by other employees who care about their organizations.

Commitment

Commitment is the feeling employees have toward achieving the goals of the organization. Employees who work under toxic leadership lose faith that their leaders will do the right thing, and they are no longer committed to the organization. Without employee commitment, organizations cannot be successful, and their survival is at stake.

In short, employee commitment is critical for organizational growth and prosperity...and that commitment diminishes under toxic leadership.

Motivation

This effect is a no-brainer. Employees who work under toxic leadership lose motivation due to the fact that their leaders only care about themselves. If bosses do not care about employees, then employees do not care about their organization...and they are not motivated to perform their jobs to the best of their ability. This creates a lose/lose situation for the employer and the employee...with the only winner being the toxic leader.

Fear

Control is a very high priority for toxic leaders. In fact, often times it is the most important aspect of the job for some of these individuals. Based on this importance, toxic leaders prefer to rule by fear because fear maintains control. Employees who experience fear are afraid to speak out against the leader due to the consequences that might prevail.

Stress

Toxic leaders create stress throughout the workplace. Part of this is planned because it helps them establish authority and maintain control. However, stress is hard on employees and can lead to physical or mental health issues. Unfortunately, toxic leaders are not concerned with employee health as long as they benefit personally.

Now you understand some of the major effects of toxic leadership, and it is rather obvious that they are all bad. However, this raises a question. If toxic leadership has all negative effects, how can employees tolerate it and work under such conditions? The next section answers that question by discussing methods of employee survival.

Surviving

This section suggests methods for combating toxic leadership and surviving the fallout. These methods include:

Control

Employees need to maintain control by not reacting emotionally to the negative actions of toxic leaders. Sometimes these leaders are looking for angry outbursts so they can implement termination policies that get rid of the offending employees permanently.

Emotional control also prevents mental and physical health issues that can result from extreme emotional reactions. Regardless of the harm done to health, employees need to react appropriately to avoid further complication of the situation.

Patience

This is similar to the control method because employees need to think before they react to the situation. Patience allows for the rational reactions that are necessary to deal with an assault from a toxic leader, and employees can gather their thoughts so they can combat the toxic leader with facts.

Typically, patience works well for employees because they have time to build cases against toxic leaders. Strong cases have a good chance of stopping this type of behavior because the toxic leaders' negative actions are exposed on a repeated basis.

Collaboration

Employees need to work together to combat toxic leadership. Rarely do "lone wolves" survive because they do not have enough power to combat leadership. However, there is strength in numbers. Collaboration with coworkers builds the necessary power to fight toxic leaders, and employees are more confident in their responses.

Collaboration is about synergy, and synergy is important for establishing strategies to combat toxic leadership. Employees can use all of the negative behavior they have witnessed to build successful cases against toxic leaders.

Summary

Toxic leaders care about themselves far more than they do about the organizations they oversee. They value control above everything else, and they use their power to maintain that control. They are not concerned about the damage they inflict on employees or workplaces as long as they personally benefit from the situation.

This book provides a broad overview of toxic leadership. It examines characteristics that make up these leaders, the tools they use to maintain their positions, and the effects that their actions have on workplaces. It also suggests ways to survive working in an organization with toxic leadership.

Congratulations! You now understand more about toxic leadership....an important aspect of organizational behavior.

Inventory Control
in Manufacturing
A Basic Introduction

Louis Bevoc

Published by
NutriNiche System LLC

Louis Bevoc books...simple explanations of complex subjects

Introduction

Most organizations need some type of inventory control. Companies that manufacture products usually have more physical items to keep track of than those that provide services, but both types of organizations have inventory that needs to be monitored. For example, a marketing company that promotes other companies products does not have to physically inventory any of those products or the raw materials used to manufacture them. However, that marketing company needs office supplies and materials for sales presentations, and stocking these items requires some type of inventory control.

A complete definition of inventory control can become quite detailed because it depends on the specific needs of individual organizations. However, for simplification purposes, inventory control for this book is defined as:

Lowest cost management of the materials required to meet organizational demands.

This book examines inventory control in manufacturing based on the above definition. Specifically, it discusses important goals of inventory control, methods for performing inventory control tasks, systems for reordering stock, management responsibilities, and ways of improving inventory control programs. The text is informational and educational, and it is written for easy reader understanding at any level.

Now that you understand the scope of this book, we can move into the major areas of discussion. Let's start by answering the following questions regarding the general concept of inventory control in manufacturing:

What is it?

Inventory control is a system that accounts for all items (raw materials and finished products) in stock at a manufacturer. It determines the location and quantity of these items so employees know what is on hand and where to get it.

Why is it needed?

Inventory control is needed a variety of reasons, but the major ones are as follows:

- It ensures finished product stock is maintained at a sufficient level. Too much inventory results in unnecessary cost and too little inventory results in unfulfilled customer orders. Inventory is expensive, but so are lost customer sales...so there needs to be a balance.
- It can be used to track raw materials or finished product usage. When an item goes out of stock, people who order it are notified so they can replenish the supply.
- It establishes reorder levels for raw materials and finished products. Reorder warnings are issued when inventory dips below designated levels.
- It detects theft, damage, and other losses. If inventory is missing but nothing was sold or produced, then there is a problem.

Why doesn't it always work?

Inventory control programs need to function efficiently to benefit the organizations that implement them. However, they do not always work properly for the following reasons:

Lack of planning

It is not uncommon for manufacturers to spend large amounts of money on inventory control software only to find that it does not meet their expectations. This happens for the following reasons:

- Management does plan for operating the system once it is live. They assume the software will run itself because they have invested a lot of money into it. The software will work, but management needs to understand what is needed to make it perform properly.
- Management does not plan for putting the right people in charge of the system. They assume employees will "fill in as needed" and take responsibility for aspects of the program that apply to their jobs.
- Management does not plan for a complete switch over to the new program. Some employees refuse to let go of old inventory control methods unless they are forced to do so. They do not trust or like the new software, so they keep doing things the way they have been doing them….and never learn the new program. Cut off dates need to be set in advance and enforced.

Regardless of the reason, planning is essential for getting inventory control systems to work effectively and produce valid information. In terms of inventory control, there is truth to the old saying, "those who fail to plan, plan to fail."

Lack of physical inventorying

This is probably the biggest reason for the failure of inventory control programs. Think of the old adage, "garbage in" equals "garbage out" because it is very applicable to inventory control. In fact, it is possible that this saying gained popularity from inventory control professionals.

If the people doing the physical inventorying do not enter accurate information, the system will not work. For example, assume 1000 boxes of pencils are in stock at a warehouse. However, the person inventorying this item only enters 600 boxes because he missed three pallets that are in a different location of the building.

This error causes a domino effect of other errors that cannot be corrected until the pencils are correctly counted. When customers buy pencils, the inventory is inaccurate…as is the case when new pencils are ordered. Re-order levels are also inaccurate, so too many or too few pencils could be kept on hand. Add this to the fact that inventory costs are wrong, and the end result is a major fiasco...all because inaccurate numbers were entered during physical inventory. Unfortunately, these inaccuracies can negatively impact the bottom lines of organizations.

Lack of customer understanding

Manufacturers that do not understand the inventory needs of their customers will not have a successful inventory control program. There must be a basic understanding of customer ordering, and this is best done by tracking trends.

For example, a meat processor's inventory control computer program is designated to reorder turkeys when inventory goes down to 500 birds. This assures a two week supply will always be on hand. However, the program does not know that at 80 percent of the turkeys are purchased two weeks before Thanksgiving...and the company runs out of birds at a critical time. Employees are upset with the computer program, but it is not the problem. Management needs to understand customer needs at this holiday and appropriately adjust reordering levels based on those needs.

Manufacturing personnel become upset when inventory programs do not perform as expected. However, often times the program is not at fault...as shown in the example above. The fault, quite simply, stems from the people in charge.

The following is a list of problems that result when manufacturing inventory control programs do not work:

- Products go missing without being noticed. This prevents mistakes and theft from being detected and rectified.
- Product shortages result from inventory trends not being noticed. This results in unhappy customers.
- Product overstocking is not detected. This results in money being unnecessarily spent and tied up.
- Product overstocking makes storage space an issue.
- Time and money are spent trying to resolve inventory problems.
- Shipping and transportation delays result from a lack of accurate information.

Based on the above, it is fairly obvious that inventory control systems need to work properly or there will be consequences. The next section expands on this thinking by discussing the goals and objectives of inventory control systems.

Goals

All programs utilized by organizations have specific goals or they would not have been implemented. The basic goals of manufacturing inventory control programs are understood by most employees, but that understanding is usually limited to the aspects that affect their specific jobs. The following is a more complete breakdown of inventory control goals for a better understanding of the need for these types of programs in manufacturing:

Track finished products

This is the most commonly known and understood goal of inventory control. Finished products need to be stored and accounted for in order to meet customer demand. Inventory control programs track the quantity and types of finished products in stock so manufacturers can be confident that they have enough to fulfill orders.

Believe it or not, many manufacturers are unaware of their finished product inventory. They have disorganized warehouses where products are not kept in common bays or designated areas. They also do a poor job of physical inventorying, so quantities being entered are wrong making every calculation that follows inaccurate. Add the fact that these companies have even less knowledge of their finished products that are stored offsite, and it is relatively easy to see why they have difficulty tracking their inventory.

Finished product accuracy is a major reason why manufacturers need inventory control. The complexity, location, and quantity of items produced by some of these companies indicate the need for computerized programs with relevant software. However, manual systems will work if the proper amount of time and effort are put forth. Either way, accurate information on finished products is important for organizational growth and survival, and that is why trend tracking is a major goal of inventory control programs.

Track raw materials

Manufacturers need raw materials to produce finished products. These raw materials are used at various points of the production process, so they must be kept on hand and stored in the facility.

The inventorying of raw materials is similar to that of finished products, except for the fact that the customer is the company itself. Raw materials are only used internally to build finished products, so one department "sells" or transfers them to another during the production process.

Quantities, location, and usage of all raw materials need to be tracked for cost and production purposes. This is done using inventory control programs, and that makes tracking raw materials an important goal of those programs.

Track trends

Organizations that turnover raw materials and finished products need inventory control for many different reasons, and competitiveness is one of those reasons. Inventory systems help manufacturers remain competitive because they generate a wealth of beneficial information. Some of that information, such as sales of individual products, is useful for tracking trends.

Unfortunately, many organizations fail to do a good job of tracking trends, and this gives their competition an advantage. In manufacturing, trends are important because they indicate the need for production during specific periods of time. For example, an ice cream manufacturer understands that sales are higher in the summer, so management must schedule production accordingly. However, before that scheduling can be done, some questions need to be answered. How much sugar, cream, cocoa, vanilla, corn syrup, and ice cream base should be kept on hand to make the ice cream? What type of cartons are needed for the ice cream and how many must be stored? How much of each flavor of ice cream should be ready for sale to customers? These questions can be answered with inventory control. Records allow the ice cream maker to look back on summers of previous years to see what raw materials were on hand and what finished products were produced, stored, and shipped. After a few calculations, raw materials can be purchased and production can be scheduled with confidence.

In short, trends help manufacturers meet customer demands while making their production processes efficient and effective. This makes them more competitive and explains why trend tracking is an important goal of inventory control.

Prevent theft

Leaders of organizations do not like to think that their employees would steal from them, but reality shows that some will if opportunities are present. In fact, most inventory theft comes from employees...and manufacturing plants are always under threat for this type of illegal behavior.

In manufacturing facilities, theft is possible in many different areas of production. Products do not have to be finished for people to steal, and that is one reason raw materials are accounted for continuously. Unscrupulous individuals stop at nothing to make money at the expense of others, and manufacturers are preferred targets because they have so many different items in inventory that can be sold for pure profit.

Theft prevention is critical to leaders of organizations, and this makes it a significant goal of inventory control systems. Since workplaces will likely never completely rid themselves of dishonest employees, this goal will likely never disappear or diminish in importance.

Prevent overages

At first glance, raw material and/or finished product overages in manufacturing plants might not seem like a major issue. After all, the material or product will get used...it is just a matter of time. Although this type of thinking might appear reasonable, it is completely wrong because stock overages cost organizations money. In fact, stock overages can cost large companies millions of dollars a year for purchasing and storage of items that are simply not needed. Additionally, space is required that could be utilized much more efficiently.

A major goal of inventory control is to prevent stock overages in order to save manufacturers money. In this respect, inventory control systems minimize costs and help organizations become more economically stable.

Prevent shortages

Raw material or finished product shortages are fairly common problems in manufacturing facilities. People order wrong quantities, order correct quantities at the wrong times, or simply do not order at all because they forgot or were unaware that stock was needed.

A major reason for shortages is uncertainty. Purchasing agents and sales people are not sure how to forecast product sales, and this causes them to underestimate. In the end, demand exceeds supply...and the end result is unhappy customers because their orders are not filled.

Effective inventory control systems prevent shortages from occurring in manufacturers. They provide information that helps people make calculated decisions about lead times and quantities of orders. This prevents mistakes from happening that hinder production and produce dissatisfied customers.

Stock shortages create headaches for manufacturers, and that is why preventing them is a goal of inventory control programs.

Inventory control systems show what happens to raw materials and finished products. They track raw materials used to manufacture finished products, locations where finished products were delivered, customers who made purchases, and prices paid for transactions. This information can then be used by management to verify that their company is performing effectively and efficiently. In short, inventory control systems ensure accuracy, and this leads to accomplishing the goals designated in this section.

Now that you understand the goals of inventory control, we can move into the next section that discusses methods manufacturers use for conducting inventory.

Methods

Every manufacturer is different, and that difference is apparent in the ways they conduct inventory. Some companies count every item in the building while others choose to exclude some items, some companies do physical inventorying on a monthly basis whiles other do it quarterly, and some companies have designated inventory control personnel while others rely on departmental employees.

Regardless of the internal differences, there are three basic methods for conducting inventory that all manufacturers follow. These methods are:

Manual

Manual inventory control is by far the most interesting method due to the creativity and variety involved. For example, some people write inventory levels on the back of paycheck stubs or production schedules while others enter the information into computerized systems. Either way, the inventory is manually entered rather than scanned or read, and it is used to track orders and purchases. That information can then be used to determine reorder levels of raw materials and finished products.

Advantages of the manual method are cost and training savings. The pencil and paper method, for example, requires very little investment and does not require employees to be trained on inventory software packages that can be somewhat complex.

Disadvantages of the manual method include lack of complexity and reliance on human accuracy. Simple input equals simple output...and this means the inventory system is not capable of generating detailed reports that track trends or provide periodic usage levels. Additionally, people make mistakes...and the manual method is held hostage to those mistakes. One wrong entry can lead to a domino effect of errors.

Bar Code

Bar coding is a preferred inventory method for many organizations because it generates accurate and reliable information that benefits personnel in all departments. Virtually all large retailers use bar coding, and major manufacturers are following their lead.

Manufacturers use bar codes for all types of inventory in their facilities. This technology allows for the tracking of raw materials to determine where they came from, where they are, where they are going, and when they need to be re-ordered. It also indicates production scheduling needs for finished products so management personnel can react according.

Advantages of bar coding are error reduction and time savings. Accuracy is not dependent on human entry, and information can be inputted in a fraction of the time required by manual methods.

Disadvantages of bar coding are cost and breakdown. Some systems are very pricey, thereby limiting the manufacturers that have access to them. Additionally, personnel become dependent on scanners...even to the point where they cannot function if those scanners are not working properly. Manual inventory is not an option because they have never done it. In short, inventory comes to a halt when scanners malfunction, are broken, or are not available.

Radio Frequency Identification (RFID)

Manufacturers that move thousands of items through their faculties need inventorying systems that are more efficient than bar coding. For these companies, radio frequency identification (RFID) is the answer. Essentially, RFID uses radio waves to collect information on products and raw materials. That information gathered is similar to that collected by bar code scanners, but it can be read from several feet away. That being said, some readers are mounted on walls or ceilings as they accurately scan all items that pass by them.

Advantages of RFID are volume and readability. Large numbers of raw materials or finished products can be scanned without the necessity of hand-held units, and these scanners do not have to have a direct line of sight to register information.

Disadvantages of RFID involve technological issues and privacy concerns. In terms of technology, there are no concrete regulations in effect, so one company's system might not be able to be read by another. This is especially troubling when the customers of manufacturers are unable to scan the items they are receiving. Additionally, these systems are difficult to program and there is a constant threat of information being intercepted. Based on these disadvantages, some manufacturers are shying away from RFID...at least until the technology gets better and the risk for problems decreases.

Now that you understand the major methods used by manufacturers to conduct inventory, let's move into specific types of inventory control systems.

Reordering systems

Different systems for reordering stock are used within each inventory method listed in the previous section. For example, one manufacturer might choose to inventory their raw materials and finished products using bar coding while another chooses manual methodology. However, both companies replenish their stock using a fixed quantity system. In other words, they reorder when stock goes below established levels....so the reorder point is always the same. Another example is when two manufacturers both choose RFID for their inventory method, but one reorders based on immediate needs such as stock outages while the other reorders based on precautionary measures such as the uncertainty of supply.

The following are different types of reordering systems used regardless of the method chosen to conduct the inventory:

Visual

This system is typically used by small manufacturers that have a good grasp of the raw materials and finished products they have in their facilities. Plant management knows from experience when they need to reorder by simply looking at the supplies they have on hand.

This system works well when competent people, such as owners, are in charge. However, other employees might not be capable of performing at the same level when the competent people are not present. In other words, this system is risky.

Fixed time

Fixed time systems base stock reordering on specific time periods rather than quantity. For example, a bakery checks wedding cake inventory at the end of each week and produces the same number of cakes that were sold during that week. If they sell 25 cakes, then they make 25 cakes. The bakery is replenishing supply based on usage over a specific period of time.

This is a rather simple reordering procedure that works well for manufacturers that have consistent sales throughout the year. However, it does not account for slow and busy sales periods. For example, the cake manufacturer needs to take into account that most weddings take place in the warmer months. If they are not careful, they could run out of wedding cakes at the beginning of May and have excessive stock at the end of September.

Fixed quantity

This system is similar to the fixed time system because it has designated reorder points for raw materials and finished products. However, the fixed quantity system is not reliant or dependent upon time frames. Reordering occurs when stock falls below designated minimum quantities.

This system is advantageous because it takes the guess work out of reordering. Manufacturers do not have to make decisions about how much stock to keep on hand because it is automatically reordered at pre-established levels. However, it also has disadvantages because those pre-determined stock levels might not always reflect actual needs. For example, a utensil manufacturer might automatically reorder raw materials for a stainless steel line of knives even thought that line is going to be discontinued. In this case, the stainless steel is not needed...but the system automatically reordered it when it hit a designated level.

Just-in-time (JIT)

The goal of this system is to reduce inventory holding costs and expose raw materials and finished products that are not used or no longer needed by manufacturers. Stock is brought in "as needed," thereby increasing inventory turnover while decreasing expenditures. JIT is very attractive to manufacturers, and it has recently become a favorite for reordering stock and supplies.

JIT is advantageous because money and space are not tied up in inventory that is not immediately needed, but it is also risky because there is always the threat of running out of stock. "Just-in-time" means stock will arrive at the point of need without anything extra. However, this is potentially hazardous because manufacturers that gamble on stock quantities might not be able to fill orders and meet customers' demands. For example, a door manufacturer might find that certain door knobs are not available when they are needed...so they are unable to fill a customer's order. This problem causes them to lose the business to a competitor who does not use JIT and has the knobs in stock.

Safety

This system is used when there is an uncertainty of customer demand or the manufacturer has difficulty producing the product. For example, a paint manufacturer makes a bacteria resistant paint that is currently being promoted by the salespeople. They currently sell 100 gallons per week of this item, but they do not want to run out of stock if customers start buying it, so they produce 1000 gallons for stock.

The safety system works well to prevent products from being out of stock, and it gives manufacturers confidence that they will be able to fulfill orders. However, it is costly due to the cash outlay, and the additional inventory takes up space. Unfortunately, the challenges involved prevent some manufacturers from using this system for their inventory.

Vendor controlled

Reordering for this system is done by vendors that sell their products to manufacturers. These vendors physically inventory their own items at the manufacturers' facilities and reorder when stock gets low. They are the manufacturers' inventory control, and they assume all responsibility for stock.

This system is advantageous for manufacturers because they do not have to use their own people to inventory and make reordering decisions. However, the other side of the coin is that manufacturers lose control of reordering, and this means money and space can be tied up based on vendors' decisions. Understandably, most vendors will not run out of their own products...but some have a tendency to overstock.

Collective

Some manufacturers use a combination of systems to reorder raw materials and finished products. This is called a collective system where inventory is classified into groups, and each group is given a level of reordering.

This system works well for maintaining proper inventory levels at companies that make a wide variety of items that are costly, consistent in sales, and difficult to produce. However, the downside is that it can be rather complicated leading to errors that cause problems for the manufacturer and its customers. For example, a pet food manufacturer classifies canned dog food (finished product) in one category, bagged dog food (finished product) in another, and lecithin (raw material) used to make both in a third category. The canned dog food uses a JIT system because it is very expensive to manufacture, the bagged dog food uses a fixed time system because sales are consistent every week, and the lecithin uses a safety system because it can be hard to obtain.

Now that you understand the various ways that raw materials and finished product are reordered, let's move on to basic management responsibilities for inventory control programs.

Management

Virtually everything in business is a gamble. Manufacturers gamble that their vendors will supply them with raw materials, their employees will produce quality products, and their customers will pay for items purchased. These gambles are worth the risk, but the same cannot be said for choosing not to implement effective inventory control programs...and those programs will only be effective they are properly managed.

The process of inventory control can be quite detailed and demanding. Larger manufacturers have entire departments devoted to this specific task, and a lot of time and money are spent making sure the information collected is reliable and accurate. That being said, it is relatively easy to understand why the management of inventory control is important.

The oversight of inventory control programs might appear to be a fairly simple process...but this is rarely, if ever, the case. Management involvement is required before, during, and after the systems are implemented because work needs to be done and decisions need to be made.

The following are specific management responsibilities in regard to inventory control:

Designating employees

This must be done before the inventory control program is implemented. If employees are going to do the inventorying, then responsibility needs to be assigned. Will a new department be established or will existing employees take on the routine tasks involved? When should the inventory be conducted? What information needs to be entered? What reports need to be generated? Who gets the information? Who is in charge of the program? Management needs to designate people for the proper functioning of the program or it will not be beneficial to the manufacturer.

Soliciting suppliers

This must be done before the inventory control program is implemented. If suppliers are going to inventory their own products, they need to be told what to do and how to do it. Which products need to be inventoried? How often should inventory be conducted? Does the inventorying need to be done on a specific day or at a specific time? Who gets the inventory information? Who makes reordering decisions? The entire procedure needs to be communicated to vendors by management or the program risks failure.

Selecting methodology

This must be done before the inventory control program is implemented. Which method or methods will be utilized? If a manual method is chosen, then how will the information be documented? If bar coding or RFID are chosen, then what information is needed? What reports need to be generated? What type of computer hardware and software is necessary? Management needs to answer these questions in order to avoid confusion and unnecessary expenditures.

Determining reordering

This must be managed while the inventory control program is running. Which type of system will be used? Can multiple systems be combined? Are there items that must be stocked at all times? Is floor space a major issue? Is money a major issue? Only management can answer these questions, and the degree of their involvement will influence the success of the program.

Monitoring inventory trends

This must be managed after the inventory control program produces information. Trends need to be continually searched for if manufacturers want to become more effective and efficient. Managers need to pinpoint areas of their business that are growing in sales so they do not short themselves raw materials and their customers finished products. Along the same lines, they need to find areas that are declining in sales so they do not accumulate excessive raw material or finished product inventories. Trends help manufacturers become more efficient and competitive...and managers are responsible for spotting them.

Now you understand some of the major responsibilities managers have in terms of inventory control. The next section expands upon this discussion by examining the ways managers can improve inventory control programs.

Improving

Raw material and finished product inventories are major assets for most manufacturers. Unfortunately, these inventories can become liabilities if they are not managed properly. That being said, inventory control programs need to be improved, and this can be accomplished by adhering to the following:

Maintain inventory records

Inventory records present problems because they are often out-of-date, inaccurate, or unavailable to the people who need them. Accurate and up-to-date records are extremely valuable for improving inventory control programs because they provide a snapshot of products that are sold, products that are in stock, products that need to be stocked, and raw materials that are needed for manufacturing. This eliminates the guesswork and time required to pinpoint organizational needs, and it improves the effectiveness of the overall inventory system.

In short, records provide information, and that information can be used to enhance the value of inventory control programs.

Generate inventory reports

Inventory control software programs are capable of generating many reports that are beneficial to manufacturing facilities. However, most managers are not fully aware of these capabilities, thereby limiting the reports they review to a select few.

Reports help managers identify trends that lead to more efficient operations. For example, they can view stock requisitions, stock returns, stock transfers, stock quantities, order picking issues, and inventory adjustments. If management takes the time to discover what they could have in terms of reporting, inventory control programs will be vastly improved.

Implement mobile devices

Technology is now capable of putting real-time inventory data on hand-held mobile devices. This allows select employees to have immediate access to important inventory information, and it lets them make faster and more accurate decisions that lead to higher customer satisfaction.

Without a doubt, mobile data is beneficial for inventory management. Add this to the fact that most people in the workforce today are fairly comfortable with hand-held technology, and mobile devices make good sense for improving inventory control programs. The only downside to this type of technology is the fact that the upfront cost makes it somewhat prohibitive.

Increase inventory frequency

This is by far the most painful method of improvement. Most people do not enjoy doing physical inventory, but it is a necessary evil of running a successful manufacturing plant. Monthly inventories, rather than year-end, provide a much clearer picture of the stock on hand and what can be done to reduce the cost associated with that stock.

Increased frequency improves the quality of inventory control programs by identifying unused, obsolete, and unnecessary stock that has no value, takes up space, and interferes with productivity. This stock can then be eliminated, reprocessed, or discounted and sold. Increased frequency is especially critical for manufacturers such as food plants that have perishable items in stock at all times.

Increased frequency also helps management identify trends more quickly in order to build upon them or take corrective action. For example, a trend might show that a supplier consistently delivers lower quantities of raw materials then were ordered. This indicates that the supplier is unreliable and might need to be put on probation or eliminated. Another example involves slow moving items. Frequent inventories bring slow movers to the forefront where they can be dealt with accordingly by trying to increase sales or eliminating them.

Summary

Inventory control is important for all organizations, but it is critical for manufacturers based and the money and space they have tied up in raw materials and finished products. Without effective inventory control programs, manufacturers have difficulty stocking the items necessary to make their products. When this happens, orders are not filled and customers are not happy.

This book focuses on inventory control from a manufacturing perspective. First, it defines inventory control and lists the major goals of inventory control programs. Next, it explores the methods available for performing inventory control tasks and explains the systems used for reordering raw materials and finished products. Then it discusses management responsibilities and examines ways that inventory control programs can be improved.

Congratulations! You now understand more about inventory control...an essential program for all manufacturers.

Quality Assurance in Manufacturing
Explaining and Understanding

Louis Bevoc

Published by
NutriNiche System LLC

Louis Bevoc books...simple explanations of complex subjects

Summary

Introduction

Some people think that quality assurance started in Japan during the 1950s due to the poor perception of the products they produced. It is true that the Japanese embraced the quality concept, but they were not the first to implement it as part of the ongoing process.

The first organized form of quality assurance took place in the United States during the Second World War. The US government did not want malfunctioning equipment or supplies in the field during the heat of a battle, so they developed procedures to check defects after items were manufactured. This concept stopped defective products from being released for use, thereby preventing many problems for American troops.

After the war, the idea of quality assurance took root with non-military manufacturers, but it was modified to develop procedures for detecting defects before products were finished. Quality checks were still performed on finished items, but procedures were also implemented during the process for preventative measures. This was beneficial for two reasons:

Customer satisfaction

Similar to the military application, defects in products were eliminated before they reached the consumer. This resulted in a higher level of customer satisfaction, less complaints, and fewer returns.

Organizational savings

Since checks were ongoing, errors were discovered before the finished product stage. This meant that products did not have to be broken down and reassembled to eliminate defects. In short, the "first loss is the best loss" mentality was implemented so products could be stopped during assembly before additional time and effort was wasted attempting to complete the process.

Today, quality assurance personnel develop procedures for making sure products meet specified requirements. This assures customers that their purchases will adhere to pre-established standards, thereby increasing their confidence that they are dealing with a credible organization.

Virtually every organization employs some type of quality assurance, and many companies have separate departments for the work involved. Employees in these departments seek to improve processes by developing procedures that assure products adhere to specified quality standards. This allows organizations to sell consistent products and remain competitive in markets that demand uniformity.

Clarification

Quality assurance should not be confused with quality control. They have similar functions and are both parts of quality management, but they are not the same. The following explains some of their differences:

Quality assurance

This process is used to make sure quality procedures are appropriate and in place for products. It assures the quality of products by establishing standards that prevent defects.

For example, a meat processing plant needs to make sure all hot dogs meet a color requirement. The quality assurance people develop a color chart that can be used as a standard. This chart is implemented in the plant as a mandatory color check on every batch of hot dogs prior to packaging.

Quality control

This process is used to verify the quality of products. It controls the quality of products using established standards that will detect defects.

Consider the hot dog example in the meat processing plant. Quality control technicians use the color chart developed by quality assurance people to check every batch of product prior to packaging. If the color does not match, the hot dogs are rejected.

Now that the difference between quality assurance and quality control is understood, it is time to move on to the next section on the implementation of quality assurance programs.

Implementation

Quality assurance programs are critical for manufacturers. They make sure procedures are in place to prevent defects, malfunctioning, and other finished product problems. Manufacturers without quality assurance programs need to implement them, and the following shows the two part process necessary to accomplish that implementation:

Part A

Below are the six steps necessary to put a quality insurance program in place. They do not complete the process, but they develop it and put it into action.

1. *Define objectives*

   Before a quality assurance program can be implemented, it needs a purpose. In other words, it needs to have defined goals and a concrete purpose. Once the objectives are defined, the organization understands the direction it needs to take, and the implementation process can begin.

   For example, a pet supply manufacturer decides to make a dog leash. They have done research and found that most leashes break after frequent use. This is a major problem for dog owners, so the pet supply company wants to make a better product.

2. *Define success*

The objectives are in place, so now the dynamics need to be defined. Which product attributes are the most important? How can the monitoring of those attributes be incorporated into the quality assurance program?

Durability is the most important attribute of the dog leash for the pet supply manufacturer, so durability must be incorporated into the quality assurance program. This is done by developing procedures designed to measure durability during the manufacturing process.

3. *Define customer base*

Who is going to use the dog leash? Is it geared for trainers or breeders? Is it meant for small dogs or large dogs?

The pet supply manufacturer wants their new leash to be geared for large dogs kept as pets by families. They are not targeting trainers or breeders, and their main customer base is determined to be middle-class suburban men and women who walk their dogs in parks.

4. *Define customer needs*

Durability has already been defined as a need, but other potential customer needs must also be investigated. Is there a color preference? Should the leash look fancy or practical? Is price a concern?

The pet supply manufacturer determines that their customer base wants dark colors to hide the dirt. They also find that a fancy look is not important, and price is not a major concern.

5. *Define quality procedures*

After the product and customer base have been defined, it is time to establish procedures for the quality assurance program.

The pet supply manufacturer decides the leash will be dark blue in color, so they develop a color chart to measure the intensity of the blue. They also decide the leash needs to easily connect to a dog's collar, so they develop a procedure to manually check the connection every hour. Last, they want to use materials that are flexible and durable, so they develop a purchasing specification for the raw material.

6. *Define quality tools*

Tools are the paperwork, software, instruments, and equipment needed to perform the designated procedures. They are provided to the employees performing quality checks on the product.

The pet supply manufacturer employees need the following tools to perform checks:

- Color chart
- Purchasing specification for raw materials
- Software to compute statistical deviations from specifications
- Tablet (computer) to record data, identify deviations from specifications, and list corrective actions

Part B

Now the program has been put into action. However, this does not complete the implementation process. The program still has to assure quality, so it is time to measure the data and react to the findings. This is done using the following four steps:

1. *Collect data*

   Data must be collected before it has any value. In this step, employees gather information from the procedural checks for subsequent analysis.

   The pet supply manufacturer collects a variety of different data. They obtain the number of leashes that did adhere to color requirements, the frequency of connection failures, and the occurrences where raw materials that did not meet specifications. After this information is gathered, it is used in the next step for analysis.

2. *Analyze data*

   This is where the collected data is analyzed. Findings are used to determine if original objectives are being achieved.

   Quality assurance at the pet supply manufacturer examines statistics and percentages to look for trends of quality related issues. The results are then analyzed and decisions are made regarding the success of the program.

3. *Adjust procedures*

   If the program is deemed successful, then it will continue on in its current capacity. However, if poor quality trends are the result of failures, then changes to the program must be made.

   The pet food supplier finds that the leash connection device is failing at a rate of two percent. Quality assurance determines that two percent is too high for this product, so a minor mechanical adjustment is made, and the frequency of the manual check is increased from every hour to every half-hour. If the failure rate stays the same or increases over the next week, the connection will be redesigned by engineers in the organization.

4. *Monitor*

If procedures have been adjusted and the quality is considered acceptable, then those procedures must be continuously monitored to assure that quality does not decrease.

The pet food supply company finds the mechanical adjustment of the leash connection device is successful. The failure rate drops to below one-half percent, and this is acceptable. Based on this analysis, quality assurance changes the manual check frequency back to every hour, and they will watch the failure rate closely to assure there is no reoccurrence.

Now you have an understanding of a basic implementation procedure for a quality assurance program. The next section focuses on the reasons that this type of program is beneficial for organizations.

Advantages

There many advantages for organizations that have quality assurance plans in place. Some of these are more important than others, so the focus in this section will be on the most significant benefits. These are as follows:

Continuous improvement

Continuous improvement employs the thinking that everything can be improved. In other words, there is no status quo and efforts are constantly made to raise the bar. Some of the changes resulting from this process are immediately apparent, while others are not so obvious and take time to transpire. Changes that transpire over time are often the preferred method of continuous improvement because they allow employees time to adjust to workplace modifications.

Of all the advantages, continuous improvement is the easiest to understand because it is the ultimate goal of every quality assurance program. This advantage is apparent after a quality assurance program has been up and running for a while because the goal of always getting better turns into reality. Designated procedures and checks continually search for process and product problems so they can be brought to light, resolved, and prevented from reoccurring. This constant vigilance means organizations continue to progress and manufacture better products.

Production

One might question how production is an advantage of quality assurance programs. After all, quality procedures seem like they would hinder production processes rather than help them. Yes, quality assurance does hinder production, but only for the short term. In the long run, it improves production because problems associated with products are identified and prevented from reoccurring. This stops defects from getting into finished products, causing those products to be reworked or reproduced...at the expense of production.

Customer satisfaction

This is likely the biggest advantage of quality assurance programs. Products are manufactured so they can be sold to customers. If those customers are not happy with the items they purchase, then they return them and/or never buy them again.

Quality assurance verifies products are being manufactured according to specifications. Procedures are designed to identify discrepancies and bring attention to them. Changes are then made to address those discrepancies and prevent them from reoccurring. These changes lead to a happier customer base, increased sales, and fewer headaches for management.

Customer returns and dissatisfaction are huge negatives for organizations. They lower profitability, increase stress, and decrease moral. Customers might not always be right, but they are always important...and quality assurance brings that importance to the forefront.

Cost savings

Most manufacturers are looking for cost savings due to the highly competitive markets that they face today...and they find those savings with quality assurance programs. How does this work? It works by measuring how effectively the products are produced. Standards and procedures increase quality and consistency, ultimately leading to better products and higher sales.

Specifically, quality assurance programs:

- Decrease employee mistakes that create waste
- Decrease employee miscommunication that leads to errors
- Decrease reoccurrence of problems that lead to reoccurring costs
- Decrease customer complaints that require resources for response
- Increase employee awareness that prevents mishaps
- Increase employee efficiency that leads to higher productive
- Increase product consistency that results in fewer returns
- Increase customer demand that drives up sales volume

Quality assurance programs cost money for personnel, equipment, supplies, and other resources. However, those resources combine to make better products and reduce misunderstanding by standardizing processes and procedures. This translates to cost saving for manufacturers, and it makes the payback well worth the investment.

Organization

Workplace organization is one of the least obvious benefits of quality assurance. The processes and procedures to control quality also dictate the manner in which production is accomplished. In this respect, they act as behavioral guidelines with step-by-step processes that are followed in the same order every time a product is produced. This prevents the chaos that can result from unstructured environments....and it keeps manufacturers organized.

Organization is a sought after aspect of every manufacturer because it leads to effectiveness and efficiency in the workplace. It keeps employees on task and prevents unnecessary or unproductive activity from occurring. In short, productivity improves as organizations get better, and organizations get better with the implementation of quality assurance programs.

Participation

This refers to employee participation. If employees sense that quality assurance programs are making their organizations more successful, then they buy into the process and begin to make quality a priority. They gain a sense of responsibility and take ownership of their jobs. This change is gradual and might not be readily noticeable, but it does happen.

People who think that employees will not buy into effective quality assurance programs over time are wrong. Successful organizations all over the world have utilized quality programs to achieve goals and objectives, and this would not have been possible without employees working together toward continuous improvement.

As you can see, quality assurance programs produce a variety of benefits. However, these programs are not without problems, and that is why challenges are the focus of the next section.

Challenges

Most good things in organizations have some negatives associated with them, and quality assurance programs are no exception. Despite all of the positive aspects, there are some shortcomings. Quality control personnel face challenges that need to be overcome before the programs they implement can become successful.

These challenges include:

Production/quality conflicts

Conflict between production employees and quality personnel is likely the most common drawback of quality assurance programs. This is somewhat expected because both departments have job-related tasks to complete, and those tasks are often opposite each other.

Quality assurance people implement programs that control the way products are manufactured, and many times this impedes the way production people want to do their jobs. Specific procedures dictate how jobs are performed, and those procedures are not always the easiest or most convenient.

The blame game

It is very easy to place blame for finished product problems on quality assurance people. This is because these problems relate back to issues that occurred during the manufacturing process. Quality assurance personnel are responsible for implementing procedures that prevent these issues from happening, so they are the most logical people to blame.

In reality, problems are always going to occur during manufacturing. People are going to make mistakes even if there are procedures in place to prevent them from doing so because procedures are not 100 percent foolproof. It is not fair to blame quality assurance for problems with finished products, but it does happen and it likely will never completely stop. This is why the "blame game" is a challenge for quality assurance people in manufacturing.

Cutbacks

Quality assurance is a very interesting concept. Many organizational leaders indicate it is one of the most important aspects of manufacturing. However, during tough economic times, it is often one of the first departments where employees are laid off. This is due to the fact that quality assurance personnel are not essential for the physical assembly of products and are therefore expendable when money is tight.

Manufacturers often depend on consistent products, and that consistency is lost when quality assurance departments are eliminated. One might think that this would indicate the importance of quality assurance personnel regardless of the financial situation. However, this is not typically the case...and it the reason why cutbacks are a challenge for quality assurance.

Stress

Quality assurance programs are capable of causing a lot of stress to people within the department. Decisions need to be made that can cause downtime in production, upset people, and make it seem like quality assurance personnel are the "bad guys" who do not care about the well-being of the organization or the people within it.

Leaders of organizations understand that quality assurance people are not out to inflict harm on the organizations that employ them. In fact, their job is to do the exact opposite. They only stop production to make the manufacturing process better in terms of quality and consistency. However, some people's perceptions of quality assurance personnel are negative...and those perceptions are their reality.

Quality assurance personnel want the best for their organizations, but their decisions can slow or halt productivity. They are well aware of the impact of their actions, and the fact that some people will dislike them. Because of this, some quality assurance personnel cannot handle the stress and end up leaving the department.

High expectations

As noted eagerly, continuous improvement means the bar is constantly being raised in terms of quality and consistency. This is great for organizations, but it can be difficult for employees...and quality assurance personnel are charged with the responsibility of making sure those employees rise with the bar.

Additionally, quality assurance people's wages are not always built into the cost of assembling products. They are tangent to the production process, and this means leadership expects them to perform at high levels in order to justify their wages.

Production training

Manufacturing typically involves a step-by-step process. That process is repeated the same way time after time in order to produce a consistent product. Some processes are simple, while others are quite complicated...and more complex processes require effective employee training.

Unfortunately, many production employees do not get the proper training they need to effectively follow the procedures developed by quality assurance personnel. They do not understand their role in the quality process, and they need to be monitored closely for mistakes and deviations. This is challenging for quality assurance personnel because they must act as "babysitters" in production situations. It prevents them from concentrating on continuous improvement because their main focus is on getting employees to adhere to current standards.

You can now see that quality assurance programs have positives and negatives association with them. Manufacturers that these programs in place need them to perform at the highest levels possible...and that is why improvement is the focus of the next section.

Improving

This section needs to be started with an "absolute must." Quality assurance personnel absolutely must NOT report to production supervisors. If this happens, the whole purpose and function of the quality assurance department are compromised. That being said, any manufacturer that has quality assurance personnel reporting to production management can immediately improve the program by simply changing the organizational hierarchy.

Even if quality assurance does not report to production management, it can be improved. The following are some ways to this:

Draw correlations

The success of quality assurance programs needs to be gauged to assure that they are effective. This is done by measuring customer satisfaction with surveys. The surveys should ask questions about specific areas that were targeted for improvement by quality assurance. For example, if a cell phone manufacturer has procedures in place to make keyboards more sensitive for texting, then a keyboard ease question should be asked.

Results of the surveys should be analyzed to see if there are any correlations between the quality programs implemented and customer satisfaction. If customer satisfaction is high, then the quality assurance programs are working and do not need to change. However, if customer satisfaction is low, then changes need to be made.

Change perception

Quality assurance personnel are not the enemy. They are there to help the company, and the changes they make help produce better products that lead to higher sales. That being said, the perception of quality assurance personnel and the procedures they implement needs to change.

This is done by:

Supplying information

Like most people, employees do not want to be kept in the dark. They want to know why procedures are in place and who will benefit from them. Skepticism results from a lack of information and quality assurance people are viewed as the reason for it. In short, management needs to inform employees of the reasons why quality assurance personnel do what they do.

Encouraging input

Sometimes the best way to get information about specific jobs is to ask the people performing those jobs. They know what needs to be done and have often figured out the best way to do it. They might need to change their ways after they give their input, but they will accept the change more readily because they will feel like they were part of the decision-making process.

Allow self-evaluation

This is probably the most overlooked method of improvement because it requires an analysis of self rather than others. It is relatively easy for employees to point out the shortcomings of their coworkers, but it is usually much more difficult to pinpoint their own faults. Most employees prefer to point out the positive aspects of their job performance rather than those that are not so positive.

Self-evaluation is another form of employee involvement, but it differs because it asks employees to evaluate their own work in terms of quality. They are given the opportunity to look at the part of the manufacturing process that they control and make suggestions for change. The changes they suggest might be small, but they indicate employees' commitment to the continuous improvement of their organizations.

In short, self-evaluation lets employees feel like they are part of the solution instead of being part of the problem.

Implement training

Proper training prevents problems from occurring. When employees are trained to follow quality assurance procedures, they make fewer mistakes and production lines run more efficiently. This means products can be produced that meet quality, consistency, and cost requirements.

The following are positives that result from employee training in terms of improving quality assurance:

Increased skills

Organizations want their workers to do their jobs more efficiently and effectively, and this requires up-to-date knowledge and understanding of the tasks they perform. That knowledge and understanding are best obtained using some form of employee training.

The most important part about increased employee skills is the fact that they benefit employees and the organization. Workers benefit by becoming more knowledgeable and valuable in their chosen profession, and organizations benefit by having more competent employees to help meet quality goals and objectives.

Increased motivation

Motivation is important in any workplace because it drives employees to perform at optimum levels. Without motivation, workers lack the desire to complete job-related tasks...and this prevents organizations from reaching their potential.

Training allows employees to learn new concepts and better understand the requirements of their jobs. This enables them to work with limited supervision, and the resulting autonomy increases their motivation to make products that meet quality standards.

Increased job satisfaction

Job satisfaction has been defined in many different ways by a variety of sources. For simplicity purposes, this book views it as employees' like or dislike of their jobs.

Training leads to workers liking their jobs because it provides information that helps them complete assigned tasks. This allows them to experience success...and that success increases their desire to produce quality products.

Increased collaboration

Many employees like to share newly acquired knowledge about their jobs. After all, this knowledge has the greatest value in the workplace because other people are working toward achieving the same goals.

Training provides employees with new knowledge, and that knowledge is shared through collaboration with coworkers. This collaboration encourages workers to think differently due to the diversity of the people involved, and the resulting ideas are beneficial for the overall quality of the organization.

Decreased absenteeism and turnover

Training can be a double-edged sword in terms of turnover. It provides knowledge, and that knowledge can be used to find a better job at another organization. However, this is typically not the case because training inspires loyalty in employees....and that loyalty keeps them working for their current employers. That loyalty also inspires them to emphasize quality in their jobs because they identify with their organizations and the products they produce.

Provide feedback

This suggestion is straightforward and simple. Feedback is essential for the improvement of any quality assurance program because employees cannot change if they do not know that they are doing something wrong. They need specific information in order to accomplish the goal of continual improvement, and that information needs to come from quality assurance personnel.

Employees also like to know when they are doing things right. This makes them feel good about their work and encourages them to continue on the same path. It also motivates workers to take ownership of the jobs they perform. When this happens, they need minimal supervision because they know what needs to be done.

In short, feedback is essential for making employees aware of how they are doing in terms of upholding quality standards.

Future

Due to ever increasing customer demands, quality assurance personnel will always be necessary in workplaces. In fact, the functions of quality departments will likely grow as organizations move into the future. That growth, however, will come with changes...so expect the following:

Increased regulatory intervention

A major role of democratic governments is to protect the people that they serve. They work for and are paid by the people of the countries they regulate, and their capacity as overseers continues to grow.

Government officials have their hands in many different aspects of organizational operations, and this shows no signs of tapering off in the future. The United States government, for example, continues to grow in size and increase spending. This allows its employees to expand their roles as overseers of organizations...and quality assurance will fall under their jurisdiction.

Increased customer intervention

Customers want to have a say in the products manufactured for them by their suppliers, especially if those products are private labeled. Two major ways they are doing this include:

Requirements (programs, policies, procedures)

Customers send specific requirements out to the manufacturers of their products. These requirements can dictate processes, specify dimensions, mandate testing, or instruct suppliers to do just about anything else that relates to the quality of the products. If manufacturers refuse to implement these requirements, then they risk losing the business.

Audits

Quality assurance personnel check the actions of production personnel, but who checks the actions of quality assurance personnel? The answer is typically nobody outside of those in top leadership positions...but that is changing, and it will change even more in the future.

Customers will conduct their own audits or contract them out to professional organizations. These audits will assure that specified quality standards are being upheld in addition to the status quo standards that are present in every type of manufacturing.

It is understandable that customers want some control over the products manufactured for them. The extent of that control is debatable, but the fact remains that it is not going to disappear...now or in the future.

Increased technology

Based on what has happened over the past few decades, it is understandable that technology will play a larger role in the quality assurance of manufacturers. This technology will come in the form of software, hardware, and equipment. For example, software will be needed for statistical analysis, hardware will be essential for portable hand-held devices, and equipment will be required for robotics.

Software, hardware, and equipment will become even more important as global competition between manufacturers increases. Remote access to all aspects of quality assurance will be required...and that requirement will be met with the advent of new technology.

Increased globalization of standards

Organizations are competing in a world market more than they ever have in the past, and this will not slow down in the future. This is great, but it will have some drawbacks. Many countries have their own standards in terms of quality, and this will need to change if they want to work with each other. There will need to be some type of globalization of quality standards. The exact nature of that globalization is yet to be determined, but it will happen...so expect it!

There is no doubt that standards will change as organizations become global, but the goal for continuous improvement will remain the same. There will always be a search for better standards than those being used. Based on this, it also makes sense that the monitoring of global standards will intensify in the future.

Increased importance on cost

Like it or not, cost is a major concern of manufacturers, and this will not change in the future. This will be bad for quality assurance personnel because their expense is often considered unnecessary for the assembly of products....so they will, therefore, be expendable. Unfortunately, some leaders will never get over the thinking that quality takes a back seat to manufacturing.

However, there is also a positive side to the importance of cost. When quality assurance departments do what they are designed to do, they actually save organizations money by reducing manufacturing errors and customer complaints (see *Cost savings* in the *Advantages* section for details). In other words, quality assurance departments provide a good return on the investment. Therefore, the cost of quality assurance in the future will not be a negative factor...as long the programs function effectively.

Increased emphasis on teamwork

One area of quality assurance that will improve in the future is teamwork. Quality assurance personnel do not always get along with manufacturing employees. Workers in these two departments tend to have different immediate priorities even though their long-term goals are the same. This cannot happen in organizations that have goals of growth and prosperity...and the future will bring about preventative change.

The reduction of conflict between quality assurance and production workers will present some challenges, but it will happen...and the first major step forward will involve empathy training. Employees will learn to understand the difficulties of each other's jobs by "putting themselves in their coworker's shoes." Once they begin to understand each other's roles, the door to teamwork will open wide.

Increased ties to safety

Quality is often tied to safety because regulated processes and procedures prevent employees from making mistakes that could be injurious or deadly. Workers are forced to stay on a proven path because there are consequences for not doing so.

A natural progression for quality assurance is to move into the area of safety management. They understand how to write programs for continual improvement, and the same thinking can be applied to safety in manufacturing plants. This is not necessarily the way it is now, but quality assurance will be involved with safety in the future.

Summary

Quality assurance is important for any manufacturing organization. It ensures that the products produced meet quality and consistency standards so customers will be satisfied. It is a proactive process that benefits organizations in many ways.

This book focuses on quality assurance of products. It describes the topic, discusses its implementation, talks about the advantages and challenges involved, notes methods of improvement, and envisions it in the future. The text is educational and informational, and it is written for easy reader understanding at any level.

Congratulations! You now understand more about quality assurance...an important aspect of any manufacturing organization.

Maintenance Programs in Manufacturing

An Introduction to Preventative, Predictive, and Corrective Types

Louis Bevoc

Published by
NutriNiche System LLC

Louis Bevoc books...simple explanations of complex subjects

Introduction

Welcome to a world that is vastly underestimated in value. It is a world where "good morning" is replaced with "I have a machine down." It is a world where employees work before, during, and after production activities. It is a world where criticism is frequent and praise is rare. It is the world known as maintenance in manufacturing.

The above paragraph might be a little dramatic, but it is a reality in many manufacturing facilities. Maintenance keeps production lines operating so orders can be filled and customers will be happy. In this regard, maintenance is one of the most important aspects of a production facility. That being said, what are the specific duties of maintenance personnel? The following is a list of their major job responsibilities:

Assembly and disassembly

When new machinery enters the facility, maintenance people are the first to have contact with it. They uncrate it, assemble it, and set it up. They are responsible for making sure all parts are included and the machine will do what it is supposed to do.

Maintenance people also disassemble machinery when it needs to be broken down for cleaning, repair, or removal. They understand the inner workings of the machines, and they know how to properly dismantle them without damaging them or creating safety risks for themselves or others.

In short, the buck stops with maintenance people in terms of assembly and disassembly.

Machine repair

Machines break down in manufacturing facilities. This happened in the past, it happens now, and it will happen in the future. However, broken equipment is not a major issue if it can be fixed...and maintenance people fill the role of fixers. They understand what needs to be done in order to get machines running properly in a reasonable amount of time. This saves manufacturers money, and it allows them to get their products to the customers who need them. In terms or machine repair, maintenance people are worth their weight in gold.

In short, machines need to be repaired and maintenance people fill that need.

Liaison

When machinery cannot be repaired, it needs to be serviced by external professionals. This means a technical person from the manufacturer of the machine needs to visit the facility to make the necessary repairs. Someone needs to be responsible for contacting that technical person and describing the problems the machine is experiencing...and that someone is almost always a maintenance person.

Describing machinery problems might seem like a relatively simple task. After all, the machine is broken, so what else needs to be said? Unfortunately, a lot more usually needs to be said. Technical people need detailed information in order to make a timely and proper diagnosis, and that information is only available from those who have a working knowledge of the machine. Typically, the only individuals with that working knowledge are maintenance people.

In short, maintenance people are liaisons who reduce the time, effort, and expense required for external repair of machinery.

Testing

How do production people know if a machine is able to meet their expectations? The answer is through testing. For example, a light intensity machine at a flashlight manufacturing company needs to measure the bulb brightness of products made on a high-speed production line. One bulb needs to be measured every six seconds in order for plant personnel to meet established production quotas. Every day before production begins; maintenance people run tests to make the light intensity machine can handle the volume.

In short, maintenance people verify machines are capable of doing what they are supposed to be doing.

Calibration

How do production people know that a machine is working properly? The answer is through calibration. For example, a scale in a meat processing plant weights weighs one pound packages of hot dogs. It is definitely capable of weighing these hot dogs, but is it producing accurate results? The only way to find out is by calibrating the scale with standard weights...and this is done by maintenance people.

In short, maintenance people verify machines are accurately doing what they are supposed to be doing.

This book focuses on the three major types of maintenance programs in manufacturing facilities known as preventative, predictive, and preventative maintenance. It examines the advantages and disadvantages of these programs in layman's terms. Maintenance terminology can be quite complex, but the text in this book is written so it is easily understandable at any reader level.

Now that you understand the scope of this book, we can move into a discussion on the three major types of maintenance programs. However, before doing this, we need to discuss the planning of these programs in order to get a better understanding of how they are implemented.

Planning

Maintenance is very important in manufacturing facilities because it affects the livelihood of everyone in the organization. Machines need to run properly because broken machinery stops production...and production is the lifeblood of manufacturing operations. In fact, production is a major reason that most manufacturing plants exist. Based on this fact, it is relatively easy to understand the importance of maintaining machines in proper working order.

Maintenance programs need to be planned before they are implemented...regardless of whether the type of maintenance is preventative, predictive, or corrective. Planning starts by defining a purpose. Will the maintenance program be proactive, reactive, or projective? If the program is proactive, then the purpose is preventative maintenance. Machines will be serviced on a regular basis to prevent problems from occurring during production. If the program is projective, then the purpose is predictive maintenance. Machine failures will be predicted so they can be managed. If the program is reactive, then the purpose is corrective maintenance. Machines will be serviced when they break down.

Surprisingly, most manufacturers do not have predictive or preventative maintenance programs in place, choosing instead to take corrective action as needed. Money and time are two major factors that cause them to opt out of predictive or preventative activities because these resources are needed in other areas. This plan might work in the short-term, but it can cause a wealth of machine problems down the road. However, regardless of the type of maintenance program chosen, the purpose of it needs to be defined.

Next, the scope of the program needs to be outlined. Questions that need to be answered include:

Who will be involved?

What people are going to perform the work and what are their designate responsibilities? In a manufacturing facility, the scope might only be applicable to one department or it might encompass the entire plant. Some maintenance personnel are highly skilled while others are not, so specific roles need to be defined. There also needs to be a manager in charge who reports to upper management.

What machinery will be involved?

Manufacturers need to designate the equipment or machinery that is going to be maintained or repaired. Some machines are purposely left off of this list because they are only serviced by representatives of the companies that manufacture them. Other machines might be left off this list because they are located outside of the physical boundaries of the plant. For example, company-owned vehicles (trucks, bulldozers, tractors, etc.) might not be serviced by maintenance personnel simply because it is more convenient and cost effective to use external sources.

What are the priorities?

Does one machine or department take priority over others in terms of repair? This is an important question because it gives maintenance personnel guidelines for allocating their time. Without a list of priorities, time can easily be spent fixing machines that are not needed until a later time. The focus needs to be on equipment that is immediately needed for production.

What will be documented?

If utilized, will routine maintenance checks of machinery and equipment be recorded? Routine maintenance is done in many plants on a periodic basis, and it is nearly impossible to remember all of the dates and times that service was performed.

A document should be available that lists all routine maintenance checks and the frequency that those checks are performed. Frequency should be based on usage (volume), safety, and manufacturer recommendations. Documentation of routine maintenance serves three basic purposes:

It indicates when maintenance needs to be conducted

Documentation shows when a machine was last serviced, and when the next service is due. This eliminates the need to rely on memory. Technology today even allows for reminders of upcoming services that can be delivered directly to smartphones or other mobile devices.

It maintains warranties

Some warranties do not remain in effect if certain routine maintenance is not performed. For example, oil might need to be changed in a machine every 200 working hours or the warranty is not valid.

It provides information for authorities

OSHA, auditors, and government agencies all request routine maintenance information when investigating injuries, validating processes, or probing violations. IF this information is not provided, fines could be levied and customers could be lost.

What is the operating budget?

Like every other aspect of business, money plays a role in maintenance planning. Many manufacturers have budgets in place that limit expenses in maintenance departments. They allocate funding for various areas such as building and grounds upkeep, machinery repair, vehicle servicing, and building renovations.

Keep in mind that budgets are great for planning, but they do not always work for maintenance because there are often unforeseen circumstances. Machinery that is critical to production simply cannot wait until the next budget renewal...it has to be fixed now or the plant will not be able to operate and orders will not be filled.

Now you understand the importance of planning for maintenance programs. Armed with this knowledge, it is time to move into the specific types of programs...starting with preventative maintenance.

Preventative maintenance

In general, preventative maintenance programs are implemented so future problems can be avoided. For example, tires on a car should be rotated every 8000 miles. This prevents the tires from wearing unevenly and needing to be replaced before the 40,000-mile life expectancy. In a manufacturing facility, preventative maintenance is also designed to prevent future problems from occurring. For example, working machine parts need to be greased on a weekly basis to avoid excessive friction that leads to damage.

Like most other aspects of business, preventative maintenance has benefits and drawbacks in manufacturing plants. These positives and negatives must be taken into consideration when deciding whether or not to implement a preventative maintenance program. The time, effort, and money invested in this type of program need to have a payback in order to be justified...and that justification can only be determined by plant management personnel.

The following are some specific advantages and disadvantages:

Advantages

Below are some advantages of preventative maintenance programs.

Risk reduction

Preventative maintenance reduces the risk that there will be failures during production. It provides insurance that production quotas will not be interfered with by broken machinery or faulty equipment. This eliminates a major headache for management personnel and allows them to focus on other areas of their jobs.

Life expectancy

Every manufacturer wants machinery and equipment to last as long as possible in their facilities. This eliminates replacement costs that can be quite significant...especially when machines are designed for a single purpose. That being said, machinery and equipment are expected to last longer when a preventative strategy is utilized because periodic servicing helps maintain them in proper working order. In terms of life expectancy, an ounce of prevention is truly worth a pound of cure.

Cost savings

When done properly, preventative maintenance easily justifies its existence economically. It helps (1) prevent maintenance personnel from fixing machines at a later date, (2) avert the need for external sources of repair, (3) avoid unnecessary downtime and the cost of unproductive labor, and (4) eliminate sluggish equipment that slows productivity. Based on these four areas of cost savings, it is rather obvious that the payback for preventative maintenance programs can be substantial.

Energy

This advantage goes largely unnoticed, but it needs to be noted. Machinery and equipment that are not serviced using preventive maintenance are often less energy efficient. They require more electricity or gas to function at desired levels, thereby increasing energy bills and wasting resources. Cost goes down and efficiency goes up when preventative maintenance programs are in place

Disadvantages

Below are some disadvantages of preventative maintenance programs.

Immediate costs

There is an up-front cost for preventative maintenance programs. Personnel need to be hired and supplies need to be inventoried. Depending on the number of people hired and the scope of the program, this can be quite expensive…and all of the costs are accrued before the first product leaves the production line. Some companies cannot afford to put out the money, and others simply refuse to do it because they believe the cost is not justified.

Management

This refers to maintenance people and preventative maintenance programs because both of them need to be managed. People require direction, and that directions needs to come from a supervisor. That supervisor also needs to make sure the program is followed and the work required gets done in a timely manner. Management of a preventative maintenance program is not a small task, and that makes it a disadvantage for manufacturers.

Volume changes

When is preventative maintenance too much or too little? This question is difficult to answer, and it can create a problem for manufacturers. For example, a program requires maintenance personnel to replace the wheels on all smokehouse racks in a turkey processing plant every six weeks. This makes sense because racks could break down during production, causing downtime. However, this program does not account for seasonal volume shifts such as Thanksgiving (when production is at a peak), and the summer months (when production is very low). In reality, wheel replacement should be much higher around Thanksgiving and much lower in the summer months…but this is not the case because the preventative maintenance program calls for replacement every six weeks.

Value

Unfortunately, some business leaders believe preventative maintenance is a luxury. As a luxury, it is one of the first areas to undergo cuts when manufacturers are experiencing financial difficulties. From a cost saving perspective, this makes little sense because the money spent preventing problems is typically less than that spent repairing machinery or equipment that has failed. However, these leaders' thinking will likely never change because preventative maintenance is regarded as a "precautionary" expenditure that is difficult to tie to actual production downtime. If the value of something cannot be directly measured, then number crunchers in the manufacturing organization will push for its elimination during tough times.

Now you understand the advantages and disadvantages of preventative maintenance. This program is beneficial for many manufacturers because it keeps equipment and machinery operating at optimal levels. However, there are some up-front costs involved, and management needs to determine the real value of this program.

Next, let's move into a discussion on a type of program that uses logic and reasoning to assess maintenance needs. That program is known as predictive maintenance.

Predictive maintenance

This is the rarest type of maintenance program used by manufacturers. Essentially, machines and equipment are examined in order to predict when maintenance should be performed. Similar to preventative maintenance, predictive maintenance is implemented to avoid future problems. However, if done properly, this program costs less than preventative maintenance because service is only performed when justified. In other words, predictions are made about the potential failure of machines and service is performed just before those failures become reality. The goal is to avoid unnecessary maintenance expenses.

Predictive maintenance is also the most difficult type of maintenance program used by manufacturers. Timing is critical because service has to be performed before the failure with sufficient warning time must be provided. Techniques include observing machine performance, ultrasound, acoustics, thermal imaging, vibration analysis, and oil analysis.

The following are some specific advantages and disadvantages.

Advantages

Below are some advantages of predictive maintenance programs:

Maintenance time

This program predicts service needs. It falls under the preventative maintenance category, but service is only performed when it is justified by the potential for equipment or machine failure. This means less maintenance effort is needed for predictive maintenance, and the end result is a savings in time and labor.

Inventory

This is likely the least known advantage of predictive maintenance. Predictive maintenance does not require an inventory of excessive machine parts because only the parts necessary for the program are kept in stock. Emergency spare parts stock no longer exists, and this results in cost and space savings.

Safety

Skill levels of personnel performing predictive maintenance are high because these individuals have undergone training and understand the machines and equipment they are servicing. As a result of their knowledge, safety levels increase throughout the plant. This safety is critical because many manufacturers work with hazardous chemicals or operate equipment that requires high pressure or temperature. It creates a win-win situation for employees and management because employees do not go through the pain and suffering associated with injuries, and management does not pay the costs associated with workers compensation.

Disadvantages

Below are some disadvantages of predictive maintenance programs.

Monitoring/testing costs

Specialized monitoring and testing devices are typically expensive. They are made for a specific task, so a higher price can be charged for them. The cost might be understandable, but it is also prohibitive for some manufacturers. They either cannot or will not spend the money necessary for the equipment, so the predictive maintenance program does not function properly.

Required skills

Every employee is not capable of performing predictive maintenance tasks. In fact, the vast majority of employees are not capable of performing these tasks because they require specific skills. In addition to having mechanical skills, people who do predictive maintenance often need training in electronics, hydraulics, or thermodynamics.

Environmental effects

Some manufacturing plants have conditions that are less than ideal for the monitoring or testing devices necessary for predictive maintenance. For example, food processors with wet or cold working environments might have problems keeping these devices working properly. The same goes for the high temperatures found in foundries or smelting plants. Along the same lines, paint manufacturers are likely to have corrosive chemicals that could do damage.

Regardless of the way the damage is done, monitoring or testing devices that are not working properly will not provide accurate information. This means calculations could be inaccurate, and the entire predictive maintenance program is jeopardized. Since it is difficult for some manufacturers to avoid destructive work environments, it is understandable why they choose not to implement this type of program.

Now you understand some of the advantages and disadvantages of predictive maintenance. This program is beneficial for many manufacturers because it analyzes machinery and predicts when it will fail. This information is then used to perform service before the failure occurs while housing fewer parts and maintaining lower labor costs for maintenance personnel. However, people need specific skills to be employed as predictive maintenance technicians, and the type of work environment can affect the data collected.

Next, let's move into a discussion on a type of program that addresses machinery and equipment failures after they occur. That program is known as corrective maintenance.

Corrective maintenance

This is the most common type of maintenance program in manufacturing plants. It is a completely reactive program, and it is necessary because equipment and machines will break down at some point. Machines cannot be expected to run forever, and constant use at full capacity typically shortens that life span.

Unfortunately, corrective maintenance is often the only type of maintenance program available in a manufacturing facility….with no predictive or preventative programs to support it. Many times this is due to cost because smaller manufacturers cannot afford to sacrifice the resources necessary to set up predictive or preventive programs. However, sometimes corrective maintenance stands alone simply because organizations do not want to invest the necessary time and effort to establish other programs. Corrective maintenance does wonderful things for equipment and machinery repair, but it needs help. Without some type of support, corrective maintenance programs can become very expensive in a relatively short period of time. This adds stress to the jobs of maintenance personnel and managers, and they might start looking for jobs elsewhere.

Advantages

Below are some advantages of corrective maintenance programs.

Initial investment

Corrective maintenance does not require the planning, time, or effort required for preventative and predictive programs. This is because corrective maintenance does not address problems before they occur; it simply reacts to issues at the time of failure. This is advantageous for manufacturers because they save on resources. In short, there is a savings on initial investment for manufacturers that choose to corrective maintenance as their only maintenance program.

Expenses

Corrective maintenance delays expenses. These expenses include the services and checks performed under preventative and predictive maintenance programs. This means machines and equipment can function for extended periods of time with little or no maintenance. This strategy is particularly beneficial for manufacturers looking for a short-term return on investment, such as that expected from machinery or equipment needed for a specific purpose. For example, a toy manufacturing company might need a machine to stitch stuffed animals for two months until they implement an entirely new process. Management does not want to put time and money into the maintenance of this machine unless it completely fails. Even if the machine breaks down, it will be "quick-fixed" or temporarily repaired because it will not be needed for the long term. In this case, the short-term return justifies corrective maintenance being the only program in effect.

Profitability

Profit is a major reason that most manufacturers are in business, and higher profits can be made by organizations that prefer to react to maintenance issues as they occur. They are willing to forego using any type of predictive or preventative programs in order to make more money. Savings from labor, supplies, and parts all lead to higher profitability...and a happier management team.

Disadvantages

Below are some disadvantages of corrective maintenance programs.

Predictability

As most manufacturers are aware, this is likely the biggest disadvantage of a corrective maintenance program. Maintenance personnel do not know when equipment or machinery will fail, and that can cause a variety of different problems. For example, parts might need to be ordered, thereby delaying the repairs necessary to get production running. Additionally, outside service might need to be called in for issues that cannot be resolved by plant personnel...and that service is typically quite expensive. When these problems mount, the cost of the corrective maintenance program can far exceed that of a program that had preventative measures in place.

Efficiency

Efficiency is important for every production oriented facility because increasing it helps keep costs down and maximizes productivity. Unfortunately, corrective maintenance programs do little for efficiency. The major goal of corrective maintenance is to keep equipment and machinery operating, but optimal levels of operation are not necessarily part of that goal. When optimal levels are not achieved, equipment and machinery do not reach their potential...and the resulting lack of efficiency causes a decline in productivity.

Urgency

As has already been stated in this book, corrective maintenance programs do not prevent problems. This makes the likelihood of problems much more probable, and those problems need to be addressed immediately when they affect production. As might be expected, most machinery problems hinder production, so repairs need to be made with no time to waste. Unfortunately, this type of environment creates a wealth of stress for maintenance personnel and managers...and that is why urgency is a negative associated with corrective maintenance.

Now you understand some of the advantages and disadvantages of corrective maintenance. This program is beneficial for many manufacturers because it minimizes expenses and raises profitability. However, repairs necessary for corrective maintenance difficult to predict, and there always tends to be a sense of urgency.

The next section summarizes preventative, predictive, and corrective maintenance programs for a better understanding.

Summary of the three types

The three major types of maintenance programs have now been described. However, their specific applications might still be a little difficult to understand unless they are compared side-by-side. Based on this thinking, a brief and concise summary is as follows:

Preventative maintenance programs are proactive, predictive maintenance programs are selectively proactive, and corrective maintenance programs are reactive.

Examples of the work performed by each type of program are as follows:

Preventative maintenance – Greasing or lubricating working machine parts, changing oil in machinery
Predictive maintenance – Measuring the amount of vibration on machines, searching for gas leaks in machinery
Corrective maintenance – repairing machinery after it has broken down, replacing broken safety covers machines

In a nutshell:

Preventative maintenance programs administer a wide variety of services that prevent failure, predictive maintenance programs do specific testing to determine services that prevent failure, and corrective maintenance programs perform services after failure has occurred.

Based on what is written in this book, it is rather obvious that maintenance programs are necessary to keep equipment and machinery functioning properly in manufacturing facilities. That being said, existing maintenance programs need to be continually updated and improved upon. This might not be easy, but it is important...and it could affect the survival of some manufacturers.

Summary

Maintenance personnel are essential for any type of production-oriented operation. They assemble, diagnose, repair, and monitor the equipment and machinery needed to fill orders and satisfy customers. In terms of manufacturing, maintenance departments are the glue that holds facilities together.

This book focuses on maintenance programs in manufacturing. First, it examines the planning that takes place before maintenance programs are implemented while discussing the people, priorities, and documentation involved. Then it analyzes preventative, predictive, and corrective programs through description and an exploration of their advantages and disadvantages. The text is educational and informational, and it is written for easy reader understanding at all levels.

Congratulations! You now understand more about preventative, predictive, and corrective maintenance...three important types of maintenance programs used by manufacturers.

Research and Development
in Organizations
An Introduction to Product-Based R&D

Louis Bevoc

Published by
NutriNiche System LLC

Louis Bevoc books...simple explanations of complex subjects

Introduction

Organizations that want to grow and prosper need new products and services. Research and Development (also known as R&D) is utilized by organizations to obtain those new products and services. The work of R&D personnel helps companies gain a competitive edge. This is important for every organization...especially those that are heavily impacted by technology.

Rewards for research and development can be very high, but there is also a large potential for failure. In fact, the majority of R&D projects fail long before they make it to the market. Organizations need successful projects in order to recoup losses on the ones that failed. In other words, there is a lot of risk involved with R&D; and this risk makes it imperative for R&D departments to be well organized and managed.

Much of the R&D done by businesses is conducted in academia. In fact, some companies contract all or most of their R&D out to academic institutions. This is advantageous because many colleges and universities have the necessary personnel, equipment, and laboratories to do the job properly. Academic R&D work is great in terms of efficiency, but the downside is that contracting companies do not learn anything from work being conducted, and they become dependent on academia for new product development. Additionally, companies that rely on academia are not the sole owners of the new products or technology that is developed, so they cannot control it from being used by other organizations.

This book is concerned with the product-based R&D work that takes place in non-academic institutions. More specifically, it examines R&D in organizations that manufacture products.

It is important to note that research and development is not the same as engineering. Some people ask why R&D is needed in manufacturing when engineers essentially do the same work. The answer is because they do not do the same work. Creativity is needed for both jobs, but engineers are an extension of R&D. R&D people develop prototype products for testing in production, and engineers convert those prototypes into items that can be manufactured in volume and sold to customers as finished products.

For the purposes of this book, research and development is defined as:

> *The creation of new products or improvement of existing products in manufacturing environments*

Now that you understand the scope of this book, let' move on to a discussion on the importance of research and development.

Importance

Innovation drives growth and prosperity, and research and development drives innovation. Astute leaders of manufacturing organizations realize the importance of innovation and they react by funding R&D projects. They realize that research and development is an investment in the future, and it is capable of transforming entire industries.

Good examples of the importance of research and development are automotive manufacturers. They are constantly on the cutting edge of technology, and they do whatever is necessary to complete in today's global marketplace. They have many people working on different vehicles that might or might not be put into production. However, the expense is justified because without innovation....automobile companies cannot compete. New automotive concepts are constantly coming into the market, and the companies that fail to produce novel ideas simply will not survive.

Other examples include food manufacturers. These companies are continually coming up with new food items for their markets. Their R&D departments develop different flavors, sizes, colors, smells, and appearances of food in order to entice consumers to make purchases. In the food manufacturing business, there truly is a "flavor of the month" that loses its appeal in a relatively short period of time. R&D people are employed to make sure new consumer interest will be consistently generated.

Manufacturers choose to invest in research and development because they understand its importance. They realize they will gain market share and a wealth of knowledge that can be used for growth and prosperity. They understand that the payback is worth the investment because R&D is needed to meet sales expectations.

Some people believe research and development only applies to large manufacturers who compete internationally. After all, these companies have the money to invest in new projects, and they can hire personnel with R&D education and experience. It is true that large companies are typically financially strong, but small companies also need R&D. Small manufacturers need new products to put on the market...regardless of the size of that market.

Small manufacturers have some advantages when it comes to research and development. For example, many of them have management personnel that have "grown up in the business." These individuals have worked a variety of different jobs in their organizations, and they take a hands-on approach to running their businesses. R&D is a natural extension of their job skills, and they are able to create new products due to their understanding of the markets where they compete. In fact, these individuals are sometimes the best choice for R&D regardless of other people's education or experience.

Research and development can be thought of as the major building block of innovation. In fact, most innovation is a direct result of the work of R&D...and this will likely never change. In this sense, R&D is a catalyst for the innovation necessary for gaining a competitive edge. This is a major reason why R&D is important, and it is also a major reason why it is an investment rather than an expense.

Research and development personnel often view problems as opportunities rather than obstacles. For example, household flies are thought of by most people as unwanted pests. They are relatively filthy and quite capable of spreading disease. However, R&D people viewed them as a business opportunity...and that is why they created fly swatters, fly strips, fly baits, and similar fly eradication devices that can are now manufactured in large volumes.

The discussion in this section would not be complete without mentioning the importance of research and development to engineering. As noted earlier, engineers are an extension of R&D. R&D people develop prototypes, and engineers make prototypes production-ready. That being said, organizations that are thought of as world class in engineering owe much of that status to R&D....and it is another reason why R&D is important. This is the way it was in the past, the way it is now, and it is the way it will be in the future.

Now that you understand some reasons why research and development is important, let's move on to a discussion on the job responsibilities of R&D personnel.

Responsibilities

Two obvious responsibilities of manufacturing R&D personnel are to "research" and "develop" new products. First, they research various aspects of a proposed product to assure that it is worth being developed.   Then they develop a prototype of the product using specifications established by management, customers, and regulatory agencies. The end goal is to get the product ready so it can be tested in production.

The above paragraph simplifies the responsibilities of research and development professionals. However, it is not all-encompassing because R&D personnel have many other job functions. For example, they get involved in sales, marketing, production, and quality employees to work on projects and come up with new ideas. They also collaborate with these individuals to uncover product trends that are of value to their organizations.

Managers who oversee the work of research and development people need to understand that a great deal of time and effort are invested in a new product before it reaches the production floor. Specifications, costs, timelines, regulatory requirements, and other aspects of the proposed product must be clearly understood before that product begins to be developed. If there is no demand in the market for the proposed product, then developing it is an unnecessary expense and a waste of time. If the proposed product is considered a viable item that people will purchase, then the next phase of work begins.

The best way to more completely understand the responsibilities of product-based research and development personnel is to list their major job functions. Essentially, these individuals are responsible for:

Researching market trends

Market research for manufacturers involves analyzing general trends of products that are selling in the marketplace. Questions are asked to understand what consumers are buying now and what they might be buying in the future. Which categories are growing? Which categories are declining? Which categories have potential? Which categories should be abandoned? Answers to these questions are used to make decisions about new products that will be developed by R&D personnel. Market research is an important responsibility of R&D personnel because new products require a significant amount of time and effort...and the cost of failure can be very high.

Researching new products

This involves researching specific products that competitors are selling. When a product sells well, it is examined to determine why it is attractive to consumers. Often times this involves purchasing the product, taking notes on its appearance, checking its performance, and disassembling it to get a better idea of how it works. This type of research provides direction for developing a competitive product...and it is a direct responsibility of R&D personnel.

Developing new products

Once market trends have been analyzed and a competitive product has been selected, it is time to develop a prototype. Research and development personnel are charged with this responsibility, and it is typically an area where they excel. They have the expertise necessary to create the prototype and deliver it to engineers for testing. In short, research paves the road to development, and development turns concepts into reality.

Shortening market time

Sometimes research and development employees are thought of as roadblocks because they have the final say on whether or not prototypes are ready to be tested in production. It is true that they hold prototypes for certain periods of time, but this holding process is necessary to assure those prototypes are ready for testing in production. R&D efforts eliminate the potential for many different mistakes, thereby preventing "back to the drawing board" situations from transpiring. In this regard, R&D personnel actually shorten the time from product conception to market by applying their expertise and knowledge to make sure prototypes function as intended.

Assessing current products

Another responsibility of research and development personnel involves assessing products that are currently being manufactured and sold. In this capacity, they ensure that these products are still functional and performing as expected. Changes or upgrades to these products might be necessary to make them more effective or efficient in their designated capacities. If R&D personnel believe that a product cannot be improved and or is no longer valuable, then they might choose to discontinue it.

Maintaining product quality

This might be the least common responsibility of R&D personnel, but it does occur in some manufacturers. It expands upon the assessment of current products by performing quality checks on those products after they are running in production. One might question why these checks are done by research and development personnel rather than quality people. The answer is because R&D people are more familiar with product specifications because they have done the research and developed the prototypes for those products. If R&D personnel do not perform the actual checks, they might play a support role for quality assurance people by collaborating with them on quality maintenance.

As you can see, research and development personnel have product responsibilities from conception to implementation and beyond. Based on these responsibilities, it is rather obvious that their work benefits manufacturers as they move into new product ventures. Next, let's examine some specific advantages that R&D personnel provide.

Advantages

The benefits of research and development expand well beyond the laboratories where prototypes are developed. They provide avenues for growth and prosperity, thereby helping organizations successfully move into the future. Manufacturing leaders need to understand the value of R&D by supporting it with the necessary funding and resources. If allowed to do what it is supposed to do, R&D has a very positive impact on organizations.

Specific advantages of research and development are listed below.

Opportunity

Without a doubt, research and development work leads to opportunistic situations. Often times this is because R&D personnel are in the right place at the right time, but it also is a result of the earnest effort put forth by these individuals. For example, they might be researching one product, when they discover a trend with another. Another example is getting an idea for a new product based on something else being made by the competition. One last example is an accidental discovery that takes place during the design of a prototype. Regardless of the way opportunities present themselves during the R&D process; their occurrence is advantageous for manufacturing organizations.

Strategy

Research and development helps organizations plan their actions in terms of sales, advertising, and marketing. Sales are grown when research and development identifies trends and specific products that are doing well. This leads to those products being manufactured and sold to the same customer base in order to gain market share. Marketing professionals rely on R&D to provide novel product designs or features that can be used to attract new customers. Last, but certainly not least, advertising departments create television, radio, and print advertisements based on products developed by R&D personnel. These ads reach hundreds, thousands, or millions of people who previously did not know that these products existed. Strategy helps manufacturers become more competitive, and R&D helps formulate strategy.

Uniqueness

If research and development personnel create a product that stands out from the competition, then they have created a product that is unique. If that product is very unique, then it can be protected with a patent. Patents prevent copycats from making the same product, and they create a somewhat monopolistic selling environment for a designated amount of time. This sales environment results in more sales, higher profitability, and a healthier organization. R&D personnel strive to created unique products, and those products can be very advantageous for manufacturers.

Profitability

Profitability is critical for virtually every manufacturer, and it only occurs after products start selling consistently. Good R&D leads to consistent selling because products are researched and developed by people who understand their jobs and their industry. When products firmly establish themselves in markets, they have the potential to sell consistently for years...and this leads to long-term profits. In short, R&D leads to profitability due to the work done with products long before they are introduced to the market.

Image

If people have a perception of an organization, then they have established an image. Image is important because it paints a picture of an organization as a whole. Positive image establishes trust with customers and the public, while negative image has the opposite effect. Manufacturing R&D helps build positive images through new product innovation that drives customer satisfaction.

The following shows how different people are affected by the image of manufacturers:

Employees

Potential employees are attracted to manufacturers with a positive image. They like the thought of working for companies that they think highly of and respect. In fact, some people will even accept a lower wage to work for these organizations rather than working for a company that they view negatively.

Current employees often choose to remain working for organizations that they view positively. They find job satisfaction because they identify with their companies, and this prevents them from looking elsewhere for employment.

Investors

Investors are enticed by organizations with positive images because it helps them believe that they will receive a return on their investments. This same thinking applies to stockholders who choose to invest in companies that they view in a positive light.

Customers

Reputation is driven by image, and people want to purchase products from organizations they deem reputable. Their loyalty is indicated by the fact that they will pay a higher price for a product from a company they respect even though the same product can be bought cheaper from another organization. Unfortunately, manufacturers with negative images can find it hard to make people think differently...and this negatively affects their bottom lines.

Cost management

Like it or not, cost affects virtually every business decision. It might not be at the top of the list, but it has to get some consideration because most manufacturers are driven by the bottom line. Cost is always a consideration for research and development decisions because R&D is an expense that involves risk with no guarantee of success. However, companies with good R&D departments actually control costs by developing new products as effectively as possible. Personnel from other areas, such as manufacturing or marketing, might know what they need to achieve...but they do not always know how to go about it in the most cost efficient manner. In the end, they spend more time and money working on new projects than R&D departments.

Tax breaks

The United States government allows companies to use certain percentages of their research and development spending as tax deductions. This book is not designed to get into specific details of those deductions, but the point is that they benefit the manufacturers that take them. In this regard, some of the money spent on R&D can be recouped, and this makes the development of new products even more attractive.

Now you understand some the advantages associated with product-based research and development. However, as might be expected, there are also some negatives associated with manufacturing R&D...and that is why the next section explores disadvantages.

Disadvantages

Effective research and development provides many different benefits to manufacturers. It helps them compete, provides them with unique market presence, enhances their reputations, and even helps their bottom lines. However, R&D also has some challenges associated with it. In fact, some manufacturers choose not to invest in it due to the following disadvantages:

Uncertainty

This might be the biggest disadvantage of research and development. Quite simply, it is never known if a new product is going to be successful. It might get out in the market and be successful, but it also might be a total flop. This risk is taken anytime R&D is conducted, and some manufacturers are not willing to accept the potential consequences.

Another aspect of uncertainty involves miscommunication. If R&D personnel do not get a clear picture of what needs to be done, then they might create something that does not work. For example, an R&D department in Arizona might be working on a new electrical component that needs to function properly for at least five years. However, they are not aware that this component has to function in a very humid area of Florida that often reaches temperatures over 100F. This environment will have a huge impact on the electrical component, and it will likely cause it to fail. In short, miscommunication can create a doomed product before it has a chance to enter the market.

Change

Research and development is not a fast process, and this will likely never change. Unfortunately, changes can occur during long periods of time...and those changes can cause the work of R&D personnel to become virtually useless. Customers might decide that they no longer want a product, specifications might be altered, the market might no longer be viable, or a better item might have been introduced. Regardless of what happens, changes that occur over time can cause products to become unwanted or unneeded. This disadvantage is not the fault of R&D personnel, but it can and does occur.

Money

How can money be a disadvantage of R&D if profitability and cost management are both advantages? The answer is because some organizations choose to view it this way...and sometimes with good reason. Without a doubt, there is an upfront cost for research and development. If that cost is not recouped, then it is a loss. Some manufacturers simply do not want to set aside money for something that may or may not work for the better of the organization. They choose to limit R&D or conduct it internally with existing management. There is a cost to using internal management for R&D, but not nearly as much as investing in an entire department. However, manufacturers must realize that their potential for large returns on new products diminishes when R&D is limited...and it can result in them becoming less competitive.

Now you understand some of the advantages and disadvantages involved with research and development. Organizations need to weigh the pros and cons before investing in R&D, and this is often a big decision. Money and time are risked if companies choose to conduct R&D, but the ability to compete is risked if they choose to do nothing. This being said, there must be ways to improve R&D...and that is why improvement is the focus of the next section.

Improving

Research and development needs to get better for it to be embraced by manufacturing leaders who are undecided about its worth to their organizations. Some ways to make it better are as follows:

Universal standards

This might be the most overlooked method of improving research and development even though it should be rather obvious. **Universal standards need to provide a reference point for all organizations that conduct product-based R&D. These standards eliminate some of the guesswork in the R&D process, thereby saving time and money that is often spent trying to establish some type of starting point. For example, a food manufacturer trying to make a honey-based salad dressing should have a Food and Drug Administration (FDA) requirement for the minimum amount of honey that must be in the product. This requirement gives a baseline for where to begin developing the product, and it evens the playing field with other food manufacturers who might otherwise choose to use far less of the expensive ingredient.**

Academia and industry collaboration

There must be a stronger bridge built between academia and industry so they can work together on product-based research and development. This collaboration should take place in educational laboratories and organizational settings with the objective being better R&D. Education is the key to developing new ways to become competitive, and organizations that participate in research are on the cutting edge of new ideas and technology. In short, theory and practical application fuel each other in the ever-changing global marketplace...and the strengthening of this relationship is necessary for improving R&D.

Better communication

As noted in the disadvantages section, miscommunication causes big problems for research and development. Fortunately, business leaders and R&D professionals are aware of this problem, but they need to work together to open the lines of communication on a more regular basis. This means decisions cannot be made without consulting everyone involved. There needs to be a plan in place that designates what type of communication will take place at each stage of the process. In terms of R&D, companies that fail to plan are essentially planning to fail.

Better communication also requires feedback after a product has been introduced to the market. Was the product successful? If not, what caused it to fail? The information gathered from constructive feedback helps improve future products by preventing mistakes from being repeated and providing greater understanding of customer needs. Feedback is valuable, but not enough of it is given in many cases.

Now you have some suggestions for improving research and development as it moves forward. This leads us to the next section that discusses the future of R&D.

Future

This section looks at the future of research and development. Not surprisingly, R&D is going to be around as long as manufacturers compete with each other. They need to develop new products in order to keep or gain market share, and this can only be done with R&D. That being said, the following specific aspects of R&D will change in the future:

Spending

Manufacturers will become more engrossed in research and development. Leaders will realize the value of R&D and the fact that it cannot be ignored if they want their organizations to grow and prosper. This means spending will increase for R&D projects. That spending will be viewed as an investment rather than a risk even though success is not guaranteed. In this regard, leaders of organizations will change their mindsets about product-based research and development. They will put money aside to make sure projects are properly completed and R&D personnel are never thought of as expendable employees.

Investment

As noted above, spending refers to the money spent internally by manufacturers. However, external funding will also increase in the form of investment. Outside investors will fund research and development projects because they will be more cognizant of the importance of those projects. Without R&D, manufacturers will not grow...and growth is necessary for return on investment.

Along the same lines, people will want to buy stock of manufacturers that are dedicated to research and development. They will understand that R&D fuels growth, and that growth increases the value of their stock. Stock purchases will create win-win situations for organizations and stockholders because the money obtained will be used to create new products that keep companies healthy and stockholders happy.

Global focus

The focus of product-based research and development will become more worldwide as companies compete in an ever-increasing global market. The research aspect of R&D will consider different customs and cultures when deciding which new products need to be developed. Additionally, technology will make it easier than it ever was in the past to transport products to any destination, and manufacturers will take advantage of that technology. In short, the face of R&D will change as the local, regional, and national focus takes a backseat to global demands.

Summary

Product-based research and development is a valuable process that is used by manufacturers all over the world. It helps them remain competitive in ever-changing markets, but that competitiveness comes with the risk of failure. However, based on the need to compete, R&D is necessary for the survival of many companies...and this will likely continue for a long time.

This book focuses on product-based research and development in organizations...primarily manufacturers. It examines the responsibilities of R&D personnel, analyzes the advantages and disadvantages of R&D departments, suggests methods for improving R&D, and assesses the general future of the concept. The text is informational and educational, and it is written for easy reader understanding at all levels.

Congratulations! You now understand more about product-based research and development...a competitive must for manufacturers all over the globe.

Supply Chain Management in Manufacturing
A Basic Introduction

Louis Bevoc

Published by
NutriNiche System LLC

Louis Bevoc books...simple explanations of complex subjects

Summary   222

Introduction

A book on supply chain management in manufacturing (SCM) would not be complete without a discussion on purchasing because manufacturers need to purchase raw materials and supplies in order to produce finished products. Not surprisingly, those raw materials and supplies do not magically show up at the doorstep...they have to be ordered by purchasing agents in a timely fashion at the best possible price.

Purchasing agents, also known as buyers, follow designated company strategies when making buying decisions. They often adhere to a just-in-time philosophy where raw materials and supplies are brought in only when needed. Excessive inventory needs to be avoided due to the money that gets tied up, and all decisions are made with cost in mind.

In the past, purchasing for manufacturers was primarily done by lower level employees. A manager told a clerical worker what was needed, and the order was placed. However, strategic purchasing has made this process a relic of the past that will likely never return. Purchasing is now done by management personnel who have a great deal of authority and responsibility, and it is a major part of supply chain management...the focus of this book.

Supply chain management is a controlled system where organizations along the entire supply chain work together to produce and deliver the best possible products at the lowest cost. Shared resources are used to assure purchasing, production, and distribution are effective and efficient while meeting established quality standards. This gives producers of products a competitive advantage in today's lean manufacturing environment.

In the global marketplace, many manufacturers rely on outsourcing and suppliers to do some of their production. This works well for getting products made, but reliance on others brings about quality concerns. Those concerns are the reason that the modern era supply chain management came into play.

Now that you have a basic understanding of the relationship between supply chain management and manufacturing, let's move on to the basic components involved with this association.

Components

In manufacturing, SCM manages the flow of goods from the purchasing of raw materials to the delivery of finished products...including the storage and of inventorying of all stock. The plan is to synchronize supply and demand while monitoring and controlling all activities along the chain. Based on this plan, it is rather obvious that good communication is critical at all levels.

SCM utilizes logistics, engineering, operations, and technology to accomplish manufacturing goals and objectives. For example, inventory levels of raw materials and finished products must always be accessible for reordering, production scheduling, and fulfillment of customer orders. Modern bar coding technology has made this possible because it has the ability to receive information about inventory that includes past and present location, quantities, and future destination.

Essentially, supply chain management in manufacturing can be broken down into three major phases as follows:

Strategical

This the planning stage. A road map for the SCM needs to be developed, and supply chain partners need to be identified. Where, when, and how will the finished products be manufactured? Who will supply the raw materials? Is another company going to manufacture part or all of the finished products? Where will the finished products be warehoused? These questions need to be answered during the strategical phase, and those answers are best achieved using collaboration from all partners in the chain. For example, companies need input from each other to figure out what makes the most sense from a logistical standpoint and which organization is most capable of manufacturing specific products.

Tactical

This is the execution stage. It involves putting the plan into effect and finalizing the details. What quantity of raw materials and finished products will be inventoried? What are the costs associated with raw materials and finished products? What are the quality specifications for raw materials and finished products? These questions need to be answered during the tactical phase, and those answers are best achieved using collaboration from all partners in the chain. For example, it might seem like the quality specifications should be set by the manufacturers, but they need input from their suppliers for realistic expectations. Along the same lines, suppliers need to communicate with manufacturers about cost so the best economical solutions can be obtained.

Operational

This is the maintenance stage. It is where the day-to-day activities are managed to ensure the supply chain runs efficiently and effectively. It entails all plant activities including purchasing, receiving, production, inventory, storage, and shipping. What types of raw materials need to be ordered? What types of raw materials need to be inventoried? What types of finished products need to be manufactured? What types of finished products need to be inventoried? These questions need to be answered during the operational phase, and those answers are best achieved using collaboration from all partners in the chain. For example, manufacturers need distributors to help them make production decisions, and they need to communicate with suppliers about fulfilling raw material needs.

The above phases are necessary components of effective supply chain management for manufacturers. However, other factors also influence SCM. These factors include environmental concerns and ethical responsibilities.

In terms of environment, production facilities are capable of creating a wealth of pollution. This pollution can contaminate the ground, water, and air…and none of it is acceptable. This concern for the environment is not new for manufacturers, but SCM raises the bar because every organization in the chain must be environmentally responsible.

Ethical responsibilities also affect SCM. Ethics are a serious issue for manufacturers that employ low paid productions workers...especially if those manufacturers compete globally. There is worldwide concern for how employees are treated, and organizations that are perceived as abusing their workers face backlash. Repercussions might be limited to verbal criticism, but they can also be much more severe....including the boycotting of products. Reduced sales can injure organizations and even put them out of business, so ethical issues do need to be addressed. Similar to environmental concerns, ethical responsibilities affect the entire supply chain.

Now you understand the major phases of supply chain management and some additional factors that affect the process. However, these components do not explain why this process is implemented by so many organizations. This leads us to the next section that discusses the goals and objectives manufacturers have in mind when they implement SCM.

Goals and objectives

Supply chain management is, to say the least, a complex arrangement. Every organization in the chain must be successful in order for it to be effective. Money, time, and human resources are required to establish relationships, define roles, implement new technology, and bring everything together for a smooth flowing system.

Sometimes the amount of work required to obtain successful SCM does not seem worth it. However, once the system is running, the benefits convince most people that their efforts were not in vain. In fact, those efforts usually pay off tenfold when goals and objectives are achieved. This raises a question. What exactly are the goals of supply chain management? The following lists SCM goals and describes their relationship to manufacturing:

Fill customer orders

This is the most basic goal of supply chain management. If finished products are not in stock, then customer orders will not be filled. The entire supply chain must work together to achieve this objective, and a week or broken link can cause a breakdown that leads to failure. Fortunately, most organizations make order fulfillment a top priority, and they tend to do whatever is necessary to achieve this objective. For example, management at a furniture manufacturer understands that a customer with a chain of retail office supply stores puts leather desk chairs on sale every June for the entire month. Based on this, they make sure they have 1000 leather desk chairs in stock at the beginning of March every year so they can fill the orders they receive.

Improve customer service

Order fulfillment is only a portion of good customer service. The other part involves meeting customer needs and expectations. In addition to filling orders, customers also want products delivered on time to specified receiving points. In other words, manufacturers must be able to ship products in a timely manner to any location, or customer expectations will not be met. For example, a dental manufacturing company that produces cavity filling compounds has a customer with 35 mobile dental labs that travel around the nation to perform low-cost dentistry on people who do not have dental insurance. This manufacturer knows they must have the compound in stock and be able to ship anywhere in the nation, so they have worked out a deal with UPS to pick up products every day at their facility for overnight delivery. This assures products will be delivered on time anywhere in the country.

Add customer value

Filling customer orders and improving customer service are both important objectives for supply chain management, but manufacturers also have to keep in mind the need to create value for their customers. Value is created by understanding and exceeding the requirements that make up customer service. For example, management at an automotive supplier understands that their customers regard just-in-time (JIT) delivery as a top priority. Rather than scheduling deliveries with lowest cost carriers on a case-by-case basis, the supplier enters into an agreement with a specific carrier that makes sure delivery trucks are available 24/7. This creates value by assuring customers that they will receive the parts they need at the times they want them.

Embrace change

Change can be difficult because it often requires people to leave their comfort zones. They have to enter unfamiliar areas causing them to fear the unknown. A major goal of SCM is to help manufacturers embrace change as they modify and adjust their behavior in different situations. Confidence is the key here, and that confidence is based on the fact that a variety of expertise is readily available with a simple email or phone call. At some point, change is going to happen to all manufacturers...so they might as well accept and embrace it for an easier transition.

Manage risks

At first glance, this might seem a bit strange. After all, why would managing risks be a goal of SCM? The answer lies in surviving workplace disruption. Over time, supply chains undergo changes...and some of those changes are catastrophic if they are not properly managed. Natural disasters, power failures, security problems, labor issues, and leadership changes are all events that can damage the flow of products and risk the survival of organizations. Risk management helps manufacturers identify, rectify, and move past disruption so they can redesign the supply chain and prevent future reoccurrences. Based on this, it makes sense that risk management is a goal of supply chain management.

Add stakeholder value

Stakeholders are people or organizations who are affected by a manufacturer's actions. This includes co-producers, suppliers, investors, communities, and government agencies. Value, similar to customer value, is created by understanding and exceeding stakeholder requirements. However, it differs from customer value because it can be driven by social requirements that are not necessarily financially beneficial to the manufacturer. For example, management at a meat processor understands the community they manufacture their products in wants a clean environment. Rather than monitoring the air quality for the smoke exhaust that exits their smokehouses, they install "scrubbers" on the exhaust stacks to reduce the amount of smoke that enters the atmosphere. This creates value by assuring the community that the air they breathe will not be polluted or contaminated.

Utilize resources

There are many different skills associated with supply chain management. Some organizations in the chain are great at production, others excel at inventory control, and still, others are highly efficient at warehousing and distribution. Every organization has specialization and expertise that helps them identify the best methods for completing job-related tasks while incorporating cutting edge technology. A goal of manufacturers is to tap into this expertise and use it for a competitive advantage.

Establish trust

In order for manufacturers to achieve a competitive advantage, organizations on the supply chain need to trust each other. This means trusting that information will be accurate, costs will be shared, and responsibilities will be fulfilled. Mutual trust benefits every organization on the supply chain, and this is why it is a goal. Unfortunately, this goal can be the most difficult to obtain because once trust is lost, it is difficult to regain.

Promote financial success

This is likely the most well-known and important goals. Supply chain management needs to increase profitability or it is not operating as intended. Manufacturers strive to reduce inventory, labor, and freight costs while increasing order accuracy, investor return-on-investment, and customer satisfaction. This leads to more efficient operations...and greater financial success. The major reason that most manufacturers are in business is to make money, and supply chain management helps them accomplish this objective.

Now that you are aware of the major goals of supply chain management, let's move on to the advantages that occur after these goals are achieved.

Advantages

If supply chain management did not have advantages, it would not be used by manufacturers. Fortunately, the advantages are plentiful, thereby making this process very attractive. The following are specific areas where SCM is beneficial for manufacturing organizations:

Quality

This advantage of SCM has far reaching effects. The quality associated with the items produced by manufacturers is one of the most important reasons those items are purchased, and that quality has been questionable over the past decade due to the changes made in many different industries. For example, some U.S. based manufacturers have exported their production to India or China in an effort to reduce costs. This makes sense financially, but it presents challenges from a quality standpoint...and SCM incorporates techniques that help overcome those challenges. Standards such as those set by ISO (The International Organization for Standardization) can be used to make products more consistent, thereby increasing finished product quality. Compliance with these standards assures customers that products meet established criteria and eliminates the need for an overabundance of quality checks during the production process. In terms of quality, supply chain management creates a win-win situation for manufacturers and their customers.

Inventory

Inventory ties up valuable resources, and this is why many manufacturers strive to keep it minimal. Supply chain management reduces money and space requirements while providing the versatility needed to accurately fill customer orders. It does this by keeping inventory at established levels based on historical data and other information provided by the chain. The success experienced is a direct result of communication between organizations involved in the process. For example, suppliers monitor raw materials and deliver only when needed, thereby creating a JIT system inventory for production. At the other end of the chain, distributors keep manufacturers abreast of sales projections and trends. This reduces worry for manufacturing buyers and salespeople, thereby allowing them to focus on other important aspects of their jobs.

Purchasing

For some manufacturers, this is the biggest advantage because substantial amounts of money and space can be saved. To get a better understanding of why this is the case, the role of purchasing agents (also known as buyers) needs to be described.

Purchasing agents are involved in many important aspects of plant operations, but their main job responsibilities are replenishing stock of existing materials and obtaining stock of new materials. This might sound fairly easy, but it is not. Many skills are required to be a top-notch buyer, and those skills typically come from experience. These skills include:

Negotiation

Buyers need the ability to work with others and create advantageous situations for the manufacturers that employ them. These advantages include payment terms, specifications, price, and guarantees. Guarantees can encompass delivery schedules, inventory quantities, product quality, and additional services provided by the vendor.

Management

Purchasing agents in manufacturing plants have a lot to manage. They need to oversee lead times, deliveries, pricing errors, and inventory levels. They also need to manage suppliers by providing them with information about changes and new requirements. In terms of management, buyers need to be astute...or they will likely let some aspects of their jobs get out of control.

Strategy

This refers to the strategy of the manufacturer rather than that of the individual purchasing agent. Management sets goals, and buyers help accomplish those goals. They monitor inventory levels, look for product losses, watch for pricing changes, and keep an eye on developing trends. Their actions affect the direction of the manufacturers that employ them, and sometimes they are the single biggest factor involved in management strategy.

Price

This is the most well-known skill required for purchasing agents. Buyers must be able to find the lowest price possible for the products or materials that best suit the manufacturer's needs. This should not be confused with simply finding the lowest price. There also needs to be value...and value is not always found in the cheapest commodity.

Essentially, price skills accomplish two objectives. They (1) improve profits and (2) make manufacturers more competitive. Profitability makes shareholders happy, and competitiveness keeps businesses operating. In short, pricing is an important skill for buyers because it directly affects the survival of manufacturing organizations.

Awareness

One might question why awareness is a skill. The answer is because, similar to a mother, a buyer's work is never done. There is a constant need to be vigilant about what is happening around them. This vigilance includes monitoring regulations, problems, policies, procedures, and changes...and reacting appropriately. As might be expected, this monitoring can never be taken lightheartedly or put to rest...and that is why awareness is an important skill of purchasing agents.

Production

Supply chain management works wonders in terms of improving production because innovation and technology lower labor costs while improving output. In SCM, every organization does what they do best and their combined efforts result in improved efficiency of the manufacturing process. Add this to the fact that organizations within the chain co-manufacture products in their areas of expertise, and the resulting production improvement becomes quite transparent. Since production is the heart of manufacturing, this advantage is one of the most important.

Distribution

It is difficult for manufacturers to be good at everything. They need to focus on getting products made that their customers need, and this means other aspects of the beginning-to-end process get less attention. Distribution is often one of those aspects, but it is not a problem with SCM because there are organizations in the chain that are logistical specialists. They make sure products get delivered to the customers that ordered them, and this relieves manufacturers of distribution related responsibilities.

Cost

The importance of cost is typically a top concern for most manufacturers. When supply chains are properly managed, there are cost savings for everyone involved. This is because each organization does its part to reduce the work required for others, thereby making the overall process more efficient. For manufacturing organizations, this maximizes efficiency from the purchasing of raw materials to the delivery of finished goods...and it results in lower costs.

Teamwork

There is little doubt that teamwork is an advantage of SCM. People work together chain-wide to make manufacturers more efficient and competitive. Below are some benefits of teamwork as they relate to manufacturing:

Synergy

This might be the biggest advantage of teams because every member of the chain can exchange thoughts and entertain other perspectives. Each organization has unique strengths that add diversity to the team, and the differing viewpoints contribute to the overall effectiveness of manufacturers. The synergy involved improves decision-making and helps the team reach goals within limited time frames.

Efficiency

Teams are able to move faster and more effectively than individual organizations acting alone. This is because they make the most of each member's strengths and talents. In areas where some companies are weak, others are strong...and their combined efforts work together to help manufacturers solve problems.

The best part about efficiency of a team is that it gets better as the team bonds. Over time, members learn the strengths of others in the group and utilize those strengths when they are needed.

Flexibility

Different organizational "personalities" on a team help the team accept change. Some companies find change challenging or stressful, while others embrace it. This is because people react differently to the same situations based on their perceptions, and those perceptions give teams the flexibility needed to accept change. This is important because change occurs frequently in manufacturing environments.

Idea generation

Companies have different experiences that add to the way their employees think about situations. Team member's individual thoughts generate unique ideas that can be bounced off the rest of the group for problem-solving. This process generates the best ideas because they are evaluated by everyone before being implemented as solutions. This improves the overall innovation of manufacturers.

Divided responsibilities

Teams divide responsibilities between group members, and this prevents individual organizations from being overloaded with work. It also allows members to support each other through cooperation and mutual understanding. In short, dividing responsibilities alleviates the stress associated with being completely responsible for a project...and this relieves the manufacturer of bearing the sole responsibility for improvement.

Risk

This advantage stems from the fact that risk is reduced when SCM is utilized. Supply chain processes and procedures help identify risk factors and determine their potential for harm. This allows manufacturers time to react and make the changes necessary to steer away from possible liabilities before they have a major impact. In short, SCM minimizes exposure to risk and allows for effective management of it.

As you can see, there are many advantages to supply chain management. It works well for manufacturers, and this is why the concept is becoming more and more popular. In fact, entire majors in college are based on supply chain management so students can enter the work world armed with knowledge about the subject. However, nothing is perfect. There are some disadvantages to SCM, and these are discussed in the next section.

Disadvantages

As with virtually every aspect of business, supply chain management has some drawbacks. Below are some of the challenges involved for manufacturers:

Complexity

This is likely the biggest disadvantage of SCM. Many different people and organizations are working toward common goals to make manufacturers more competitive, and this creates a wealth of opportunities for mistakes and problems. Supply chain management has great value for manufacturers, but the problems that result from the components that make up the chain offset some of that value.

Time

The Rolling Stones sang a song about time being on their side. Unfortunately, this is not always the case for SCM. Manufacturers invest massive amounts of time into managing the supply chain. They have to make sure their suppliers are performing at expected levels by measuring important variables such as quality and cost. A balancing act is required because quality must remain high while cost is minimalized. Every partner on the chain needs to be assessed, and this takes time. If SCM was eliminated and the entire manufacturing process was internal, a lot less time would be required.

Trust

Trust is a goal of SCM, but it is a goal that is not easily achievable. In fact, trust can lead to a complete breakdown of supply chain management systems. This is especially true for global manufacturers.

One important aspect of trust involves manufacturers' relationships with their suppliers. They need to believe their suppliers will perform as expected because deviations from expectations are expensive. In short, manufacturers are at the mercy of their suppliers, and this is bad if those suppliers have issues or are unreliable.

Foreign laws

Theft is an unfortunate reality for organizations that operate internationally. The global marketplace is very attractive, but laws in the United States do not protect manufacturers from being taken advantage of in other nations. Loss of intellectual properly is the biggest concern in foreign markets. Protection for patents and trademarks might not exist, and this can cost manufacturers millions of dollars in research, attorney fees, and lost market share. One might think that this threat would deter many manufacturers from competing globally, but this is typically not the case. Apparently, the risk is well worth the reward in the minds of the decision makers.

Uncertainty

Similar to foreign laws, there are other factors that present challenges to manufacturers that utilize SCM in the global marketplace. Please consider the following:

- Nature can create a wealth of problems. Areas susceptible to earthquakes, tsunamis, and volcanic eruptions can lead to disastrous situations that nobody predicted. The entire infrastructure of a nation can be destroyed along with the manufacturer's supply chain.
- Political climate is a threat because new administrations can completely change the rules upheld by their predecessors. If this happens, current ways of doing business are no longer valid...and neither is the supply chain of the manufacturer.

- The economy can suddenly become unstable. If this happens, organizations can go out of business. Obviously, the bankruptcy of a partner would hinder the manufacturer's supply chain as a whole.

You can see that the above disadvantages can spell disaster for supply chain management. That being said, there need to be methods for improving SCM, and those methods are discussed in the next section.

Improving

Supply chain management has a lot of upside potential, and this is why more and more manufacturers are implementing it as a part of their everyday process. However, regardless of the benefits of SCM, there is always for improvement...as long as manufacturers are willing to make the effort.

The following are some suggestions for making SCM better:

Involve employees

This might seem like a rather obvious way to improve SCM, but it is often overlooked. Management tends to forget that their own workers are part of the supply chain, choosing instead to focus on other organizations for improvement. Employees work for the most important link in the chain, and their involvement in the process will help strengthen that link. Additionally, their specific jobs might give them insight into valuable ways to improve the chain as a whole...and this is beneficial to everyone in the system.

Improve technology

No manufacturer is 100 percent up to date in terms of technology. Computerized systems automate and simplify many aspects of the supply chain process, but cost limitations often prevent their implementation. However, one investment that is worth the money is radio frequency Identification (RFID). Manufacturers that move thousands of items through their faculties need inventorying systems that are more efficient than bar coding. For these organizations, radio frequency identification (RFID) is the answer. Essentially, RFID uses radio waves to collect information on products and raw materials. That information gathered is similar to that collected by bar code scanners, but it can be read from several feet away. Large numbers of raw materials or finished products can be scanned without the necessity of hand-held units, and these scanners do not have to have a direct line of sight to register information.

Encourage innovation

Manufacturers have a wealth of innovative capacity at their fingertips...if they choose to tap into the talents of the organizations within the chain. These companies have expertise in specific areas that can be used to simplify production and get products to market faster and more affectivity. In short, manufacturers can improve SCM by leveraging the innovative skills of other chain members.

Utilize information

Similar to innovation, manufacturers have a lot of information available from the supply chain that they do not utilize. Detailed data analysis gives them the ability to effectively manage their supply chains from start to finish. Communication with suppliers opens the door to information that can be used to determine customer needs, increase competitiveness, and improve the supply chain performance. This information can also be used to develop standards. Manufacturers must avoid the "do your best" mentality because this reduces accountability. Standards give suppliers goals and direction for continuous improvement...and this betters SCM as a whole. In short, information is readily available if manufacturers decide to use it.

Review performance

Performance reviews of organizations in the supply chain can be a very time-consuming process...and that is why some manufacturers avoid it. However, if performance is not reviewed, then weak links cannot be identified and the right partners will not be put in place. Manufacturers need to invest time and effort into the continuous review of companies in the chain so they do not end up in difficult situations that are challenging to resolve. In short, a plan needs to be in place to measure performance, implement improvement strategies, and make the changes necessary to make the chain better. In terms of performance reviews, "those who fail to plan, plan to fail."

Analyze returns

Virtually every organization that manufactures products can expect to get some of those products returned by customers. Unfortunately, many returns are the result of faulty quality...something that should have addressed in the supply chain. Manufacturers need to spend time analyzing their returns to see exactly where the problems stem from so they can address them in the chain. However, this is typically not the case. Most manufacturers assume there will be a certain percentage of returns, so they ignore them when they come back to their facility. This is a wasted opportunity because, if given the proper attention, returns can improve the supply chain by pinpointing areas where changes need to be made.

Summary

Supply chain management is being embraced by many manufacturers today. It is especially valuable for those who compete globally because it involves an international chain of organizations that work together to produce the best products at the lowest cost. This gives manufacturers a competitive edge in a world where profit margins are lean and competition is fierce.

This book focuses on supply chain management in manufacturing. First, it examines phases of this system and the factors that affect it, next it explores goals and objectives established by management, then it analyzes advantages and disadvantages in the chain, and last it suggests ways to improve the overall process. The text is informational and educational, and it is written for easy understanding at all reader levels.

Congratulations! You now understand more about supply chain management...an increasingly popular concept for manufacturers worldwide.

Human Resource Management
A Basic Introduction

Louis Bevoc

Published by
NutriNiche System LLC

Louis Bevoc books...simple explanations of complex subjects

Introduction

Human resource management (also known as HRM) was first visualized when managers begin to realize the significance of people in organizations. Employees, not equipment or machinery, were the most important aspect of workplaces, and their efforts were directly related to the success of the business. Frederick Winslow Taylor expanded upon this thinking early in the 20th century, thereby popularizing the concept of workforce productivity. Human resources (also known as HR) departments followed as a means of developing and managing workforce productivity, and that is how the field of HRM came into being.

Today, HRM involves the management of human resources in order to help organizations meet established goals and objectives. HR personnel find people for jobs, educate them through training, provide them with relevant policies and procedures, and evaluate their performance.

The above paragraph is a rather broad description, and it needs to be expanded upon for better understanding. More specifically, HR people oversee and are involved with the following:

Recruitment

This is likely the most well-known area of HRM because most people associate HR departments with the hiring process. HR personnel select candidates, interview them, and make decisions about whether or not they are a good fit for the organization. This might seem like a relatively simple and straightforward process, but there is actually a lot of work that goes on before, during, and after the interview. This work consists of:

Specification

Every job that needs to be filled must have some type of pre-determined specifications. This requires the job to be analyzed in order to establish the skills, education, experience, and personality required for the best job fit. This is especially important for newly developed jobs because there is no information available. However, specifications on existing positions should also be reviewed for outdated information.

Strategy

This refers to the strategy used to promote job openings. Who is the job geared toward? Will the job be open to internal candidates only or can anyone apply? Will websites, social media, trade magazines, newspapers, and/or outside agencies be utilized to promote the opening? Answers to these questions provide a method by which potential candidates can be viewed for potential interviews.

Selection

This refers to the ways that the candidate pool is reduced during the interview process. Questions in the interview are designed to uncover information that might not show on a resume. Leadership and interpersonal abilities are brought to light, and specific personality testing is sometimes utilized.

Interestingly, many HR departments take the personality aspect of job fit very seriously because people's traits have been found to predict their behavior at work. Testing is utilized to determine how individuals work alone, work in teams, and work in specific environments. In other words, it shows how potential employees will fit into the culture of the organization. While personality testing is not completely reliable, it does provide insight into the selection process that cannot be obtained by reading resumes or interviewing candidates.

Planning

HR personnel are involved in the planning aspects of organizations, thereby ensuring that the goals and objectives of the company are achievable. This involves employees' identification with their workplace, and it important because employees who identify with their organization are more committed toward its goals. For example, a vegetarian who supports animal welfare probably does not identify with the goals of a pig slaughterhouse. However, that same individual would likely identify with the objectives of an animal shelter for abused pets. In short, there needs to be a plan to make sure the people are committed to the organization that employs them.

Planning also involves understanding employee behavior in the workplace. For example, turnover should be analyzed for patterns that might exist. This information can be used to find causes of absenteeism and low morale that were previously unknown. In short, risk factors need to be identified so they can be eliminated or minimized. This provides leadership with the confidence that their organizations will operate more efficiently over time.

Compensation

This refers to the compensation employees receive for the work they perform. Pay, benefits, vacations, personal days, sick days, and retirement all fall into this category. HR personnel typically do not determine employees' compensation, but they are a critical part of the process because they assure compensation decisions made by management are accurately implemented.

Training

Training is a process where information is provided for educational purposes. Employees acquire knowledge and skills that can be used for enhancing their job performance. They get better at their jobs, thereby becoming more efficient and effective. Additionally, training leads to employees requiring less direct supervision. They are able to do their work with minimal guidance do to the autonomy that training instills. This means supervisors can focus on other aspects of their jobs without the threat of employee mistakes being made due to misunderstanding or lack of knowledge.

One benefit of training that largely goes unnoticed involves psychology. Training improves attitudes and increases morale because employees feel empowered due to the attention paid to them. They realize that they are more than just a "face in the crowd," and their jobs have an impact on the well-being of the organization. Attention also works well for increasing employee commitment. They feel an active part of the organization, and this makes them more committed toward its goals and objectives.

In short, many benefits stem from an educated workforce. Employees grow and progress as they become more independent. This benefits supervisors and organizations. Anyone who has taken on a new work project that is confusing understands the importance of training, and HR people are always at the center of it.

Evaluation

All employees are evaluated by people in higher positions. Sometimes that evaluation is informal, such as an evaluation by an owner of a small company. Other times it is a documented formality that occurs on a regular basis. Either way, evaluations are a method of determining the worth of employees to their organizations. Promotions, demotions, and terminations are often based on them, and wages are adjusted accordingly.

HR personnel are usually an active part of the evaluation process. They might have a supervisor present at the review, but they make sure a structured format is followed to address important aspects of the employee's performance. This format ensures that an employee is meeting expectations in a timely and effective manner. If expectations are being met, then the review can be rather brief. However, if expectations are not being met, then the review can last substantially longer and include an improvement plan that details specific requirements and time frames for completion.

HR monitors the process of improvement plans in order to assure employees are doing what is expected of them. This process might appear to be derogatory because people's shortcomings come to the surface and are dwelled upon...but that is simply not always the case. In fact, improvement plans can be very constructive, and their benefits include the following:

- They help employees achieve goals that they were unable to accomplish alone.
- They document success that builds employee confidence.
- They help employees realize that they have more to contribute to the organization.
- They allow employees to maintain their jobs while paving the way for future compensation increases.

In short, employee evaluations are important because help organizations accomplish goals and objectives. HR people are responsible for much of this process, and this makes their department a significant part of the organization.

Legalities

This is where high levels of expertise are required because mistakes can be very costly to organizations. HR people uphold policies and procedures, including disciplinary action and terminations, and must understand the legal aspects of situations or they risk the possibility of lawsuits. For example, HR might terminate an employee for stealing based on witness accounts of the situation. However, if there is no video of the actual theft, then it might be hard to prove in court if the employee files a lawsuit. If the company loses the lawsuit, they might have to hire the employee back with retroactive pay in addition to paying attorney fees on both sides. If the company wins the lawsuit, they still to pay their own attorney fees. In short, it is much better to understand the legalities involved and avoid firing someone without the necessary proof or documentation.

Now you understand some of the major aspects of business that involve HRM. Let's expand upon this discussion by examining the specific goals of HR departments.

Goals

HR departments have a lot of responsibility in organizations. Essentially, they are involved in every aspect of business. Even CEOs have their wages, benefits, bonuses, and other perks monitored by HR personnel. So far, the role of HRM has been described in general. However, there are also specific goals that need to be accomplished including the following:

Compliance

One of the major objectives of HRM is to help organizations avoid legal problems and the fines associated with them. They diligently work to keep companies in compliance with all applicable rules and regulations. As noted in the introduction, this means taking disciplinary action for situations that subject organizations to lawsuit risks. However, it also entails making sure government rules and regulations are followed. For example, there are many OSHA (Occupational Safety and Health Administration) requirements that companies must adhere to or risk the consequences. The United States Department of Labor established OSHA in 1970 with the sole purpose of enforcing laws in industrial and commercial businesses. These laws were created in response to the workplace injuries and fatalities that occurred in the US. Companies that do not adhere to the rules can be fined...and those fines can exceed six figures if the findings are severe enough. HRM safety specialists promote safety awareness in workplaces when employees are working around dangerous machines or hazardous chemicals. Their goal is to keep organizations in compliance with OSHA guidelines so workers are safe and lawsuits and fines are avoided.

Along the same lines, HR departments work to comply with all labor and wage laws. There are state and federal laws that apply to minimum wage, overtime, child labor, right to work, family medical leave, and other work related issues. HR personnel need to understand these laws with the goal of keeping their organization in compliance.

HRM also has a goal of preventing discrimination and harassment. They strive to uphold equal opportunity requirements, promote diversity, and prevent problems from occurring. Accomplishing this goal saves money, but it also has an effect on the perception of organizations. The public does not like it when they read about organizations that allow discrimination or harassment. This activity is illegal, and it results in the company being perceived as unethical.

One last HRM objectively applies to unionized facilities. Grievances related to seniority, overtime, wages, job responsibilities, and other aspects of work need to be addressed...and HR people have a goal of resolving them as quickly and efficiently as possible. They want rules in the contract followed, and they also want to minimize costs to their employer.

Commitment

This is one of the most difficult goals of HR personnel because it is based on individual perception...and every individual is different. HRM wants all employees to be committed to their jobs and their employer. This helps organizations run more efficiently, and it relieves some of the stress experienced by HR people.

To encourage commitment, HR personnel get involved with employees and their supervisors. They work with employees so their voices are heard. Workers who have attention paid to them are more committed to their jobs because they feel like they are an active part of the company. This is supported by the now famous Hawthorne Studies conducted by Elton Mayo and Fritz Roethlisberger in the 1920s. These studies show that, regardless of the work environment, employees are more productive and engaged when management pays attention to them and involves them in decision-making processes. HR personnel also work with supervisors to improve their communication skills and help them become more empathetic toward employees. Emotional intelligence research started by Daniel Goleman has shown that supervisor empathy is critical for getting employees to become more productive and committed.

In short, the goal of HRM is not just to hire people who are qualified and have the right fit. It is also to get those people involved and make them feel a productive part of the workplace so they become committed to their jobs and their employer. Committed employees tend to remain with their organizations for long periods of time...and longevity fuels the prosperity of organizations.

Classification

This goal involves the classification of job responsibilities and job titles. It is much more important in large companies where employees do not wear a variety "different hats," but it also has application in some small organizations. Essentially, HR personnel design job titles and related tasks by working closely with management. This leads to clearly define jobs that neatly fall into place on a hierarchy chart that provides a visual image of the company's authoritative structure.

A hierarchy chart is often a part of conducting business in the United States. Leaders want to know who is in charge of the companies they are working with, and they also want to know who is responsible for making sure their needs are met. Sometimes this process can be rather informal, such as a brief introduction and a handshake, but is never that simple in Asian nations such as Japan. In Japan, a person's title has huge importance, and it should never be disrespected. In fact, it is so serious that the Japanese even place an emphasis on the way their business cards are treated. There are designated places for storing business cards...and a person's wallet or purse is not one of those places. This makes classification one of the biggest goals of HRM in Japan, and that is unlikely to change in the near future.

Teamwork

Teams are important in a wide variety of business aspects today, and that why many companies are built around a team concept. Teams are able to move faster and more effectively than individuals acting alone. This is because they make the most of the individual member's strengths and talents. In areas where some people are weak, others are strong...and their combined efforts work together to solve problems.

However, there are also downsides to teams. Sharing ideas and concepts with others is not always easy. In fact, it can be quite challenging for some people. This is because people differ professionally and personally. Differing opinions, beliefs, and values can lead to conflict...and that conflict is dysfunctional if the attacks turn personal and members focus on position instead of principle.

HR professionals have a goal of making teams the best that they can be. They advise management personnel on best practices for selecting team members and assigning roles. Business priorities and employee skills are taken into consideration, along with an understanding that workers have personal preferences when working with others on group projects. In short, teams are critical for idea generation and problem-solving, and that is why HR personnel have an objective of finding the right fit for members.

Diversity and Ethics

Many organizations, especially those that are global, are made up of employees with a wide variety of backgrounds, skills, experiences. This diversity is good for improving organizations as a whole, but it can lead to legal and ethical concerns. People with different cultural values, customs, religious beliefs, and social norms can offend each other without even knowing it...especially if the organization is global. Bribery, for example, may be considered unethical in the United States, but it is an accepted practice in some other nations. Along the same lines, derogatory treatment of women in business might be acceptable in certain areas of the globe, but it is illegal in the United States.

HRM has a goal of making organizations diverse while upholding ethical and legal standards. They make sure that employee differences are understood and respected. This is done using awareness programs that include emails, newsletters, manuals, or programs that address culture, spirituality, customs, and social norms of the different groups of people that need to work together to accomplish organizational objectives. Achievement of this goal is critical because it prevents conflict and workplace violence that can potentially be fatal.

Improvement

Like many departments in organizations, HR personnel have a goal of continuous improvement. They want to get better so their company runs more effectively and efficiently. However, unlike other departments in organizations, the improvements made by HR personnel are geared toward bettering every area of the business. For example, the quality control department of a food manufacturer puts an entire day's production of potato chips on hold because they do not meet quality standards. As a consequence, the production department needs to work overtime to remake the product. The action taken by quality control personnel looks good for their department, but it hurts the production aspect of the business. At the same time, the HR department of the food manufacturer announces a training program geared to improve the active listening skills of supervisors. This program helps all supervisors understand the needs of their employees so the organization can operate more efficiently.

HR personnel attempt to improve all areas of companies including recruitment, training, legalities, ethics, compensation, safety, and healthcare. These areas need to progressively get better for the organization to grow and prosper...and that is why improvement is a goal of HRM.

Now you understand some of the major goals of HRM. That being said, there needs to be a method in place for achieving those goals. That method is HRIS...the next section of discussion in this book.

HRIS

HR functions need to be managed effectively, and that management can be done using Human Resource Information Systems (also known as HRIS). HRIS allows users to view data for HR processes including attendance, payroll, disciplinary action, benefits, bonuses, training, and job classification. It typically consists of a software program that is custom designed to meet the specific needs of an organization. This program is continually updated as the organizational changes, and it is the most important system used by HR personnel.

The following are specific functions of HRIS:

Recruiting

Recruiting is an important aspect of HRM that requires the attention of HR personnel. This makes sense because good recruiting finds employees who can take the organization to the next level. However, if HR people are not careful, they can end up spending their entire day on recruitment issues. This means other aspects of their jobs get ignored...and that is not good for the organization.

With HRIS in place, much of the HR labor that was previously needed for recruiting is freed up for use elsewhere. These systems allow candidates to submit resumes and attachments from anywhere in the world that has internet access. HRIS then searches resumes for key information and classifies candidates based on priorities. This eliminates the work required for resumes received via mail, fax, email, or websites. Classification can be done using education, experience, skills, location...and even public speaking or writing ability. The software handles much of the selection process, and this is a big help for those involved in HRM.

Administering and self-governing

Administration of payroll and benefits is a problem for many HR departments, and HRIS provides a solution by streamlining these processes. Everything is done electronically, thereby eliminating paperwork and providing a permanent record of all transactions conducted.

The best part about this procedure from an HR standpoint is the fact that employees can select benefits, alter tax information, choose retirement plans, and make changes to any of their choices by themselves. They simply log into a website and start entering information that best meets their needs. HR personnel are available for help or consultation, but the time they spend administering information is drastically reduced when compared to the traditional ways of the past.

Scheduling, tracking, and reporting

This is likely the most critical function of HRIS because scheduling, tracking, and reporting are all important aspects of HRM. Examples of this importance include the ability for attendance to be monitored, vacations to be scheduled, injuries to be documented, and data to be analyzed. Additionally, notifications of events, meetings, conferences, deadlines, and other organizational happens can be issued and received by anyone. This allows organizations to pinpoint problems, identify needs, and prepare budgets.

In terms of reporting, HRIS has virtually unlimited capabilities. With a few clicks, reports can be generated that would take hours to research using traditional methods of the past. For example, five years' worth of data on peak periods of absenteeism, turnover rates per department, hours worked for employees, and supervisor bonuses as a percentage of base salary can be collected and put into a report. HRIS produces valuable information in a short amount of time, and this is very beneficial for HRM.

So far, only the positives regarding HRIS have been discussed. Unfortunately, there are also some negatives associated with it. Some disadvantages or HRIS include:

Expense

Cost is a factor for virtually everything in business...and HRIS is no exception. These systems require an initial outlay of cash, and there are also costs for maintenance and updates. Additionally, IT people need to be on staff to oversee the system, and these people can be rather expensive. If cost is a concern, then a cloud-based system might be a better solution for managing HR functions because clouds do not require as much money for implementation or operation.

Security

This is likely the biggest downside of HRIS. Confidential information is stored in these systems, and the release of that information to unauthorized people can create nightmares for organizations. To combat this problem, most companies have different levels of access for employees...depending upon their job and rank in the hierarchy. However, no security system is perfect, and sensitive information always has the potential to be leaked.

Now you understand some of the disadvantages of HRIS. However, typically the positives usually outweigh the negatives, and that is why so many organizations utilize this type of system.

Based on what has been written in this book so far, it is rather obvious that HRM is important to organizations because it offers a variety of benefits. However, as might be expected, there is also a downside to employing HR personnel...and some of the negatives are discussed in the next section.

Disadvantages

Unfortunately, HRM is not the "land of milk and honey." It presents some problems in organizations that can fester over time, and if those problems are not addressed they can lead to severe consequences.

The following are some disadvantages associated with HRM:

Security

As noted in the previous section, security is an issue with HRIS systems. Security is also a big concern with HRM as a whole...even if sensitive information is stored on something as simple as an excel file. This is due to the fact that electronic data is vulnerable to viruses that can shut down or even wipe out systems. More importantly, hackers can penetrate systems and do serious damage. Personal information, including social security numbers and bank accounts, can get into the hands of unscrupulous individuals who will stop at nothing to profit at the expense of others. Preventative programs must be in place or there will most likely be some type of breach of security. Unfortunately, many preventative programs prove to not be effective enough to deter illegal activity.

Most of the security issues discussed so far stem from people who are not employed by the organization. However, there are also internal threats from employees. When employees are involved, the system is usually breached for information gaining purposes, and the action is more unethical than illegal (with the exception of embezzlement). For example, unauthorized employees who access payroll systems can find out what their coworkers are paid and spread that information around the company. This is never good for the organizational because it can create jealousy and feelings of inequity because some employees are always paid more than others.

Mistakes

HR employees are capable of making mistakes just like everyone else. However, HR mistakes are often noticed by everyone...such as forgetting to issue bonus checks on the day they were designated to be distributed to employees. There are less noticeable errors such as spelling employee names wrong or entering their tax information incorrectly. While this does not upset the entire workforce, it does negatively impact the affected individuals. Too many mistakes make the HR department appear incompetent or incapable...and this damages the entire concept of HRM.

Objectivity

Objectivity is often lacking in HRM because statistics are the main source of evaluation. Managers often base important employee concerns such as promotions, raises, and bonuses, on numbers rather than looking at the situation objectivity. They do not get to know their workers personally and do not see their accomplishments that are not quantifiable. For example, team-oriented employees are willing to let others take credit for accomplishments, while selfish employees only credit themselves. Statistically, selfish employees look better on paper...but this is often not the reality of the situation. Along the same lines, college degrees indicate achievements, but they do not necessarily reflect a commitment to the goals of organizations or the effort put forth on jobs. Non-college educated employees can be better suited for the needs of organizations. In short, statistics paint a good picture of accomplishments, but sometimes they do not tell the entire story.

Technology

HR employees become so reliant on computer systems that they are unable to do their jobs if those systems are not working. This means data is not accessible and the functions of HRM come to a halt. It is also a major headache for employees who want to enter benefit or retirement information when the system is down.

Another problem with technology is the fact that it can be quite complex. Programs might be capable of performing many different functions, but those functions are virtually useless if HR employees do not know how to perform them in order to access the information. Technology might require outside consultants or training, and both of these are additional expenses.

As you can see, there are some negatives associated with HRM. The combination of these negatives might prevent organizations from hiring HR personnel in the future simply because the rewards do not justify the effort and risk. Supervisors might be told to handle HR related tasks for their departments or outside services might be contracted to do the work. This leads to the next section that discusses HRM in the future.

Future

Critics of HRM believe it will become obsolete in the future. They argue that software will replace HR personnel, and HR departments will no longer exist. However, there are also people who believe technology will enhance HRM and take it to new levels. When this happens, HR personnel will be added rather than deleted. So, what exactly is the future of HRM? Time will provide a complete answer to this question, but the following will be major factors:

Temporary employees

This refers to contract employees and seasonal employees who work for temporary employment agencies. They work for companies on an "as needed" basis with no guarantee of permanent jobs. These workers are defined as follows:

Seasonal employees

These employees work for specified periods of time (usually 120 days or less), typically during the peak business periods of organizations. They often fill jobs that do not require a high level of skill, but this is not always the case. However, regardless of the skill level, seasonal jobs are critical for obtaining goals established by the organizations that need help.

Many different types of food manufacturers use seasonal employees. Examples include turkey processors at Thanksgiving, ice cream manufacturers in the summer, and candy makers at Christmas. In this role, temporary employees are hired as production workers to help produce enough food products to meet customer demands. These jobs usually do not require a high degree of skill, so employees with a variety of different backgrounds are utilized. In some cases, the people filling these jobs do not even know how to speak English. The jobs are so simple that they can be shown what to do using non-verbal communication. An example includes putting six packaged turkeys into a carton and putting that carton through a tape machine. The employee performs this same process all day long, so specific training is not a factor for the job.

Some organizations require training for all employees...even those that are seasonal. Retailers need seasonal employees during the Christmas season due to the increased shopping demands of their customers, but those employees need some understanding of the company and the jobs they are performing. For example, a clothing store in a mall needs to train associates on how to stock items, assist customers, and operate cash registers. These skills are not natural for everyone, and many people need training. This training is even more critical in the food court area of the same mall. For example, employees who cook food need to be trained on proper finished product temperatures or someone could become ill due to food poisoning.

One last type of seasonal worker is often referred to as a "permanent" seasonal worker. This term appears to contradict itself, but it makes sense because these seasonal workers repeat the same job every year. A lawn care service is an example of an organization that needs this type of temporary help. Lawn care companies call the same people year after year to work for them during the summer months. Fishing vessels also employ the same seasonal workers every year. These individuals are out at sea for a few months, and then they live off the money they earned until the next season.

Contract employees

Contract employees stand out from seasonal employees because they have skills that are needed by organizations. Many of these individuals are temporary employees because they choose to be...not because they cannot find permanent work.

Examples of temporary employees who bring valuable skills to organizations include accountants, lawyers, engineers, scientists, and a broad range of consultants. These individuals contract their services out to companies that need help in specific areas, but do not want to hire permanent employees.

Some contracted employees want to be hired as permanent employees, while others prefer working under on a contractual basis. Full-time permanent employees receive health, vacation, holiday, and/or retirement benefits as part of their compensation, but contract employees do not receive any of these perks. However, contract employees have the freedom to control their own destiny, and this is very appealing to some people...especially those who are no longer working out of necessity.

In short, organizations that utilize temporary workers are not responsible for the HR aspects of those workers employment. The temporary agency that sends the worker out for jobs handles all HR related aspects of the employment.

In the future, the use of contract and seasonal workers will increase; thereby reducing the workload for HR personnel. This will ultimately impact HRM professional in companies because their services will not be needed as much as they were in the past.

Remote employees

Employees want to work remotely for work-life balance reasons. Work-life balance involves employees' ability to accomplishing work-related goals while enjoying their lives outside of work. This is important because time is limited, and different things need to take priority at different times in life. People need to work in order to sustain a certain lifestyle...but they also need the time to enjoy that lifestyle.

Telecommuting provides millions of people the opportunity to work from just about anywhere in the world. It helps them find work-life balance and reduce some of the stress in their lives. This is important because excessive stress can lead to fatigue, anxiety, irritability, and deteriorating physical health.

Employees experiencing positive work-life balance are able to step away from their jobs and enjoy life. They worry less, and this helps them go to sleep without thinking about work related problems. In the morning, they are ready to meet new challenges.

Work-life balance also helps organizations to hire the best Job candidates. If employees work remotely, then they can be hired from all over the world because it does not matter where they live. However, the best people want to be well-compensated for their efforts...and work-life balance is an important part of that compensation.

Telecommuting promotes the work-life balance necessary for happy employees, and happy employees are typically less stressed than those who are unhappy. That being said, remote employees will become a larger part of workforces and their HR needs will be handled by internal HR personnel. This means HRM will become more important in companies that promote working remotely.

Diverse employees

In the future, people of all different colors, ages, religions, and backgrounds will work together in organizations all over the world. Teams will benefit the most from this diversity because the combined skills, knowledge, and cultural understanding of members create synergy that cannot be found in homogeneous teams. Differing viewpoints will contribute to the overall effectiveness and improve decision-making, and this will work well for complex projects that involve innovative thinking.

Diversity will also help employees gain a better understanding of each other's roles in the workplace. Subconscious barriers of cultural judgment and racial intolerance are broken down as employees become more empathetic towards their coworkers.

Organizations high in diversity will rely on HRM for keeping their workplace effective and efficient. Unique needs will need to be addressed by HR personnel, and this will increase their importance to a level not yet experienced.

Specialized employees

In the past, temporary employees were mostly used for unskilled factory jobs. This has changed, and it will change even more in the future. Temporary agencies will have demands placed on them for employees with specialized skills. Organizations will be looking for temporary help in positions including:

- Architects
- Artists
- Executives
- Human resources personnel
- Researchers
- Trainers
- Translators
- Writers

The progression into more skilled temporary workers will not be difficult because it will come gradually. However, regardless of the speed of implementation, the basic functioning of temporary employment agencies is going to change because they will be taking on more HR functions. In short, the role of specialized employees will increase, thereby reducing the need for internal HRM.

Cost

Probably the biggest factor that will determine the role of HRM in the future will be cost. If it is less expensive to outsource HR functions, then organizations will do so. Add this to the fact that future companies specializing in HR services will be better than they ever were in the past, and it will make sense for many businesses to outsource.

Summary

Organizations today rely on HRM more than they ever have in the past. This is partially due to finding the right people, providing them with policies and procedures, training them if necessary, and evaluating their performance on a regular basis. However, it is also due to the fact the world is becoming a global marketplace...and companies must adapt in order to compete. They cannot ignore the differences in the people they employee because everyone needs to work together in order to achieve organizational goals and objectives.

This book focuses on HRM in organizations. It explores the roles of HR personnel, examines departmental goals, discusses the implementation of HRIS, and touches upon the future of this concept. The text is informative and educational, and it is written for easy reader understanding at all levels.

Congratulations! You now understand more about human resource management...a critical aspect of developing and managing workforces.

Risk Management
in Organizations
A Basic Introduction

Allison Shearsett and Louis Bevoc

Published by
NutriNiche System LLC

Louis Bevoc books...simple explanations of complex subjects

Introduction

Organizations experience a wide variety of risks, and leaders need to make decisions based on the potential rewards or consequences of those risks. They do this by implementing programs known as risk management. These programs are designed to reduce uncertainty in organizations when the effects of something that might happen are unknown. This is important because negative effects can compromise the goals and objectives of organizations...and they can even lead to businesses shutting down.

Uncertain times have led many companies to stop forecasting or predicting their future. Economic downfalls, terrorist threats, environmental concerns, and political changes have all impacted the way business is conducted, and this has led to leaders being more discrete about their short-term and long-term plans. Uncertainties have also resulted in leaders choosing to focus more on risk management than they have ever done in the past. They try to identify the most significant risks in their organizations and act accordingly with programs designed to reduce or eliminate them.

Essentially, any actions that reduce or eliminate risk fall under the umbrella of risk management. These actions help organizations secure their future by warding off potential problems before they occur. Risk management allows companies to make business decisions with confidence, and it also provides options when potential problems become reality. Organizations that make decisions without evaluating risk are gambling...and that gambling can lead to their demise.

Risk management programs also play a big role in protecting organizations from potential catastrophes. These programs are put in place for decision-making that identifies potential danger and works toward preventing or eliminating it. In short, they help organizations achieve goals and objectives while controlling the risks involved.

Now that you understand the concept of risk management, let's move to a discussion on the six basic steps involved.

Six steps

Essentially, risk management programs involve the six steps listed below. A meat processing company is used as an example for each step.

Assemble

This step involves assembling the risk management team. Care needs to be taken when selecting people because there should be a mixture of job responsibilities and personalities that allow the team to identify and analyze risk from multiple perspectives without bias. Work experience is also important because veteran employees typically have knowledge that is worth its weight in gold...and new employees often make suggestions that were previously never considered. The goal of the selection process is to make sure the team is heterogeneous so members do not all think the same. Diversity is the key to assessing risk in any situation.

Example

A meat processing company decides to implement a risk management program. They start by assembling a risk management team that consists of the plant manager, quality manager, sales manager, distribution manager, and office manager.

The plant manager and quality manager have been with the organization for more than 15 years. They have seen the company go through growth phases, and they also understand what they need to do when sales slow and times get tough. They have a very good grasp of the processes, policies, and procedures that are utilized for manufacturing meat products. In short, their experience is very valuable because they understand many of the risks involved when running a production facility.

The sales manager does not fully understand plant operations, but she is well aware of customer needs. She has only been with the company for six months, but prior to this job, she worked for a competitor for seven years. She sees risks involved with product being out in the field...particularly those that involve food safety because the last company she worked for had a product recall due to bacterial contamination. This experience causes her to perceive the risk of recall as very serious.

The distribution manager has been with the meat processing company for over three years. He understands finished product storage, inventory, and transportation. He perceives product loss, damage, and theft as the biggest risks in his department because he has the unfortunate experience of seeing all three of these problems occur while product is stored or transported to other locations. His finished product perception makes him a valuable member of the risk management team.

The office manager understands record storage, customer service, accounting, and payroll. She realizes embezzlement and other white collar theft are potential issues. She also knows the risks involved with calculating employee hours worked, paying invoices, or collecting money owed to the company. She views risks from an administrative standpoint, and her perception adds diversity to the risk management team.

Identify

This is where risks are realized. Each team member identifies and documents the risks that they see in their organization. Their perception is valuable because everyone perceives things differently.

This procedure should not take place in meetings because (1) some team members are more dominant than others and (2) there is potential for groupthink. Each member needs to think independently and document the risks they determine to be important. This asynchronous process gives all members flexibility so they can fit their thinking into their routine work schedules.

Example

The risk management team members at the meat processing company think about risks from their perspectives and identify them as follows:

Plant manager

Risks identified: power, productivity, nature, inventory, staffing, attendance

More specifically:

- *Power* refers to the risk of power outages
- *Productivity* refers to the risk of losing manufacturing productivity
- *Nature* refers to the risk of natural disasters (tornados, high winds, lightning strikes, earthquakes, etc.)
- *Inventory* refers to the risk of overstocking or understocking raw materials
- *Staffing* refers to the risk of having the right people for the jobs
- *Attendance* refers to the risk of people not showing up for their jobs (due to strikes, sickness, vacations, etc.)

Quality manager

Risks identified: allergens, bacteria, metal, chemicals, flavor, appearance

More specifically:

- *Allergens* refer to the risk of exposing people to ingredients that give them allergic reactions
- *Bacteria* refers to the risk of product being contaminated with disease-causing bacteria
- *Metal* refers to the risk of product being contaminated with metal
- *Chemicals* refer to the risk of product being contaminated with chemicals
- *Flavor* refers to the risk of product having an off taste
- *Appearance* refers to the risk of color and shape being wrong

Sales manager

Risks identified: product recalls, price, new products, service, quality, availability

More specifically:

- *Product recalls* refer to the risk of product being recalled back to the company for consumer safety once it has been shipped
- *Price* refers to the risk of customers not buying product because it costs too much
- *New products* refer to the risk of the company not producing the new products necessary to compete
- *Service* refers to the risk of customers not being happy with the service provided to them
- *Quality* refers to the risk of product not meeting acceptable quality standards

Distribution manager

Risks identified: transportation, delivery vehicles, drivers, accidents, inventory, nature

More specifically:

- *Transpiration* refers to the risk of lost or damaged product during transportation
- *Delivery vehicles* refer to the risk of delivery vehicles not running properly when needed
- *Drivers* refer to the risk of driver shortages
- *Accidents* refer to the risk of drivers getting into accidents
- *Inventory* refers to the risk of inventory being inaccurate, stolen, or lost.
- *Nature* refers to the risk of bad weather that prevents delivery of products

Office manager

Risks identified: customer satisfaction, employee ethics, theft, attendance, payables, receivables

More specifically:

- *Customer satisfaction* refers to the risk of customers not being satisfied with products or service
- *Employee ethics* refers to the risk of unethical employee actions
- *Theft* refers to the risk of white collar theft
- *Attendance* refers to the risk of employees missing excessive time at work
- *Payables* refer to the risk of suppliers not being paid
- *Receivables* refer to the risk of customers not paying their bills

Analyze

Now the team gets together to categorize the risks that have been submitted by individual members. Some risks overlap and can be combined in the same category, others need their own separate category, and still, others are eliminated. These categories define the type of risk and its potential impact on organizational goals and objectives. They also create a solid structure that helps facilitate the next step of the process (evaluate).

Example

The risk management team members at the meat processing company reduce the identified risks to the following categories:

Natural disasters

This includes inclement weather, tornadoes, earthquakes, lightning, flooding, snow drifts, and flooding.

Food safety

This includes product recalls, product spoilage, and product contamination.

Customer satisfaction

This includes price, delivery, order fulfillment, and quality.

Employee attendance

This includes delivery personnel, production personnel, and replacement personnel.

Finances

This includes payables and receivables.

Employee ethics

This includes unethical and illegal employee actions.

Inventory

This includes shortages and overages of finished product or raw materials

Evaluate

After risks have been categorized, it is time to rank them in order of importance. Typically this is done by evaluating each risk for its potential to occur and consequences that can result. Some risks are important enough to be quickly addressed in the next step while others can be moved to the backburner.

This step is sometimes considered the most difficult because inaccurate evaluations can lead to unanticipated problems...essentially defeating the purpose of the risk management team. However, there is a need for an order of importance, and evaluation addresses that need.

Example

The risk management team members at the meat processing company establish the following order of importance:

Employee attendance

Why? Employee attendance is a threat virtually every day. It is hard to get everyone to show up for work, and productivity is hindered on a fairly regular basis. For this reason, employee attendance ranks first on the list of important risks.

Food safety

Why? The meat processing company has not had a recall, and they have only had one complaint of a customer getting sick. However, the potential is there and the consequences could be devastating. Allergens are also present in the plant, and there is a risk that they could contaminate products without being listed in the ingredient statements.

Customer satisfaction

Why? Sales are critical for the meat processing company. A large reduction in sales volume could risk the survival of the organization.

Finances

Why? Vendors must be paid for their services or they will discontinue being vendors, and the meat processing company must get paid in order to have money to operate. Based on this, financial risk potentially threatens the well-being of the organization.

Inventory

Why? Raw material and finished product inventory outages affect the fulfillment of customer orders, and inventory overages tie up money that could be used elsewhere. There is a risk with inventory, but it is not major.

Natural disasters

Why? Tornadoes and flooding are threats that can occur with little or no warning. These weather disasters are a long shot, but they do present a minimal risk.

Employee ethics

Why? Unethical and illegal concerns have not been a problem in the past, but the potential for their occurrence does exist on a small level. For this reason, employee ethics receives the lowest ranking in terms of risk importance.

Address

Once risks have been categorized and ranked, it is time to address those that have been determined to be the most important. This is commonly referred to as response planning, and it is where the treatment begins. This treatment involves reducing the risks to acceptable levels using strategic planning and contingency planning. The goal is to minimize the probability of negative risks (strategic planning) while determining ways to address the problems that result when risks become reality (contingency planning).

Unfortunately, contingency planning often faces two major obstacles. These obstacles are:

Motivation

Contingency planning is essentially a backup plan that goes into effect if the strategic plan is not successful. Many risk management teams put so much time and effort into their strategic plan that they think it will be successful regardless of the circumstances. They simply believe that they will not need a contingency plan, so they are not motivated to create one.

Urgency

In reality, there is a low probability of a situation that will require a contingency plan. Yes, there are circumstances that create a crisis, but those circumstances are viewed as few and far between....so contingency planning moves to the bottom of the list in terms of importance. When something is a low importance priority, it tends to never get done properly because there is no sense of urgency.

Example

The risk management team members at the meat processing company establish the following risk reduction measures as part of their strategic plan:

Employee attendance

On the job training is conducted at the plant, and this reduces the risk of employee missing work due to injuries. Job rotation is also ongoing; thereby allowing employees to learn each other's jobs and function as backups.

Food safety

A HACCP program is in place to address food safety in the plant. It pinpoints critical areas of meat processing in order to assure meat is safe when it leaves the plant. Additionally, all employees are educated on food safety and food defense. They are trained when they start with the meat processing company and on an annual basis.

Customer satisfaction

Surveys are sent to customers to assess their satisfaction. These surveys allow respondents to provide detailed information about why they are not happy.

Finances

All accounting and office personnel undergo initial and annual financial training specifically geared toward the meat processing company. This assures fewer mistakes will be made in the office.

Inventory

Employees conduct month end inventory to reduce the risk of error, and weekly meetings are held between manufacturing, distribution, and purchasing personnel to discuss shortages and overages.

Natural disasters

The plant roof is inspected annually for damage, and the plant walls are constructed to withstand 70 MPH winds. This assures building security under severe weather conditions.

Employee ethics

A written ethics policy is given to all employees when they are hired. They must (1) pass a written test that shows they understand the policy and (2) sign off that they are in possession of the policy.

As part of their contingency plan, the risk management team members at the meat processing company establish the following to reduce problems that occur when risks become reality:

Employee attendance

A contract is established with a temporary staffing firm if the company experiences employee shortages. This firm can provide up to 100 employees within one hour of being contacted by the meat processing company.

Food safety

Mock recalls are conducted to assure all affected product can be recalled. These recalls trace all raw materials to original sources and all finished products to end users. A law firm has also been contracted to handle interaction with the government and others if a recall becomes public.

Customer satisfaction

A policy is in place that refunds customers the product purchase price if they are not satisfied with for any reason. Customers merely need to show proof of purchase, and they will be promptly refunded.

Finances

Internal audits are performed for all major financial discrepancies, and a contracted CPA firm is available for consultation.

Inventory

Internal investigations are performed for all major inventory discrepancies, and a contracted CPA firm is available for consultation.

Natural disasters

Local authorities (police, fire, utilities) are contacted to assess the situation and recommend a course of action. These individuals are trained in natural disaster response, and they have access to resources that are not available to the meat processing company.

Employee ethics

Internal investigations are performed for all unethical or illegal activities, and a contracted law firm is available for consultation.

Monitor

At this point, the risk management team has identified, analyzed, evaluated, and addressed important risks in their organization. However, the program still needs to be monitored to assure that it is working properly.

In this step, questions need to be asked. Is the program working as intended? Are the established controls still effective? Will the established controls be effective in the future? What are the weak points? What needs to be changed? If the program has been successful, then it can be left as is without change. However, if the program has failed or the future points towards its failure, then changes need to be made.

Example

The risk management team members at the meat processing company monitor the program as follows:

Employee attendance

Employee attendance is monitored using an employee attendance system that has a two-fold effect. It rewards employees with good attendance and disciplines those with poor attendance. Additionally, the fill-rate of the temporary employer is tracked. If the fill rate falls below 80 percent, then other temporary employment services are explored as an option.

Food safety

Trends are tracked for all food safety deviations from the HACCP plan. Established trends require the meat processing company to make changes to processes and procedures to prevent future reoccurrences.

Customer satisfaction

Data from customer surveys is collected and analyzed for trends. Any negative trends require changes to be made to prevent reoccurrences.

Finances

All accounts payable and accounts receivable errors are documented. If a trend develops, then action is taken to determine why that trend occurred and how it can be prevented from reoccurring.

Inventory

Inventory outages and overages are tracked and documented. If a trend develops, then meetings are held to determine why the problem occurred and how to prevent a reoccurrence.

Natural disasters

All damage is documented on a list. Management reviews the list to find weak points that can be made stronger to prevent a recurrence.

Employee ethics

Unethical employee behavior is documented and disciplinary action is taken to prevent a reoccurrence. This discipline can involve employee termination and/or legal action.

Now you understand the premise of a risk management program and the basic steps involved in establishing that program and putting it into action. Let's expand on this discussion in the next section by describing the two major types of risk management.

Types

This section simplifies two rather complex types of risk management so they can be understood by most people. These types are quantitative and qualitative, and they are broken down as follows:

Quantitative

Quantitative risk management determines the cost of catastrophic situations by establishing the probability of occurrence and the potential consequences resulting from that occurrence. It classifies and evaluates the impact of problems on organizations and their employees. In short, it determines the cost of lost productivity, replacement of assets, and damaged reputation using statistical analysis. For example, the meat processing risk management team might use a continuous variable commonly known as return on investment (ROI) to determine the standard deviation (variance) of a financial risk. First, they identify the threats that produce the biggest estimated losses, and then they determine appropriate measures to reduce those losses.

An advantage of quantitative risk management is the results are objective. Personal bias is not a factor because statistical analysis is used to determine risk. However, a disadvantage of quantitative risk management is the complexity of the process. Calculation of results can be difficult and cumbersome.

Qualitative

Qualitative risk management does not utilize statistical analysis and is therefore used by many small organizations. It uses relative values to determine potential loss if a problem occurs. In short, it awards scores for the probability of problematic situations and the need for action to minimize the risk involved. For example, the meat processing company is located in rural Kansas. The risk management team might evaluate the probability of a hurricane as insignificant and the need to take action to reduce the risk as very minor. Along the same lines, they might evaluate the probability of employees missing work as very likely and the need to take action to reduce risk as major.

Advantages of qualitative risk management include ease of calculation and implementation. The method is relatively simple to understand and implement in most organizations. However, a major disadvantage is personal bias. Lack of statistical analyses allows employees the ability to manipulate results based on their perceptions of situations.

Quantitative and qualitative types of risk management have both experienced success and failure, but each type has a goal of identifying risks and reducing or eliminating them. That being said, there must be ways to improve risk management in general...and that is why improvement is the focus of the next section.

Improving

Risk management programs provide many benefits to organizations. This makes sense because if they were not advantageous, then they would not be implemented. However, these programs are not foolproof and they can always be improved. Suggestions for improvement include:

Follow the program

Some risk management teams try to implement risk management programs without following the six basic steps. These steps are essential for the success of risk management because they promote continuous improvement of predictive power. For example, the risk management team at the meat processing company might decide not to evaluate the importance of each risk that has been categorized. They believe all risks are equally important, so there is no point in evaluating them individually. This might appear to be a rational decision, but it is a mistake because equal risk importance is not the reality of their situation. It is much more likely for employees to miss work than it is for bad weather to damage the building. Ranking these two risks as identical is doing an injustice to the organization in terms of preparing for problems that might occur in the future.

Define roles

Risk management is dependent on a team, and each member needs to contribute in a unique way. If two members have the same responsibilities, then the team is not performing at a peak level and success will be negatively impacted. For example, if three members of the meat processing company's team are all assessing risk from a production standpoint, then the overall team effectiveness is reduced because other areas of the operation are not considered. Team members must have a goal of increasing predictive power for all organizational risks...and this starts by defining roles.

Ask open-ended questions

Many questions asked by team members are closed ended and they fail to produce the detailed answers required to create a successful risk management program. For example, the president of the meat processing company might ask the office manager if she believes white collar embezzlement is a risk. This question will get a "yes" or "no" answer, but it could generate much more valuable information if the president asked the office manager to explain why she does or does not see white collar embezzlement as a risk.

Principle not position

This is related to the "define roles" suggestion discussed earlier in this section. Risk management personnel need to focus on "principle not position" by doing what is best for everyone involved. For example, individual team members at the meat processing company need to step back in order to view the organization as a whole. Risks need to be identified based on the good of the organization, not the department or the individual. This can be difficult, but it is possible and it will achieve the best results.

Leadership commitment

This suggestion is rather simple. Commitment to a risk management program needs to start at the top of the organization...but unfortunately, this is not always the case. In many instances, commitment is only found at the lower levels of organizational hierarchies. This creates situations where employees are not encouraged to move forward with thoughts and ideas, and their motivation to implement and maintain a risk management program fades over time. For example, if the president of the meat processing company does not show interest in the risk management program, then the team will follow his lead the program will never be useful. In short, risk management programs without leadership commitment do not have the necessary support to take root and prosper.

Realize opinion limitations

It must always be remembered that risk management is based on opinions...and everyone on the risk management team has an opinion. Their opinions are shaped by their education and experiences...and those opinions can be bias. Diverse make-up of team members helps prevent similar thinking and opens the door to new ideas, but it does little to change opinions. For example, the meat processing company put together a fairly diverse team. However, all of these people harbor feelings that result in their individual preferences. In this sense, opinions are a limiting factor of risk management because they are naturally slanted toward personal thoughts, experiences, ideas, and concerns.

Another problem with opinions is the fact that it is impossible to predict whose opinion is corect. If organizations knew the risks they were going to face in the future, they would not need a risk management team. They would simply prepare based on what they know is going to happen. For example, If the leadership at the meat processing company knew that the only risk they will face in the future is food safety, then they would forego the risk management program and focus their efforts on preventing food safety problems. In short, risk assessment is about the future...and the future cannot be predicted with 100 percent assurance based on people's opinions.

Now that you understand some ways for improving risk management, it is time to move on to the last section that discusses the future of this interesting concept.

Future

What does the future look like for risk management? This is an interesting question because risk management is about the future...so it is essentially asking what something that predicts the future will look like in the future. Regardless of the irony involved with this question, the answer is "very good." However, there will be some changes due to the impact of a few factors.

The following factors will impact the future of risk management:

Regulatory agencies

Not surprisingly, regulatory intervention is going to increase in the future. Government agencies will have goals of protecting consumers, and they will achieve those goals by implementing new rules and regulations. When this happens, organizations will find themselves facing even more risks. Those risks will need to be reduced, and that reduction will be accomplished using risk management. In short, regulatory agencies will continue to make changes...and risk management will address those changes.

Technology

Technology impacts virtually every aspect of an organization. This impact is often for the better, but it does lead to increased risk. For example, a technological advancement that makes something easier has a risk of failure that can leave an organization helpless. Along the same lines, complex technology runs the risk of employees not understanding how it works. Technological risks will certainly be present in the future, but they will be minimized if organizations utilize risk management. This means the advent of technology will lead to an increase in risk management programs for organizations all over the world.

Globalization

Global competition has become the norm for many organizations. They sell their products and services internationally, and they have no intention of changing this strategy in the future. In fact, more and more companies will jump on the global bandwagon because there is great potential for growth and expansion. However, global competition brings about changes in social norms, politics, ethics, and the environment that create new risks. These risks need to be reduced...and risk management achieves that reduction. Risk management programs will need to modify their approach, but they will help prevent many global risks from becoming reality.

Culture

People in management typically base their decisions on the values and beliefs of their employers. Those decisions help some organizations grow and prosper, but they also drive other organizations out of business. It is impossible to predict with 100 percent accuracy whether future decisions will be right or wrong, but it is a known fact that those decisions will create risk....and that risk needs to be addressed. In the future, the culture of organizations will create risk that will be minimized by risk management programs.

Summary

Risk management is an appealing concept due to the uncertainty that exists in many organizations. It is more important today than it ever was in the past, and that importance appears to be growing. Based on its popularity, risk management is taking center stage in the thought processes of leaders all over the world.

This book focuses on risk management in organizations. It introduces six basic steps for development and implementation, describes major types of methodology, suggests methods of improvement, and examines the future of this interesting concept. The text is informational and educational, and it is written for easy reader understanding at all levels.

Congratulations! You now understand more about risk management...a useful program for predicting and protecting the future of organizations.

Behavior Based Safety in Manufacturing

A Basic Introduction

Louis Bevoc

Published by
NutriNiche System LLC

Louis Bevoc books...simple explanations of complex subjects

Introduction

Safety has long been a concern of management and workers in manufacturing facilities because injuries cost a lot of money. More importantly, some injuries cause production workers pain and suffering that cannot be alleviated with monetary compensation because no amount of money is worth the loss of health that cannot be restored.

The above paragraph is true, but it leads to a question. If safety is a concern, then why do some manufacturing employees expose themselves to risks that could endanger their health and well-being? Sometimes it is because supervisors coerce them to behave unsafely. However, this type of management behavior is changing as the consequences for such actions become more and more severe. Coercion aside, the following are some major reasons why manufacturing employees gamble with their safety:

- *Probability*

   Risky behavior sometimes has a low probability of negative consequences. For example, if an employee understands the mechanics and functionality of a machine that he is cleaning, he can override the safety with limited risk that he will injure himself. In other words, he can ignore the safety because he believes the odds of getting hurt are in his favor.

- *Shortcuts*

   Risky behavior sometimes saves time. In manufacturing facilities, time is often very important because more time means higher levels of production...so employees resort to shortcuts. For example, an employee moving product from a lower level to a higher level drives her forklift with the forks five feet off the ground. She knows that, for safety reasons, she should lower the forks to the floor when moving, but she wants to save the time it takes to continually raise and lower them.

- *Simplicity*

   Risky behavior sometimes makes a job easier...and most employees want their jobs to be easier. For example, an employee overrides the safety of a production mixer so he can keep the lid open and watch product as it is mixing rather than having to stop the machine to open the lid and view the product.

Based on the above, it can be assumed that employees will behave safely if that safe behavior is easy or simple. Along the same lines, they will not behave safely if that type of behavior is difficult or challenging. Either way, the behavior becomes habit...and habits are difficult to change. Behavior based safety (also known as BBS) teaches employees about the consequences of their behavior so they develop good habits.

An important feature of BBS is that it extends beyond rank-and-file employees to supervision. It forms a safety partnership between employees and supervision where everyone watches their own behavior and that of their coworkers. It is based on management-employee relationships and is most dependent on workers trusting those in higher positions.

In a nutshell, BBS adheres to a protocol where an activator leads to behavior that produces results. The protocol is broken down as follows:

Activator

This is a condition that influences the way an employee behaves. It is the reason that an employee chooses to exhibit safe or unsafe behavior (the next part of the protocol). An example of an activator is a production employee who needs to produce a certain amount of product in order to properly do his job at a manufacturing plant.

Behavior

This is the employee's reaction to the activator. In other words, it is the action they take after being stimulated to do something. Using the activator example, the employee chooses to use safe or unsafe behavior in order to meet his production quota.

Results

These are the benefits or consequences that result from the behavior of the employee. Safe behavior is beneficial while unsafe behavior is consequential. In the activator example, unsafe behavior might cause the employee to get injured; thereby preventing him from accomplishing his production goal.

Based on the above, it can be seen that activators tell employees that they need to behave in certain ways, and results are the outcome of that behavior. In other words, activation is motivation, behavior is motivation-based action, and results are action-based consequences.

Now that you understand a little about safety and its relationship to BBS, it is time to move on to the next section that focuses on the basic principles of BBS.

Underlying Philosophy

The following are essential principles of the behavior based safety process in manufacturing:

Prevention

This might be the most important principle, and that is why is listed first. It needs to be accepted and understood by all employees that every injury, regardless of the type of seriousness, can be prevented...and safety is the key.

Along the same lines, every safety risk needs to be identified and adequately managed. "Adequately" is the key word because inadequate management does not reduce or eliminate the problem.

Management driven

In order for BBS to work properly, everyone has to be involved and take on some type of responsibility. However, management is still legally, ethically, and financially responsible for the safety of all employees in the manufacturing facility. That being said, the BBS process is management driven...and this will likely never change.

Trust

Trust is essential for the BBS process to work as designed. People need to trust each other to watch out for everyone's safety. However, this process is management driven, so most of that trust involves production employees trusting those in higher positions. This is important because once trust is lost...it is difficult to restore.

Safety is profit

If safety is viewed as an expense or cost, then the BBS system will not work properly. The prevention of injuries needs to be thought of as adding to profitability because it makes good business sense to have safe manufacturing workforces. In the long term, employee health and welfare show up on the bottom line as black rather than red...and this makes all stakeholders happy.

Safety is paramount

Safety can never take a backseat to production. Instead, it needs to intertwine with production so each is dependent on the other to make the manufacturing facility the best that it can be. Along the same lines, safety cannot be compromised because it is more difficult than taking shortcuts. It needs to be viewed as helping an organization get better, rather than bogging it down.

Safety is not optional

All employees need to be aware from their first day of employment that they do not have a choice when it comes to safe behavior. Safety is a condition of employment, not an option that can be chosen based on discretion.

Training is necessary

All employees need training for BBS or they cannot be expected to embrace and follow the program. Education is essential, and it cannot be put on hold due to time restraints or other issues. In most workplaces training involves:

- Educating managers on how to observe and take action to prevent unsafe employee actions

- Educating employees on how to observe and take action to prevent their own unsafe actions
- Educating employees on how to observe and take action to prevent unsafe coworker actions
- Education managers and employees on how to take action by giving constructive feedback on their observations

Employees have safety responsibilities

It is imperative that all manufacturing employees understand their responsibilities with regard to safety. They need to make sure that their coworkers behave safely, and part of this responsibility involves stopping unsafe operations. They cannot stand by and watch their coworkers engage in unsafe behavior; they have an obligation to get involved and halt unsafe processes or procedures.

Now that you understand the thinking behind BBS in manufacturing, it is time to move into the next section that describes the BBS process as a whole.

Process

This section describes the process of BBS, and it is the crux of this book. The following are steps that need to take place in order for BBS to be successful using a manufacturing example:

Identify unsafe behavior that needs to be improved

This is more than just identifying the safety issue. It involves finding the root cause of the problem. For example, if an employee is behaving unsafely while operating a machine, then the reason for her unsafe behavior needs to be determined. It could be due to any of the following:

- She Is being pushed for production quotas.
- She has not been trained and is unaware that her behavior is unsafe.
- She is told to ignore safe behavior.
- She chooses to ignore safe behavior.

Instead of telling her to "stop doing that," an understanding of the root cause needs to be determined so it can be addressed for the prevention of future safety violations.

Develop a list of ideas that can be utilized to correct the unsafe behavior

Management determines that the root cause of the employee's actions is her supervisor telling her to ignore safe behavior. Her supervisor believes the risk for injury while operating her machine is low, and safe behavior takes time that could be spent putting out higher levels of production. Based on this determination, there needs to be clarification of management's safety expectations. The list of potential corrective ideas to do this is as follows:

- Reprimand her supervisor to correct the problem and prevent a reoccurrence.

- Meet with her supervisor to correct the problem and prevent a reoccurrence.
- Meet with all supervisors to correct the problem and prevent a reoccurrence.
- Meet with all employees to correct the problem and prevent a reoccurrence.

Select the best idea from the list

Management chooses "meet with all supervisors to correct the problem and prevent a reoccurrence" as the idea they want to put into action. It is selected because supervision is the root cause of the problem, and her supervisor's behavior needs to be addressed. However, it is a known fact that all supervisors take some shortcuts and need to be made more aware of the importance of safety, so they can also benefit from the meeting.

Develop an action plan for the idea

When developing an action plan, it is important to understand that BBS uses positive reinforcement to (1) change employee behavior that is unsafe and (2) support employee behavior that is safe. Positive reinforcement differs from negative reinforcement as follows:

Positive reinforcement

Positive reinforcement increases safe behavior by focusing on non-mandatory employee efforts. In other words, it encourages workers to willingly perform above minimum standards by recognizing them for their efforts. The goal is a win-win situation where employees and the manufacturer both experience success. For example, employees who notice unsafe behavior on production lines are awarded gift certificates when they inform their supervisors.

Unfortunately, positive reinforcement does not exist in some manufacturing facilities. Employees are not recognized for their safety minded actions regardless of the effort they put forth. For example, an employee always reminds other workers to lock out machines when inspecting or cleaning them, but he never receives management praise or credit for "going the extra mile." When this happens, the employee-management relationship is minimal and trust diminishes.

Negative reinforcement

Negative reinforcement is fear based. If the employees comply, they are not disciplined...but their efforts are not recognized. The focus is on complying with a standard because compliance leads to success. This method often works to increase safety, but the only winner is the company. Employees fear repercussion for non-conformance, so they comply. For example, employees are told that they will avoid disciplinary action if they wear appropriate gloves when operating a drill press. They comply and wear the gloves to avoid punishment for not wearing them.

Some manufacturers believe only in negative reinforcement. They threaten disciplinary action for unsafe behavior, and employees comply out of fear. For example, management might threaten employees with suspension or termination if they fail to wear safety goggles while working on a lathe. This causes the employee-management relationship to deteriorate quickly...and employees lose trust in their bosses.

As noted earlier, the action plan is to have a meeting with supervisors to discuss the problem. In this meeting, management explains the safety issues that they have observed, and they explain why this behavior is unsafe. They share their ideas for change and ask for suggestions in order to create a safer manufacturing process and prevent future safety problems from occurring. Once an agreement is reached, it is time for the implementation phase.

Implement the action plan

This is where ideas become reality. At the manufacturing facility, all supervisors meet with their employees to explain the new safety policies, protocols, and procedures. They offer training to any employee who would like to go through it, and they express confidence that their employees will perform their jobs with safety as a top priority.

Evaluate the success of the action plan

The changes made to the manufacturing facility need to be monitored for success. This is done when management directly observes employee safety behavior and reviews documented safety violations and work-related injuries. When employees perform their jobs safely, they receive feedback in the form of praise or rewards. This is an important part of the BBS process because it assures the plan is effective and continues to work as expected using positive reinforcement as a motivator.

Now let's examine a complete example that can be used as a model for manufacturers. The BBS process below was implemented in a paper towel manufacturing plant. It has real-world application and can be used as a model for building other BBS programs.

Wilson Paper Supply
Behavior Based Safety Process

Scope

Wilson Paper Supply (as known as the company) is a paper towel manufacturing plant located in Chicago, IL. The company employs 250 people including 190 production employees. Nick VanDeer is employed as the company's safety manager and oversees all safety related operations, including a safety team that consists of the plant manager, the quality control manager, and the office manager. The safety team meets once per month to discuss safety concerns in the facility.

Safety problem

The safety team has identified forklift driving in the warehouse as unsafe behavior that needs to be improved. There have not been any documented injuries, but employees have complained to management on three separate occasions that forklift drivers are exhibiting unsafe behavior. It appears that it is only a matter of time before someone gets hurt.

Specific issues with forklift drivers include:

- They sometimes fail to yield for employees walking through the warehouse.
- They sometimes drive forklifts at unsafe speeds.
- They sometimes drive outside the yellow lines that they are instructed to stay within.

Root cause

After interviewing the forklift drivers, the team has determined that the problem is not due to lack of knowledge or misunderstanding. The drivers understand the rules, but they have limited time to get their work done and subsequently do not always follow them.

Potential solutions

The following are potential solutions for correcting the forklift driver's unsafe behavior:

- Terminate the drivers who have exhibited unsafe behavior.
- Threaten to suspend forklift drivers who violate safety rules.
- Meet with the forklift driver's to discuss their unsafe behavior.
- Meet with other managers to discuss the forklift driver's unsafe behavior.
- Meet with all employees to discuss the forklift driver's unsafe behavior.

Chosen solution

The team decides to meet with the forklift drivers to discuss their unsafe behavior. This gives the safety team an opportunity to explain the reasoning behind the rules, and it allows the drivers to ask questions or request clarification. Management and the other employees are not needed in this meeting because the drivers' individual behavior is the specific issue that needs to be addressed.

Action plan

Upon meeting with the drivers, Nick VanDeer (safety team leader) starts by explaining to the forklift drivers that some employees have expressed concerns to management about unsafe forklift driving. Nick describes the mentioned driver actions below and explains why they are unsafe.

- *The drivers sometimes fail to yield for employees walking through the warehouse*

Employees often need to cross over forklift paths, so management has designated specific crossing areas. Management realizes the time is important at the paper towel manufacturing plant and drivers want to be efficient at their jobs...but employees should not have to fear accidents when crossing at designated areas.

- *The drivers sometimes drive forklifts at unsafe speeds*

  Employees work alongside forklift drivers in some areas of the plant, so management has posted yellow "SLOW" signs in those areas. Again, management realizes that time is important because drivers want to optimize their performance, but employees should not have to worry about being hit by a forklift that is going too fast to stop in time.

- *The drivers sometimes drive outside the yellow lines that they are instructed to stay within*

  Employees need to move around to different areas of the plant, so management has drawn yellow lines on the floor to separate forklift paths and employees. Management realizes that it virtually impossible to stay within the yellow lines 100 percent of the time, but employees should not have to fear getting hit by forklifts when they are in their designated areas.

After explaining the safety issues, Nick asks the drivers for suggestions on what could be done to create a safer work environment. One driver suggests that the shipping manager should stop pushing them so hard to get their work done. Nick agrees this is a good idea, but he says that this is not the shipping manager's fault because he is being pressured by the salespeople to fill last minute orders. However, he can initiate some changes to prevent this from happing on a regular basis. Another driver suggests an incentive program where drivers are rewarded for safe behavior. Nick says safe behavior is expected by all employees, but he can come up with something to help them in this area.

The meeting adjourns, and Nick promises to get back with the drivers the next day with potential resolutions to the problem.

The following day, the safety team again meets with the drivers. Nick proposes the following solutions:

- *Salespeople will be required to put in their order one day before they need to be filled.*

  The sales manager will meet with all salespeople and explain to them that safety is a top priority, and rush orders are creating an unsafe work environment. Understandably, this is not always possible...but it is definitely an area that can and will be improved.

- *Drivers will earn one extra vacation day for every four months that they go without an accident or a complaint.*

This means the drivers have an opportunity to earn three paid vacation days per year for practicing safe behavior based on written documentation and evaluation by their coworkers.

The drivers agree with Nick's proposal, and the action plan goes into effect at the start of the next work week. Nick expresses confidence in the forklift drivers' ability to be successful, and he tells the drivers that he will share the results with them via an email to their manager at the end of each month.

Evaluation

One year after the BBS process has been implemented, the results are analyzed and it is found that the process is successful. Forklift drivers are practicing safe behavior, and this is verified by the following:

- *Ongoing discussion with plant employees has yielded no complaints since the BBS process was implemented.*

- *All drivers have been awarded at least two vacation days since the BBS process was implemented.*

- *Tracking of sales data indicates rush orders are down 75 percent since the BBS process was implemented.*

Follow-up

For the next two years, the safety team meets every six months to discuss forklift driver safety. They review sales data and employee complaints regarding forklift driver safety. Additionally, they have one forklift driver and two plant employees attend the meeting to voluntary discuss the ongoing success of the BBS process. After each meeting, positive feedback is given about the success that is continually being experienced.

Benefits

There are many benefits that stem from BBS. Some of these benefits documented, such as reduced work-related injuries, while some are not documented, such as improvement of employees' attitudes.

The following are all positives that result from BBS:

- *Elimination of current practices of unsafe behavior*

  This is the major reason for the implementation of BBS. Once up and running, BBS eliminates existing unsafe behavior and replaces it with safe practices.

- *Prevention of future unsafe behavior*

BBS puts safety first. Safety does not take a backseat to production in manufacturing plants, and this means it is at the top of every employee's agenda. The workers' mindsets prevent them from taking safety risks; thereby preventing unsafe behavior in the future.

- *Reduced documented injuries*

  This benefit is documented. When safety is at the forefront, unsafe behavior decreases....and so do workplace injuries. This is one of management's favorite benefits because the reduction is quantifiable.

- *Reduced OSHA intervention*

  Fewer workplace injuries lead to fewer visits from OSHA officials. This means OSHA violations are reduced...as are the cost of their fines. This is also high on the list of favorite benefits for management because it equates to fewer headaches and expenses...especially in manufacturing facilities.

- *Increased morale*

  Rewards and positive reinforcement are both a part of successful BBS processes. People's morale is raised when they are acknowledged for their good actions, and that acknowledgment comes from rewards. Positive reinforcement also raises employees' morale; thereby making them more likely to perform at peak levels.

- *Avoidance of the "blame-game"*

  BBS does not place blame on any one individual. The goal is to improve safety as a whole by making everyone aware of unsafe behavior. Rather than place blame on their coworkers, employees watch out for each other creating a win-win situation for the company and the people employed by it.

- *Open two-way communication*

  BBS is all about management-employee communication regarding safety. This opens the door for candid discussion about other issues; thereby creating an environment of open two-way communication.

The above benefits of BBS show that the system is worth implementing. However, as might be expected, there are also some negatives associated with this concept. The following section focuses on the challenges involved with BBS.

Challenges

If you ask critics, they will tell you that there are many challenges associated with BBS. In fact, all one needs to do is search the Internet, and they will find their share of negative comments. The scope of this book does not allow for listing all of those comments, but it does extract four major criticisms as follows:

- *Employees are rewarded for not reporting unsafe behavior*

  BBS has been accused of creating a very contradictory situation because it rewards employees for not reporting unsafe behavior. For example, if production workers know that they will receive a bonus for plant-wide reduced injuries, then they will not report certain injuries. In other words, the BBS system ends up doing what it was supposed to prevent. The injuries are still there, but they are covered up because employees would rather have the added compensation.

- *Unsafe behavior is not always the cause of injuries*

  Many manufacturing plants have old or poorly maintained machines in operation. These machines break down regularly; thereby creating unsafe situations that have nothing to do with employee behavior. Regardless of their safe practices, employees get injured due to circumstances that are out of their control.

  It might seem like a simple fix to this problem is to invest in new machinery. Yes, that works, but it is often easier said than done. Some manufacturers simply do not have the money to invest....so they keep the old machinery operational for periods of time that far exceed normal expectations. If this is the situation, then BBS is nothing more than a grand illusion.

- *Supervisor limits*

  Most organizations that implement BBS expect supervisors to do more work in terms of safety observation. In theory, this sounds great...but it is often not realistic. Manufacturing supervisors are increasingly expected to do more with fewer resources, and their time needs to be spent on other important issues. In short, supervisors do not have the capacity to operate BBS processes as intended....so the processes ultimately fail.

- *Union opposition*

  Some unions strongly oppose BBS because they believe the process encourages employees to get into conflicts and disagreements about safety. It is not a production worker's job to tell another production employee that they need to change their unsafe behavior. Union employees are supposed to unite and work together, not "rat-out" each other and become quarrelsome.

  Some unions also believe that management tends to see BBS as "cure-all" that absolves them of their own safety responsibility. They simply pass that responsibility on to their employees, and the employees argue among themselves until they find a resolution.

Finally, some unions believe managers see BBS as a way to save money in their departments. Rather than spend money to fix equipment and machines, they spend time changing employees' unsafe behavior. This might work for a short period of time, but it ultimately ends up making manufacturing workplaces more unsafe.

Summary

Behavior based safety is a process that works to eliminate and prevent unsafe behavior. It uses positive reinforcement by rewarding employees who perform above minimum standards; thereby benefiting workers and the organizations that employ them.

This book focuses on behavior based safety in manufacturing. It introduces the topic, discusses its underlying principles, and provides a real world example that can be used as a model for manufacturing facilities. The text is informational and educational, and it is written for easy reader application and understanding.

Congratulations! You now understand more about behavior based safety...an important aspect of many manufacturing operations.

Labor Unions
in Organizations
Types, Structures, Advantages, and Disadvantages

Louis Bevoc

Published by
NutriNiche System LLC

Louis Bevoc books...simple explanations of complex subjects

Introduction

First, a point needs to be clarified about this book. It does not support or oppose unions in workplaces, nor does it argue any position on the topic. It is written for readers to gain a better understanding of union types and structures, and it introduces them to union advantages and disadvantages from an employee standpoint.

Labor unions have lost some power in recent years, but they are still fairly common in businesses across the United States. Certain areas of the country, such as the Northeast and Midwest, have larger percentages of unionized companies, but unions can be found in every state.

Unions represent workers in a variety of different industries in matters involving wage and benefit negotiations, working conditions, and disagreements with management over contract stipulations. However, the most prominent unions today are rooted in the public sector. This is partially due to the fact that unions in private industry have been attacked by special interest groups for having attained too much power of over the past half-century.

Unions are established in organizations after being voted in by employees. A majority of worker votes is needed to solidify the existence of a union, and that union then has the sole authority to negotiate all conditions of employment for its members.

The process used for negotiation is called collective bargaining. Collective bargaining differs from other business negotiations because it is mandated and governed by a variety of external laws and provisions. Collective bargaining also differs from other types of negotiations because the parties involved must continue working together after finalizing the contract. Management and union representatives need to resolve disagreements based on the stipulations of the contract, and this can be difficult if personnel on either side dislike each other.

Typically unions negotiate the following for employees:

Wages

Most workers want to earn more money...and that is why wages are critical for unions to negotiate. A union's goal is to increase employee wages to a level that the union perceives as fair. Once wages are negotiated and finalized, they become part of the union contract. The contract must be followed by management or the company could face legal action to mandate compliance.

Benefits

Unions negotiate all employee benefits, and this can be more involved than many people might think. Benefits negotiated can include any of the following:

- *Health insurance*

This is insurance for the general health of employees and their families. It generally provides coverage for all health issues except those related to eyes or teeth, and it includes many different types of specialists.

- *Dental insurance*

This is insurance for the teeth related health of employees and their families. It includes generalists and different types of specialists.

- *Vision insurance*

This is insurance for the eye related health of employees and their families.

- *Life insurance*

This is insurance for employees if they die. If they pass away, the money from the insurance is given to their designated beneficiaries.

- *Long-term disability insurance*

This is insurance for employees if they become disabled for long periods of time.

- *Short-term disability insurance*

This is insurance for employees if they become disabled for short periods of time.

- *Paid sick days*

This is pay that employees receive when they are sick and cannot come to work.

- *Paid personal days*

This is pay that employees receive when they need time off for personal reasons. It is in addition to paid vacation and paid sick days.

- *Paid vacation*

This is pay that employees receive when they take time off for vacations.

- *Paid holidays*

This is pay given to employees when they do not work on designated holidays.

- *Paid pregnancy leave*

This is pay given to employees who miss work due to pregnancy.

- *Pension programs*

  These programs provide income for employees after they retire.

- *401K programs (including company match)*

  These are tax-deferred retirement programs that employees can contribute to during each pay period. The money they contribute is sometimes matched by their employer.

- *Profit sharing programs*

  These programs provide money in addition to regular pay, but they are based on the profitability of the organization.

- *Gain sharing programs*

  These programs provide money in addition to regular pay, but they are not based on profitability of the organization. Instead, employees need to meet designated goals in order to receive payouts.

- *Bonus programs*

  These programs give money to employees at the end of a specific amount of time-based on performance.

- *Stock ownership programs*

  These programs allow employees to purchase stock below the market value.

- *Work-life balance programs*

  These programs are designed to help employees find a balance between work and personal life. An example is telecommuting.

- *Employee discount programs*

  These programs are discounts given to employees for designated products or services.

From the above list, it's rather obvious that the term "benefits" has many different applications.

Job Security

Workers want job security with their employer, and that is one of the reasons they vote unions into their organizations. Unions prevent "at will" employment (situations where employees can be terminated without establishing "just cause") and make it harder for employers to terminate employees for reasons that are illegitimate or superficial. Some of these reasons include:

- *The employee is not fast enough*
- *The employee is not working hard enough*
- *The employee did not listen to instructions*
- *The employee is not friendly*
- *The employee does not fit in*
- *The employee is not well-liked*

Employees guilty of the above infractions might ultimately be terminated in the long run, but union contracts have formal procedures in place that need to be adhered to before the termination can take place. These procedures include warnings and suspensions that follow a specific progression.

Working Conditions

Unions fight to improve workplace safety and overall working conditions. Some of their actions include:

- *Regulating workplace temperatures*

    Unions try to assure workplaces are heated or air-conditioned if working temperatures are a concern. For example, job shops in Minnesota should be heated in the winter, and assembly plants in Florida should be air conditioned in the summer.

    However, there are limitations to union intervention regarding workplace temperatures. Extreme hot and cold environments cannot always be controlled due to mandatory requirements or the nature of the situation. For example, smelting plants are going to be hot due to the environment, and meat freezers need to be cold for food safety reasons. In these situations, unions are not able to fight for changes...so instead they work toward getting employees more frequent breaks.

- *Regulating workplace lighting*

    Employees need to be able to see what they are doing in order to perform their jobs properly and prevent accidents from occurring. Unions do research to discover recommended lighting levels, and then they work towards forcing companies to comply with those recommendations.

- *Requiring safety equipment*

    Some jobs require safety gear such as special shoes, helmets, or gloves. Unions designate gear that is needed to keep employees safe and then work towards forcing companies to supply that gear.

- *Requiring cleaner work areas*

  Clean work areas are often needed for productivity and safety reasons. Unions push organizations to maintain work areas in a clean or sanitary manner so the conditions are better for their members.

- *Requiring periodic breaks*

  Unions want to make sure employees are well rested in order to properly perform the functions of their jobs. They work toward getting companies to supply frequent or longer breaks for their members.

Now that you have a basic understanding of what labor unions attempt to do for employees, let's move into the specific types of unions that exist in the United States.

Types

Unions reached their peak in the mid-20th century. Membership has declined since that point, but unions still influence the way many organizations operate and conduct business.

Essentially, there are three types of unions in the United States. These unions are:

Industrial

Description

Industrial unions generally represent workers in specific industries, regardless of the jobs they perform. They have more members than craft unions because craft unions are limited to individual trades or skills.

Types of industries that elect industrial unions include:

- *Transportation*
- *Distribution*
- *Warehousing*
- *Construction*
- *Food*
- *Chemical*
- *Power*

Industrial unions are considered better unions than craft unions due to the following:

- Industrial unions have greater bargaining power during contract negotiations because they have more members than craft unions.
- Industrial unions have more leverage during strikes because they have more members than craft unions.

- Industrial unions remain united at all times. This is not the case for craft unions because they are most concerned about the well-being of their own members.
- Industrial unions are not divided. Craft unions tend to fight over jurisdiction and the right to strike.
- Industrial unions members do not cross picket lines. Craft union members often have the freedom to cross each other's picket lines. In fact, some craft union contracts require members to cross picket lines of other unions.

Craft

Description

Craft unions typically represent workers in a specific trade or occupation. This includes workers in skilled trades.

Occupations that elect craft unions include:

- Electricians
- Millwrights
- Plumbers
- Welders
- Pipefitters
- Machinists

Craft unions are considered better unions than industrial unions due to the following:

- Craft unions are able to get higher wages for specifically skilled workers. Industrial unions have to negotiate the group as a whole, so skilled workers lose to compensate unskilled workers.
- Craft unions fight harder for every worker because memberships are smaller. Industrial unions have large memberships and workers might not get left out.
- Craft unions control apprenticeships, and they can create a shortage of skilled workers in order to drive up wages. Industrial unions do not have apprenticeships to control, and they cannot drive up wages by creating shortages of workers.
- Craft unions control apprenticeships, and they can select the best individuals to assure the union continues. Industrial unions do not have apprentices to control, and they cannot select the best individuals to assure the union continues.
- Craft unions control the content of jobs and the skills needed to perform those jobs. Industrial unions cannot control the content or skills of their member's jobs.

Public Sector

Description

This is the largest type of union in the United States. It represents government workers, regardless of their job.

Workers in public sector unions include:

- Police officers
- Firefighters
- Postal workers
- Sanitation workers
- Teachers

Public sector unions are considered better unions than industrial unions or craft unions due to the following:

- Contract negotiations are based on government budgets...and governments rarely ever go bankrupt or shut down. Craft union and industrial union negotiations are based on the financial stability of private corporations...and private corporations go bankrupt and shut down on a regular basis.
- Public sector unions have national exposure and often get public support or sympathy nationwide. Craft unions and industrial unions rarely get public support or sympathy on a national level.
- Public sector unions are growing in membership as craft unions and industrial unions decline in membership. This gives public sector unions more negotiating power than craft unions or industrial unions.

Now that you have an understanding of the three basic types of unions, let's move into the structure of unions in general.

Structure

Unions have similar structures, but those structures are tailored toward the goals and objectives of the specific union. For example, a craft union for teachers would have a mission that is different from that of an industrial union in a food processing plant. The teachers' union might have a goal of reducing class sizes, while the food processing union wants to add more employees to the workforce.

Along the same lines, a police officers' public sector union would have a different mission than an electricians' craft union. The police officers' union might have a goal of increasing protective equipment for officers on the streets, while the electricians' union has an objective of eliminating holiday work.

Unions of the same type can also have differing objectives. Consider two types of occupations in the public sector unions - firefighters and sanitation workers. The firefighters' union might want members to work a maximum of one weekend per month, while the sanitation workers' union wants to reduce the maximum weight of refuse they are required to lift from 40 pounds to 35 pounds.

In short, goals and philosophies of different unions reflect the needs of their members. However, the structure of all unions can be broken down into four major areas. These areas include the general membership, executive board, executive officers, and committees. Each area is described below and broken down into smaller components for a more detailed understanding.

General membership

General members are the reason unions are formed. They are the beneficiaries of union activity, and their needs rank above all other concerns. They are also the most powerful decision-making force within the union, and they control its destiny. However, this power comes with responsibilities that involve understanding union objectives and getting involved with union actions.

Below is a closer examination of the role of general membership within the union:

Benefits

- They are entitled to union education and training.
- They are entitled to union grievance support.
- They are entitled to union legal assistance when necessary.

Power

- They elect people to important union positions including the executive board and executive officers.
- They approve policies and procedures regarding union management.
- They approve changes in union leadership.

Responsibilities

- They need to understand the by-laws and constitution of the union.
- They need to participate in internal and external union activities.
- They need to pay dues for their union membership.

Executive board

This is the next level up from general membership on the union's hierarchical ladder. Members at this level make sure that approved policies and procedures are implemented and carried out in the manner designated by the general members.

The executive board plays an important role in the union because it ensures the general member's wishes are adhered to properly. Without this board, the guidelines voted in by general members would be essentially useless, and anarchy could be the end result.

Additionally, the executive board considers the general members to be shareholders in the union. Similar to a board of directors in a business, they report on all union activities so general members are kept abreast of internal and external happenings.

Executive officers

This group consists of the president, vice-president, secretary, treasurer, auditors, chief steward, and stewards. Once elected by the general members, they are responsible for the daily functioning of the union. This entails being involved in virtually every aspect of daily operations to assure the union works for members in order to attain higher wages, better benefits, and improved working conditions.

Each officer has specific responsibilities in regard to union operations, and those responsibilities are as follows:

President

The president is the main person responsible for the daily operations of the union. If the union is not achieving designated goals or objectives, then the president is responsible. In short, the president is accountable for the union's maintenance, growth, and prosperity.

Other responsibilities of the president often include:

- Acts as chief external union communicator
- Acts as chief internal union communicator
- Acts as chief union negotiator
- Acts as chief union arbitrator
- Oversees union executive board meetings
- Oversees union finances (P&L, budgets, expenses, etc.)
- Directs union executive officers
- Directs union general membership
- Signs important union documents

Vice-president

Similar to the vice-president of the United States, the vice-president assumes the president's responsibilities if he or she is unable to do so. He or she also handles other tasks assigned by the president.

Other responsibilities of the vice-president often include:

- Acts as chair of the grievance committee
- Acts as advisor to chief steward and stewards
- Coordinates union benefits
- Coordinates union training

Secretary

The secretary is responsible for all clerical duties. This involves maintaining and storing all records, files, and data related to union activities.

Other responsibilities of the secretary often include:

- Writes or records minutes at union meetings. Minutes are official records of union actions that are permanently filed.
- Writes official union letters.
- Opens union mail (letter, bills, etc.) and delivers to appropriate officers

Treasurer

The treasurer handles many financial aspects of the union's daily operations. He or she monitors union funds for accuracy and discrepancies and maintains all financial transaction records. In short, the treasurer is a safeguard for union funds.

Other responsibilities of the treasurer often include:

- Prepares budget
- Manages assets
- Assures dues are collected
- Arranges for audits

Auditor

The auditor conducts audits of union financial activities over specific periods of time. This assures that monetary transactions are consistent with the goals and objectives of the union. In short, the auditor is a safeguard for making sure union finances reflect the goals of the organization.

Specific aspects of union financial activities examined during an audit often include:

- Wages
- Expense reports
- Credit card charges
- Allowances
- Receipts
- Disbursements
- Government reports
- Union reports
- Record maintenance

Chief steward

A chief steward assists lower level stewards in their daily activities. These individuals are typically seasoned union officials, and they serve the role of a mentor.

Other responsibilities of the chief steward often include:

- Educates new stewards on handling grievances
- Identifies member concerns and creates plans of action for addressing
- Oversees steward committee meetings

Steward

The steward is on the front line for member grievances. These individuals receive the grievances and process them using the standard union protocol.

Other responsibilities of the steward often include:

- Educates members on union policies and procedures
- Organizes union meetings with members
- Serves as union contact for disputes with company management

Committees

Unions have a variety of committees that utilize members from all levels of the hierarchy. These committees have different functions, but essentially they are designed to provide members with guidance, direction, and understanding in regards to union policies and procedures.

The following are examples of committees that are often formed by unions:

Organizing committee

This committee coordinates the efforts of the organizing process. It involves employees at all levels of the union, and it requires member commitment.

Education and training committee

This committee educates members on union programs, policies, and procedures. In short, it educates employees on their rights and responsibilities as union members.

Budget/finance committee

This committee serves as a watchdog over union money to assure it is used appropriately.

Legal Committee

This committee is in charge of any legal actions that take place within the union.

Information committee

This committee provides the union with the information needed for negotiations. Members do research to gather facts and data that can be used to support the union's position.

Negotiation committee

This committee represents the union in negotiations with management. They establish goals based on the feedback they receive from members.

Grievance committee

This committee works to resolve disputes and conflicts between members and management.

Community services committee

This committee gets the union involved in the community to support causes they deem worthwhile.

Retirees committee

This committee has a dual purpose. First, it organizes retirees to gain their support for the union. Then it gives back to the retirees by supporting community service programs that they value.

Now you have a basic understanding of union types and their structure. Let's expand upon that knowledge in the next section by discussing the pros and cons of unions from an employee perspective.

Advantages

Unions are advantageous to employees for the following reasons:

Better wages and benefits

Unions fight for improved wages and benefits for their members. This often results in better compensation packages than workers who perform similar jobs in non-union plants.

Right to grievances

Union employees have the right to argue their position if they feel they have been wronged by the company. They simply file a grievance with the union steward, and the union fights on their behalf. Employees in non-union companies do not always have the option to argue their position because management's decision is final.

Strength in numbers

Unions have an advantage based on the number of members they have fighting for a common cause. In short, it's easier for a group of people to get a company to change than it is for any single person.

Secured jobs

Management in union companies cannot fire workers for any reason. A strict protocol must be followed in order to terminate an employee, and this provides job security for union members.

Disadvantages

Unions are disadvantageous to employees for the following reasons:

Devaluation of high performers

Many people believe that higher performing employees deserve higher pay. This is not possible in a union environment because workers at the same level are compensated equally.

Abuse

Unions were necessary when workers started to organize many years ago. Workplace conditions were often terrible, and management had no restrictions on how employees were treated. However, those type of workplace conditions are few and far between in the modern world because laws are in place to prevent them from existing. Today's unions often end up fighting for those members who abuse their protection. Some union employees are aware that companies have great difficulty firing them, and because of this, they abuse the system so it works to their advantage.

Problems with seniority

Unions reward employees based on seniority. Skills and qualifications are not taken into account when positions become available, and this means the best people are not always chosen for the job.

Loss of jobs

Unions do a good job increasing wages and benefits for their members. However, these increases can put financial burdens on companies that cannot be overcome. When companies shut down because they are no longer profitable, everyone loses...including union members.

Summary

Labor unions have been a hot topic of discussion in the United States for many years because once voted in, they have sole authority to negotiate all conditions of employment for their members. They represent members in matters involving wages, benefits, working conditions, and disagreements with management over contract stipulations. Although unions have lost some power in recent years, they are still fairly common in organizations across the United States.

This book helps readers gain a better understanding of union types, structures, advantages, and disadvantages. It does not support or oppose unions in workplaces, nor does it arguing any position on the topic. The goal is simply to educate readers about unions so they can formulate their own opinions.

Congratulations! You now understand more about labor unions...an important aspect of organizational behavior.

Nonprofit Organizations
A Basic Introduction

Louis Bevoc

Published by
NutriNiche System LLC

Louis Bevoc books...simple explanations of complex subjects

Introduction

Many people start businesses in order to generate income. They sell goods or services to make money as a reward for the time and effort they invest in their livelihood. These businesses are designed to earn profits, and they are regulated by the government based on their for-profit status.

A nonprofit organization (NPO) is not the same as a for-profit company. NPOs generate income, but that income is not for the investors, shareholders, owners, or employees. The money left after bills are paid is reinvested back into the efforts of the organization. In other words, it helps the organization maintain its status and promote its cause. NPOs are regulated by the government based on their nonprofit status, and they must serve the public in some manner.

NPOs are specifically classified as such by the Internal Revenue Service (IRS). This means they are granted tax-exempt status and usually money donated to them is tax deductible. Additionally, all financial information is required to be made public so anyone who donates can see how their money is being used.

Workforces of NPOs are generally established for humanitarian, environmental, freedom, or religious reasons. They further a cause by promoting an idea, belief, or concept that appeals to people's emotional or spiritual needs rather than a product or service that has value in a specific market. Unlike for-profit operations, NPOs rely on donations and grants from individuals, organizations, and governments.

NPO workers are rewarded differently than employees in for-profit companies. For-profit businesses financially compensate the vast majority of their employees, and people work at these organizations so they can earn a living. NPOs have limited numbers of paid employees with most people volunteering their time and effort. These individuals identify with the cause of the NPO, tend to work tirelessly, and their reward is the success of the organization. Since the volunteers work for free, they are generally never fired. If they stop working for the cause, it is usually by their own choice.

This book focuses on nonprofit organizations. It explores types, economic influences, advantages, disadvantages, trends, and the future of this business concept. The text is informational and educational, and it is written for easy understanding at any reader level.

Please note that this book does not discuss specific legalities of NPOs. It touches upon their tax status, but it is not intended to be used as a legal reference for those who are considering opening or are involved with nonprofit businesses. It does not go into any detail on issues such as the tax-exempt requirements, tax deduction of donations, or the sub-listing of 501(c) classifications. People interested in the legalities of NPOs should read books that are geared toward that subject.

Now that you understand the scope of this book, let's move on to the next section that examines specific types of NPOs.

Types

It would be very difficult to list every type of NPO because they vary so much in composition and cause. However, the major types are listed below.

Advocacy

These groups are the most political of the different types. They have a goal in mind, and they will generally do whatever is necessary to achieve that goal. Sometimes their goal is to influence people so they make choices that reflect the group's effort, and other times it is to change or repeal something that is already in effect. Often known as political action committees or special interest groups, advocacy NPOs lobby hard using supporter funds to achieve their objectives.

One problem with advocacy NPOs is they sometimes resort to illegal activities to achieve goals and objectives. They are so intent on furthering their cause that they have been known to commit crimes including bribery and fraud. They also get involved in non-violent activities (also known as civil obedience) to bring attention to the ideas supported by their organizations.

Association

These NPOs are organized in order to bring people together who share a common interest. That interest can be education (parent-teacher associations), experience (war veterans), finance (credit unions), lifestyle (condominium associations) or something secretive (masons). Associations often involve rituals or other activities unique to the people in the NPO. For example, fraternities (educational associations) sometimes have a handshake that is used to greet and identify brothers. The handshake is only divulged after a person becomes a member....and it is not to be discussed or used with any non-members.

Charity

Charitable NPOs collect money for select causes. Many times this is for health concerns (muscular dystrophy), catastrophic circumstance (earthquake), social inequality (foundations), or animal protection (animal shelters). These organizations are almost entirely funded by outside donations, and they have extremely dedicated personnel.

One problem associated with charitable NPOs in the fact that that part of the money received is spent on overhead and marketing costs. This portion of revenue varies depending on the organization, but some people believe that not enough goes to the designated cause. This is not necessarily illegal, but it does bring about ethical concerns.

Cooperative

Cooperative NPOs are formed when people work together to achieve a common good for everyone involved (such as the Dairy Farmers of America). Farmers often form cooperatives for financial reasons such as lowering the seed prices for crops or raising the quality of feed for animals. The power of these individuals functioning as a unit benefits everyone in that unit. These NPOs are typically funded by members or outside donations from individuals, organizations, or the government (in the form of grants).

Recreation and socialization

These NPOs include country clubs, hiking groups, and hobbyists. They form when people seek others who share common recreational, personal, or social interests in order further those interests. Members typically want to obtain knowledge, add to their collection, socialize, exercise, or relax. They might meet at someone's home, a sports facility, or an outdoor park. However, regardless of where they meet, they do it for mutual interest reasons. An example is a chess club that rents out library space for monthly tournaments or a bike club that meets at a designated destination to ride for a pre-determined number of miles.

The biggest positive about recreation and socialization NPOs is the fact that money is not typically a concern. They are almost always funded by the members themselves, and those members usually work somewhere else to earn money in order to make a living. They have expendable income that they voluntarily give to the NPO, and they become part of it for enjoyment purposes rather than furthering some type of cause. For this reason, they do not need to be continually contacted for donations by those who do the organizing.

Religious

Religious NPOs are quite common in America...partially due to the separation of church and state reference in the *First Amendment to the Constitution of the United States* that allows for freedom of religion. These organizations unite members of specific faiths for spiritual purposes, and they are often self-funded. The Jonah Project is an example of this type of NPO.

Unfortunately, these types of NPOs come under scrutiny by the government due to the fact that the financial aspects involved can be abused. High ranking members sometimes compensate themselves rather than putting the money back into the organization to further its cause.

Now you understand some of the major types of NPOs. However, classification goes a step further because some of these organizations are public (for example credit unions) while others are private (for example home associations). Since these two categories make a difference in operating strategies, private and public NPOs are discussed in the next section.

Public vs. Private

Each type of NPO can be further classified as public or private. The major difference between the two is that public NPOs receive donations from the general public, while private NPOs received financial backing from a few select contributors.

The following is a more detailed description of public and private NPOs:

Public

As noted above, public NPOs receive funding from the general public. They offer perks for certain types of paid memberships, such as discounts on products or services from organizations that also support the NPO. In this situation, one hand essentially washes the other and both parties feel good about contributing to a noteworthy cause.

An example of a public NPO is St. Jude Children's Research Hospital started by Danny Thomas in 1962. This charitable organization has received donations from people and organizations all over the world. American Lebanese Syrian Associated Charities (ALSAC), another non-profit charity, is responsible for fundraising of the Children's hospital that totals almost 2 million dollars per day. Obviously, this amount of money would be difficult to collect from a few select donors, and that is one reason why St. Jude is a public NPO.

Private

As noted above, private NPOs are funded from a few select sources. In fact, some small private NPOs are entirely funded by one wealthy donor who is interested in bringing attention to the cause. These types of organizations usually do not look for contributions from the general public, but that could change if the need arises. Private NPOs also have lower operating costs than their public counterparts because far less money is spent on marketing or fundraising activities. This is advantageous because a higher percentage of each dollar is used directly for the cause, and it is a reason why some people choose to support private rather than public NPOs.

As you can see, public and private NPOs differ in the ways that they are funded. However, both types of organizations have a goal of furthering the cause for which they were established. Next, let's looks at the advantages and disadvantages offered by all types of NPOs...starting with the advantages.

Advantages

NPOs offer many different advantages. Some of these advantages are external and visual, such as the ability to solicit funding from individuals who believe in a specific cause; and some of them are internal and less transparent, such as the satisfaction those individuals receive from giving.

To simplify matters, NPO advantages are broken down as follows:

Identification

NPOs all have some type of cause, and they receive funding because people or organizations identify with that cause. Interestingly, that identification is for different reasons. For example, three different people donate money to an NPO that services the needs of war veterans. The first person donates because her father and grandfather were war veterans. The second person donates because he has read that veterans often do not receive proper medical care. The third person donates because he wants a tax deduction and helping veterans seems like a noble cause. The reasons for each of these individual donations are not the same, but the all believe they are giving to a worthwhile cause. In short, each of these individuals identifies with war veterans and finds it advantageous to give to them.

Variety

Variety is often thought of as the spice of life...and that type of thinking can also be applied to people's jobs. After all, they spend a large percentage of their waking day at work, so their jobs should have variety in order to make them interesting.

People who work for NPOs experience a great deal of variety. In fact, the diverse nature of their responsibilities often makes their work more enjoyable than any other job they have ever done. They are usually assigned to multiple projects at the same time, and these projects allow them to make decisions on a moment's notice. This provides ample opportunity for growth...the type of growth that is simply not possible in many for-profit organizations.

In short, NPOs are not looking for specialists who prefer one specific type of job responsibility. They search for people who like to multi-task and enjoy new challenges...a type of environment where opportunities for learning are virtually endless.

Communication

This is an advantage that many people, including NPO employees, do not readily recognize. Workers at NPOs regularly get to discuss organizational happens with the top people or person in the organization. This is due to the fact that NPOs usually have flat hierarchies with one or two levels of management. Heads of these organizations do not distance themselves from the rank and file employees, and this makes communication much better. Unfortunately, the same cannot be said for many for-profit organizations where CEOs are never found meeting or socializing with lower level employees.

Commitment

People who work for NPOs find a lot of satisfaction, regardless of whether they receive compensation or volunteer. They are supporting a cause they view as justifiable and necessary, and this makes them feel good about their efforts. When they feel good about their efforts, they identify with the organization and its goals...and this helps the organization function more efficiently and effectively. In short, NPO employees are committed to their workplaces thereby creating a win-win situation for employees and organizations.

Knowledge

Contrary to what some people in for-profit businesses believe, NPOs place a very high priority on business skills. They search for people who believe in the cause and have worked in for-profit organizations so they can tap their minds for the knowledge within. When these individuals are brought on board, they combine their strengths to make the NPO the best it can be in regard to accomplishing goals and objectives. Smart leaders of NPOs recognized the need for knowledge, and they know it can be found in the for-profit sector.

The advantages of NPOs are many, but there are also some associated disadvantages. These disadvantages typically do not discourage organizations from becoming or remaining non-profit, but they do exist...and they are discussed in the next section

Disadvantages

As most people who have worked for NPOs understand, there are disadvantages for these types of organizations. Similar to advantages, some disadvantages are external and visual, such as the technology that is available for people to do their jobs. However, other disadvantages are not as easily seen, such as the frustration experienced by workers or volunteers who cannot see themselves making progress toward furthering the cause.

To simplify matters, NPO disadvantages are broken down as follows:

Frustration

One NPO disadvantage is the fact that it can be difficult to pinpoint progress or achievement on a small scale. For example, a group of animal rights activists is picketing outside of a store that sells mink coats. After the store owner calls the police, they are forced to leave the properly...and this raises questions. Did they have any success with their actions? Were they noticed? These questions are hard to answer because it is difficult to determine if anyone was impacted by the picketing. This can be demoralizing to the picketers unless they realize that their efforts are for the greater good of the cause. In other words, it can be challenging for these individuals to look past their immediate situation to see the success of the organization as a whole....and this can be frustrating.

Technology

This disadvantage can be minimal or substantial based on the importance of technology to the NPO. If state of the art technology plays a big role in furthering the cause, then this disadvantage can be paralyzing. For example, sophisticated software might be necessary for an NPO to implement data, track trends, formulate reports, and determine course of action. However, that software can be expensive...especially if it needs to be continually updated. Since the NPO relies on donations to operate, that money might simply not be available. This prevents them from reaching the level that they need to be in order to complete their designated goals and objectives, and it could lead to failing to secure the funding necessary to continue their efforts in the future.

Funding

Funding controls every NPO, and donors are the sole source of that funding. Contributors who decide not to donate can stop an NPO dead in its tracks. This is similar to for-profit organizations relying on sales, but donors are usually much scarcer than customers. For-profit businesses can diversify their customer bases to include a variety of outlets for their products or services. NPOs usually do not have this opportunity because only a select few people or organizations have an interest in their cause.

Additionally, there is a constant need for NPOs to solicited funding. Customers of for-profit organizations often return without prompting because they like the product or service they have purchased. However, this is rarely the case for NPOs. If donors are not contacted, then they often choose not to donate again. They need to be reminded of their importance to the organization and the importance of the organization's cause to those impacted by it.   This means time and effort must be continually dedicated to fundraising, and that takes away from doing other work that furthers the cause of the NPO.

Structure

As noted in the advantages sections, communication in NPOs is often better than that in for-profit organizations because much of the management is done at ground level without the multiple layers organizational hierarchy found in many companies. Unfortunately, this type of organizational structure is not all good. A major negative associated with it is the fact that there is no leadership at lower levels to implement the plans made by higher-ranking personnel. Every rank and file employee has essentially the same amount of authority, and this can result in nobody taking charge. More importantly, it can lead to internal conflict over who has authority. If that conflict becomes dysfunctional, then personal attacks can result where the combatants focus on position rather than principal...and nothing constructive gets accomplished.

In a nutshell, for-profit organizations typically have lower levels of managers that are in charge of departments, teams, or groups. This allows tasks to be delegated to subordinate levels of authority so they implement and complete them. NPOs, on the other hand, are flat when it comes to management. This is understandable due to cost factors, but it also hinders goals and objectives from getting accomplished. When goals and objectives are not accomplished, NPOs are unable to further their cause...and this makes people think twice about donating their hard-earned money.

Turnover

Turnover is a concern for many different types of organizations, but it is particularly threatening for NPOs. This is due to the fact that NPOs have a special set of factors that do not apply to profit based entities.

Turnover factors for NPOs are as follows:

Safety

For example, a man who works for a forest preservation NPO has his life threatening by loggers who make a living harvesting lumber from trees. He determines his efforts are not worth the potential consequences, so he stops volunteering for the NPO.

Second thoughts

For example, a man who works for a forest preservation NPO realizes that native people in isolated areas cannot feed their families without hunting wild game and gathering fruits from the forest. He decides that he cannot consciously tell these people to discontinue their current way of life, so he chooses to stop volunteering for the NPO.

Pressure

For example, a man who works for a forest preservation NPO dreads calling people and asking them for their financial support. These people have told the man to quit calling, but the head of the NPO tells him to continue doing so because the funding is desperately needed. He reaches a point where he simply cannot make another solicitation phone call, so he chooses to stop volunteering for the NPO.

Now you understand some advantages and disadvantages of NPOs. Let's expand on the discussion by examining the impact that the economy on these organizations. This is an interesting subject because some of this impact is not as transparent as it might appear at first glance.

Economic impact

Most people know that the economy has an impact on for-profit businesses. When the economy gets worse, people tend to forego unnecessary expenses and many businesses are negatively affected. These businesses see reduced sales resulting in less profit and, in worst case scenarios, this leads to their demise.

The economy also has an impact on NPOs. In fact, this impact is often bigger than that on for-profit businesses because NPOs are hit twice as hard. Please consider the following as support:

For-profit organizations

If the economy is bad, then sales for many different types of businesses start to decline. This is due to the fact that people have less expendable income so they limit their spending to essential goods and services. Organizations that suffer the worst include restaurants and companies involved in the vacation business because people tend to eat at home and avoid going on trips in order to save money. Sales decline as demand for the products and services decrease and some organizations end up in financially troubling situations.

When the economy is good, for profit organizations tend to do better. The demand for their products and services increases because people have extra money that they are not afraid to use for items that are not necessarily essential. This leads to businesses becoming profitable, and they are able to grow and prosper.

NPOs

Some NPOs are hit with a double whammy when the economy sours. People have less expendable income...and financial support for a cause is typically one of the first things to go. This is understandable because NPO support is a non-essential expenditure. However, many times the demand for NPO services increases as donor contributions decrease. For example, the services of an NPO that feeds the hungry and shelters the homeless will be needed more as the economy tanks and people lose jobs. However, there is now less money to support those services...and that lack of funding prevents them from achieving their objectives. Obviously, this is not the case for every NPO. The demand for the services offered by other types of NPOs does not necessarily increase as the economy gets bad, but donations still decrease...and this means the NPOs have less money available to continue working at the same level.

When the economy is good, NPOs are at a peak for productivity. They get more donations because people are not afraid to give their money to a cause that they deem worthwhile. Additionally, fewer people are out of work so there is less need for services that help people during difficult times. Along the same lines, the demand for the work done by other types of NPOs typically does not necessarily increase, but the additional money from funding allows them to do more to further their causes.

Now you are aware of the impact the economy has on NPOs and the reasons it affects them differently than for-profit organizations. With this in mind, let's move forward into the next section that discusses the things NPOs need to do in future in order to weather economic storms, promote their cause, and reach new levels of growth.

Future

This section deserves some attention because NPOs will need to change in the future in order to thrive and survive. The following gives some insight into the type of changes that will take place:

Results driven investments

In many ways, people who give to NPOs are "investing" their hard-earned money in those organizations. Yes, they believe in the cause or they would not be supporting it. However, like other investments, they write a check and monitor the performance of that investment. In NPOs, that performance is usually determined by accomplishments that show results. As might be expected, those results are analyzed and the donor makes a decision on whether he or she wants to "reinvest" in the future.

Results have always been important to donors, but that importance is going to increase substantially in the future. NPOs will be compared against each other to determine which ones are performing best in the minds of those contributing. Results, rather than cause, will be the biggest factor determining the destination of expendable income.

Educated donors

Donors will conduct research on the NPOs that receive their contributions. Social media and the internet have made this relatively easy, and the use of these tools will increase in the future because donors will be very comfortable with technology. This increased level of education will mean that donors will become more selective about which organizations receive their contributions. They will not give less money, but the money they contribute will need to be justified by the NPOs receiving it.

Increased staff

People will realize that the infrastructure of NPOs is important in order to run those organizations effectively. Funds will be put aside to hire management personnel who are in charge of completing tasks, and this will not be frowned upon by donors. In fact, donors will realize the value of management and contribute even more money. Unfortunately, this will not be all positive because hierarchical charts will increase causing a lack of communication. Also, the percentage of volunteers will likely decrease...and sometimes volunteers are the most dedicated personnel because they believe most in the cause.

Narrowed marketing

NPOs will realize that they have a specific market that provides them with most of their funding. That being said, they will focus on that specific market and move away from trying to entice others in the population to donate. Marketing money will largely be spent on the renewal of current donors rather than the search for new people willing to contribute.

Marketing money will also be spent on corporate donor solicitation. Corporate giving is important for public image, and CEOs are beginning to take advantage of this fact. They will donate more money to charitable causes in the future in order to establish credibility in the eyes of consumers. In short, the leaders of companies will utilize NPOs as their own marketing tool, and this means that corporate giving has only begun to reach its full potential.

Competition

This refers to the competition between NPOs for the funding that is available. It takes into account the thinking that people will become more educated and organizational leaders will work toward establishing positive perceptions of companies. All donors will be looking for "more bang for their buck," and this means competition between NPOs will increase. NPOs will need to find ways to stand out from the rest of the pack in order to get the funding necessary to further their causes. This is possible, but it will take creative thinking and hard work. Unfortunately, NPOs that fail to distinguish themselves from the competition will likely dissolve.

Expect the unexpected

Every company needs to expect the unexpected, but this thinking is more applicable to NPOs than it is to most other organizations. NPOs are scrutinized by the public and governmental agencies for ethical and legal reasons, and this means the laws regulating them could change at any time. NPO leaders need to be ready for this with strategies that can be used to maintain status and continue furthering causes under a variety of different circumstances. In short, NPOs need to plan because those that "fail to plan, plan to fail"

Summary

NPOs can be found all over the United States. They further specific causes, are funded by donors that support those causes, and sometimes have an impact worldwide.

This book focuses on NPOs. It explores specific types, investigates advantages and disadvantages, analyzes the economy's impact, and discusses the future of these businesses. The text is informational and educational, and it is written for easy reader understanding at all levels.

Congratulations! You now understand more about the nonprofit organizations that play a critical role in bringing attention to important causes.

Thank you for reading this book
For questions or comments please contact:
info@nutriniche.com